EXECUTING THE CONSTITUTION

SUNY series in American Constitutionalism

Robert J. Spitzer, editor

EXECUTING THE CONSTITUTION

Putting the President Back into the Constitution

Edited by
Christopher S. Kelley

State University of New York Press

Published by
State University of New York Press, Albany

Printed in the United States of America

For information, address State University of New York Press,
194 Washington Avenue, Suite 305, Albany, NY 12210-2384

Production by Judy Block
Marketing by Susan Petrie

Library of Congress Cataloging-in-Publication Data

Executing the Constitution : putting the president back into the Constitution / edited by Christopher S. Kelley
p. cm. — (SUNY series in American constitutionalism)
Includes bibliographical references and index.
ISBN 0-7914-6727-9 (hardcover : alk. paper)
ISBN 978-0-7914-6728-2 (pbk. : alk. paper)
1. Executive power—United States—History. 2. Constitutional history—United States. 3. Presidents—United States—History. I. Kelly, Christopher S., 1964– II. Series.

JK511.E93 2006
352.23'5'0973—dc22

2005021345

ISBN-13: 978-0-7914-6727-5 (hardcover : alk. paper)

10 9 8 7 6 5 4 3 2 1

I dedicate this book to my father,
Thomas Kelley,
the smartest person I know

Contents

Preface

This book was a labor of love. It enabled me to bring together a group of extraordinary scholars, some established and most soon-to-be. They made this project very simple to edit and a complete joy to read.

I want to thank all of the contributors who took time out of their busy schedules to contribute to the book. Every one of these contributors has a heavy workload, yet none hesitated when I asked them if they would contribute their time for this book.

I would like to thank Robert Spitzer, who not only contributed to the book but also worked with me in soliciting SUNY Press for publication. He answered all of my questions regarding how to solicit a proposal regardless how ridiculous the question was. Bob is a true friend and scholar.

I would like to thank the Department of Political Science at Miami University in Oxford, Ohio, and in particular the chair, Ryan Barilleaux, for giving me the time and the space to work on this book. Ryan has been a very good friend and mentor, and without him none of this would have been possible.

Nancy Kassop was instrumental in making suggestions to the introduction and the conclusion that improved the structure and the content of each. Not only is she an outstanding scholar, but she is also a wonderful editor.

Richard Pious has been a great source of inspiration for this book. He was one of our team leaders in 2001 when many of the contributors of the book came together in Washington, D.C., as part of the Supreme Court Historical Society summer scholars program. Dick has always been accessible and has helped me work through and formulate numerous ideas.

My very good friends Mark Sachleben, Andrew Dudas, Kevan Yenerall, and Mark Morris have never faltered in pushing me in my scholarly pursuits. Everyone should be so lucky to have a group of friends such as these fine gentlemen.

I would like to thank all of the individuals at SUNY Press who made this book possible: Dr. Michael Rinella, the acquisitions editor for agreeing to take this manuscript in the rough draft pages; Judith Block and her staff of editors for their work in preparing this book for final publication; and finally Susan Petrie for her help in marketing this book to as wide an audience as possible.

The greatest amount of support came from my family. My niece, Mandy Hans, helped me edit a number of the chapters. She provided a great deal of assistance in making sure that everything was grammatically correct and even more important, that each of the chapters she read made sense to her. My parents, Thomas and Bonnie, have never doubted what I can accomplish. I owe everything to them. Finally, my wife, Sandy, has been very instrumental in providing the moral support needed in taking on a project such as this. And my daughters, Megan and Zoe, give me the reason for getting out of bed in the morning. They are the best daughters a father could ask for.

Introduction

Christopher S. Kelley

The George W. Bush administration has clearly renewed scholarly interest in the use and abuse of presidential power. Following the close election of 2000, experts widely believed that President Bush would have to govern from the middle if he wanted to get anything accomplished. Bargaining and persuading, we are often told, is at the center of presidential power.

President Bush, however, tested the limits of presidential power from the start. He moved to revoke several controversial executive orders the lame-duck Clinton administration made, he issued an executive order putting into place the White House Office of Faith-Based and Community Initiatives, and in response to the energy crisis in the western United States, he formed an energy task force that worked in near secrecy. This was before the events of September 11, 2001. After September 11, President Bush was given wide latitude to act unilaterally to protect the country from the threat of terrorism. The Department of Justice pushed the controversial USA PATRIOT Act through Congress that gave law enforcement and the executive branch a great deal of power to conduct investigations and make arrests. The president's lawyers made aggressive interpretations to give the president wide discretion to hold U.S. citizens as enemy combatants, therefore holding individuals without benefit of habeas corpus relief. And the president used the authorization he was given in the fall of 2001 to fight terrorism and wage war against one semisovereign state (Afghanistan) and one sovereign state (Iraq).

The war with Iraq has been the focal point of the president's problems, and it has been the starting point from which President Bush has been called the new "Imperial President," a reference to Arthur Schlesinger's work on the state of presidential power at the time of Watergate. In fact, John Dean, who was President Nixon's White House counsel, has suggested that the Bush presidency ". . . may be the *most* imperial presidency our history has yet seen.[1]

In the last two years of President Bush's first term in office, he found himself enmeshed in all sorts of controversies involving the overexpansion of presidential authority. To name but a few, a suit was filed in federal courts challenging the secrecy of Vice President Cheney's Energy Task Force, and legal challenges were raised with regard to President Bush's detention of unlawful combatants. In two high-profile instances, President Bush asserted the right as commander in chief to detain U.S. citizens without the right of hearing charges against them or without benefit of counsel. And, as Anthony Lewis has documented, advanced by the attorneys who work in the White House Office of Legal Counsel the aggressive interpretation of constitutional and international law made a mockery of established constitutional and international legal precedent.[2] All of these arguments centered on an expansive, constitutional interpretation of presidential power.

And just like that, pundits and scholars alike began to focus on the meaning of presidential power. The Bush administration, it seemed, had come out of nowhere and in wild-eyed fashion was testing the limits of presidential power. But had it?

PRESIDENTIAL UNILATERALISM

After Watergate, the U.S. presidency was assaulted by the Congress, the media, and the U.S. public, which all sought to reign in a system they felt had become abusive. Beginning roughly with the Reagan administration, the executive branch was staffed with individuals committed to reasserting presidential power. To do this, the presidency was forced to turn to the U.S. Constitution. The Reagan administration engaged in numerous high-profile clashes with the Congress and the courts over its assertions and interpretations of presidential power. In fact, Attorney General Edwin Meese III caused a major stir when he spoke at Tulane University and defended the president's prerogative to interpret the Constitution independently, despite what the Congress or the courts said.[3]

The administration of George H. W. Bush continued the tract of aggressively asserting presidential power. For instance, the Congress refused to confirm President Bush's nominee to head the Office of Information and Regulatory Affairs (OIRA) until the administration agreed to allow the Congress a role in how the regulatory process worked. Rather than capitulate, the Bush administration simply created a regulatory council (the Council on Competitiveness) within the Executive Office of the President that the vice president chaired. The "Quayle Council," as the Council on Competitiveness came to be called, was extraordinarily effective in ensuring that all regulations the executive branch agencies developed were cost effective to business, much to the chagrin of the Congress.

The Bush administration also got creative in how it used the signing statement to win battles lost in the legislative process. The Reagan administration successfully had the signing statement added to the legislative history section of the *United States Code, Congressional and Administrative News* (USCCAN). At the time, Attorney General Edwin Meese argued that it was done "to make sure that the President's own understanding of what's in a bill is the same . . . or is given consideration at the time of statutory construction later on by a court. . . .[4]

In 1989 President Bush vetoed a foreign operations bill that contained an amendment by Rep. David Obey (D-WI) that "prohibited the sales of arms or aid to any foreign government to further U.S. foreign policy objectives if the U.S. would be prohibited from the same kind of influence."[5] A subsequent bill contained the Obey amendment again, and the president signed it. However, when he issued his signing statement, he pointed to a "colloquy" on the Senate floor as the authoritative legislative history for the bill, and would thus construe the meaning of a section of the amendment narrowly. The "colloquy" that President Bush pointed to in his signing statement was actually an alternative legislative history the Republicans in Congress crafted as a backup for the administration if the Obey amendment became law. The purpose, as Charles Tiefer points out, was to supplant "congressional legislation on a central and hotly contested issue."[6]

The Office of Legal Counsel in the Clinton administration issued two opinions[7] that underscored Attorney General Meese's argument that the president had the right to *independently* interpret the constitutionality of law. After the Republicans took control of the Congress in 1995, President Clinton simply turned inward to govern, turning to executive orders, memoranda, and signing statements, leading to the now-famous quote by Paul Begala: "Stroke of the Pen. Law of the land. Kind of cool."[8]

CALLING ATTENTION TO CONSTITUTIONALLY ORIENTED POWER

Many presidential scholars have not detected the unilateral actions of those administrations that preceded the George W. Bush administration because the predominant focus on the presidency—the Neustadt paradigm—neglects to study the importance of a public law approach to the presidency. But this has not meant that many scholars have not used a public law approach or that they have tried to call our attention to its importance.

Most recently, Kenneth Mayer wrote the lead article in the spring 2004 issue of *PRG Report*, the newsletter of the Presidency Research Group, in which he advocated challenging what the Neustadt paradigm has told us about the presidency and renewing our "focus on the explicit legal foundations of presidential action."[9] As Mayer correctly notes, since taking office, many of the more significant actions the Bush administration took were actions rooted in unilateral assertions of constitutional power.[10] By delegating the importance of the legal foundations of presidential power to the law journals, presidential scholars trained in the social sciences have neglected the importance of a public law approach to understanding presidential power.[11]

Richard Pious, long an advocate of a public law approach to studying presidential power, both countered a Neustadt-only approach and highlighted the value of a public law approach to understanding presidential power in a special 2002 issue of *Presidential Studies Quarterly*.[12] He argues that simply looking through the lens of "public approval ratings, the number of seats the president's party holds in Congress, and the length of time the president has been in office," we are often left with no explanations of success or failure.[13] An example to highlight this is President Clinton's ability to turn around his presidency in 1995 by failing to get a budget passed by the Congress.

Instead, by taking a public law approach, or in Pious's argument one that emphasizes prerogative power (defined as an expansive reading of constitutional powers), we can understand why a president "imposes tight secrecy, [confines] his deliberations to a small group, . . . [and] issues proclamations, executive orders and national security directives."[14]

THE RICH LINEAGE OF THE PUBLIC LAW APPROACH

The Neustadt approach to the presidency, often referred to as the "modern" or "strategic" presidency, has long emphasized the soft aspects of power—bargaining and persuading—and not the aggressive interpretation of constitutional powers.

As influential and important as Professor Neustadt's work is, the political environment of the 1970s, 1980s, and 1990s have made bargaining and persuading extraordinarily difficult for the president. This prompts some presidential scholars to advocate a return to the constitutional roots of the office—what Pious referred to as the "fundamental and irreducible core of presidential power."[15] Hence a president, still expected to lead, found reaching out to the Congress or the public post-Watergate nearly impossible and was forced inward toward the powers the Constitution vested to the presidency.

Thus, in the late 1970s to the present, a disparate but growing number of presidential scholars began investigating unilateral presidential actions such as "administrative clearance," "executive orders," "executive privilege," "presidential proclamations," and "parallel unilateral policy declarations." A nonexhaustive list of some early presidential scholars offering a counter to the Neustadt approach includes scholars such as Louis Fisher, who has written numerous influential books and articles examining separation-of-powers issues;[16] Robert Spitzer and his work on the presidential veto;[17] Richard Pious and his continuing efforts to build a cohesive theory around prerogative power; Mark Rozell and his focus on executive privilege; and Ryan Barilleaux and his focus on things such as parallel unilateral policy declarations.

Although some of the other scholars advocating a public law approach to the study of the presidency have invariably been missed, the point remains that it is not something that has sprung forth in the Clinton and Bush presidencies. It has a rich theoretical lineage of which we should all be cognizant.

Recently, the public law approach has enjoyed a greater recognition. For instance, the 2002 Neustadt Book Award went to Kenneth Mayer's book on executive orders, *With the Stroke of a Pen: Executive Orders and Presidential Power*,[18] and another book examined all types of new unilateral presidential powers referred to as "power tools."[19] William Howell titled his book *Power without Persuasion* to illustrate the variety of unilateral actions that presidents take because of the highly polarized political environment of the last thirty years or more.[20]

Clearly, contemporary presidential scholars are recognizing the established voices of Pious, Spitzer, Fisher, and others who have been urging presidential scholars to add the public law approach to our methodological repertoire. In fact, Pious, Spitzer, and Fisher draw from the work of Edward Corwin, whose constitutional approach to the study of the presidency in the 1940s and 1950s was the dominant approach.

What this book hopes to achieve is twofold: First is to expose the reader to a burgeoning group of scholars who use the Constitution to explain the development of presidential powers as strategic tools for chief executives from Richard Nixon to George W. Bush. For example, Christopher Kelley discusses how presidents have come to rely on presidential signing statements to protect the prerogatives of the office as well as to advance their own policy preferences. Graham Dodds explains how presidents have used executive orders across successive presidencies to exert presidential control over the administrative state—influence that extended to the independent regulatory agencies in both the Clinton and the George W. Bush administrations.

Second, all the authors use from Nixon to George W. Bush as their period of analysis. This period saw a fundamental shift in U.S. politics in general and for the presidency in particular. During this period, one president resigned, another was impeached, and still another won the Electoral College but lost the popular vote. Furthermore, the political climate during this period has become especially hostile for the president—the influence of the political party has declined, the relationship with the Congress has been poisoned, and the news media have treated each president during this period in a more negative rather than positive tenor of coverage. Yet our president is still expected to lead. Leadership has required the presidency to become very creative, and this creativity is found in the number of "power tools" forged out of the ambiguities of Article II of the Constitution.

PLAN OF THE BOOK

The chapters in this book are organized by theme rather than in chronological order. The first two chapters are more abstract, emphasizing the public law approach to the study of the presidency. The chapters that follow are organized around particular instruments recent presidents have used to gain leverage over the Congress and the courts. The book finishes with an examination of foreign policy and how presidents have continued to exercise greater unilateral control over foreign policy ventures.

In chapter 1, Richard Pious sets the tone of the book, arguing that presidential scholars need to mix their approaches to understanding the presidency rather than simply adhering to one approach. He urges a public law approach integrating one of several methods in understanding the presidency. This not only helps us to understand the executive branch, but also alerts us to instances in which the president may overstep the bounds of Article II power and act unconstitutionally.

The chapters that follow take Professor Pious's challenge and explains ways in which presidents have pushed the boundaries of presidential power to succeed in what occasionally has been a hostile political environment, to the point of abusing executive power in the name of protecting the office of the presidency.

Professor Ryan Barilleaux examines how and why recent presidents have exceeded the limits of presidential power and what effect this has had on the political system, something he refers to as *venture constitutionalism*. He argues that in the past, presidential scholars have been limited in their examination of presidential power, either by examining discrete instances of unusual presidential actions such as President Jackson's move to take money from the Bank of the United States or by establishing good cop/bad cop scenarios of how some expand power for good whereas others expand it for personal or selfish reasons.

The next three chapters examine the use (or misuse) of particular presidential instruments employed to gain leverage over the legislative process.

Graham Dodds examines the use of executive orders that enable a president to accomplish administratively what cannot be accomplished legislatively. Professor Dodds argues that the use of executive orders is not necessarily new, but the number presidents of both political parties used for strategic purposes is something that has stemmed from the political environment of the last thirty or thirty-five years. What is interesting about Professor Dodds's study is the connection between each administration from Nixon through Clinton to use the executive order to give the president control over the administrative state—something today that reaches not only executive branch agencies such as the Environmental Protection Agency, but also extends to independent regulatory agencies such as the Federal Communications Commission.

Christopher Kelley examines the "understudied" use of the presidential signing statement, which on its own is nothing more than a written and/or verbal statement the president makes after he has signed a bill into law. On its own, the signing statement has not drawn a great deal of interest because most presidential scholars have viewed them as nothing more than a presidential news release. However, beginning with the Reagan administration, the signing statement was used for deliberate political and constitutional reasons, which allowed the president either to advance his policy preferences by interpreting vague or undefined sections of a bill advantageous to the president's position or to nullify sections of a bill that the president independently determines to be unconstitutional.

Mark Rozell turns our attention to the subject of executive privilege, which he argues has always been a part of the presidency, but since the Nixon administration the use of the privilege has become more frequent due to the highly polarized political environment. Professor Rozell first examines how the use of executive privilege has developed over the course of the last thirty-five years, arguing that when a president wanted to withhold something from Congress, more often than not the executive branch would use a term other than executive privilege to do so. Professor Rozell then focuses on the George W. Bush administration and argues that the administration from the beginning sought not only to use executive privilege, but also expand its use into new areas, thus setting an important precedent for future presidents.

Robert Spitzer turns to the concept of the "protective" pocket return veto, which he argues is an "aggrandizement" of presidential power that presidential scholars have largely missed. Professor Spitzer explains that as a matter of custom, presidents and Congress agreed that the pocket veto would be used only at the end of a session of Congress—or after sine die adjournments. The Reagan administration broke this agreement, arguing that a president had the right to execute the pocket veto at any point during the legislative session. Furthermore, the George Herbert Walker Bush administration escalated the situation with the use of the "protective" pocket return veto, which involves returning the bill to Congress and at the same time issuing a pocket veto of the bill. The result was to take the qualified veto that the Founders gave to the president and make it absolute.

Kevan Yenerall puts a twist on the normal study of the rhetorical presidency by placing presidential rhetoric within the confines of presidential power. He looks at how recent presidents—in his chapter, Clinton and Bush—have used rhetoric in support of unilateral executive action. By using case studies, Professor Yenerall shows how Presidents Clinton and Bush rallied the public in support of their executive orders, memorandum, and signing statements to create what he terms the *rhetorical branch* inside the executive office.

The next two chapters examine the president's relationship with the federal courts. In the first chapter, George Thomas examines the question of whether Ronald Reagan was the sort of transformative president who brings about a fundamental change of a regime—in this instance, the New Deal regime of President Franklin Roosevelt. Professor Thomas argues that Reagan's use of judicial appointments, the Department of Justice, the Office of Legal Policy, as well as executive orders and signing statements shifted constitutional thinking in legal terms. Professor Thomas finds that the number of Supreme Court cases in the 1990s that challenged congressional interference in the activities of the states was a direct result of the regime President Reagan established in the Court in the 1980s.

In the next chapter, similar to Professor Thomas, Kevin McMahon argues that presidents have attempted to extend presidential influence into the courts by using their appointment powers, the threat of court-curbing legislation, as well as the powers of the Department of Justice. The motivation for doing this varies—it can range from being ideologically driven to seeking to implement the president's constitutional vision. He concludes that presidential and legal scholars who look only at ideological reasons for appointing individuals to the bench fail to capture the larger reasons for presidential appointment politics.

The final two chapters examine presidential power in the area of foreign policy. In the first chapter, Michael Cairo argues that presidents no longer even hint toward sharing power over war with the Congress, that instead they exercise unilateral control in what he deems to be a "triumph of the imperial presidency." Cairo looks at the Clinton and George W. Bush administrations and the strategies they have employed to exclude Congress from decisions concerning the use of force. Cairo highlights how both Clinton and Bush have used international agreements as the means to use force without consulting Congress, which is an interesting counter to Richard Rose's[21] thesis that international commitments have worked to diminish presidential power.

Patrick Haney et al. focus their chapter on how President Clinton sought to undermine Helms-Burton from the moment he signed it into law, arguing that in Clinton's signing statement, the president worked to retake presidential power that was lost in the legislative battle over the bill. The president was forced to sign the bill after Cuba shot down an airplane that carried Cuban expatriates in international waters. Thus where the president lost influence in the legislative process, he gained it back by the language he used in his signing statement.

In both the Cario and Haney et al. chapters, the authors argue that presidents have abused their constitutional authority by using unilateral means to undermine authority lost in the constitutional process.

Hopefully this book will jump-start a discussion among presidential scholars around some extremely significant powers recent presidents developed that have gone unstudied in any systematic way. I certainly do not wish to suggest that the public law approach should be *the* approach to study presidential power. Rather, if we remain cognizant of the different approaches to presidential studies, we will better be able to understand for ourselves, our students, and the public why presidents do the things that they do.

NOTES

1. John Dean, "The U.S. Supreme Court and the Imperial Presidency: How President Bush Is Testing the Limits of His Presidential Powers," http://writ.news.findlaw.com/dean/20040116.html. Dean has also taken his argument to book form. See *Worse than Watergate: The Secret Presidency of George W. Bush* (New York: Little, Brown, 2004). See also Robert Byrd, *Losing America: Confronting a Reckless and Arrogant Presidency* (New York: Norton, 2004).

2. Anthony Lewis, "Making Torture Legal," *New York Review of Books*, July 15, 2004, http://www.nybooks.com/articks/17230 (accessed August 2, 2004).

3. Edwin Meese III, "The Law of the Constitution," *Tulane Law Review* 61 (1987): 979–89.

4. Quoted in Marc N. Garber and Kurt A. Wimmer, "Presidential Signing Statements as Interpretations of Legislative Intent: An Executive Aggrandizement of Power," *Harvard Journal on Legislation* 24 (1987): 367.

5. Charles Tiefer, *The Semi-Sovereign Presidency: The Bush Administration's Strategy for Governing without Congress* (Boulder, Colo.: Westview Press, 1994), p. 38.

6. Tiefer, p. 40.

7. Walter Dellinger, "The Legal Significance of Presidential Signing Statements," Memorandum for Bernard N. Nussbaum, Counsel to the President, November 3, 1993, http://www.usdoj.gov/olc/signing.htm; Walter Dellinger, "Presidential Authority to Decline to Execute Unconstitutional Statutes, Memorandum for the Honorable Abner J. Mikva, Counsel to the President, November 2, 1994, http://www.usdoj.gov/olc/nonexcut.wpd (both accessed August 15, 2000).

8. James Bennet, "True to Form, Clinton Shifts Energies Back to U.S. Focus," *New York Times*, July 5, 1998, p. 10.

9. Kenneth Mayer, "The Return of the King? Presidential Power and the Law," *PRG Report* 26 (Spring 2004): 1.

10. Mayer, p. 11.

11. For example, the entire October 1993 issue of the *Cardozo Law Review* was devoted to the study of the Unitary Executive, which takes an expansive view of the take care and oath clauses of Article II to push presidential power.

12. Richard Pious, "Why Do Presidents Fail?" *Presidential Studies Quarterly* 32 (December 2004): 724–42. Unfortunately for Pious and his argument, his thesis had to compete with numerous theses, including one by Richard Neustadt, on the appropriate way to study the presidency. Pious's argument may have been lost among the cacophony of competing voices in this special issue of *Presidential Studies Quarterly*.

13. Pious, "Why," p. 731.

14. Pious, "Why," p. 734.

15. Richard Pious, *The American Presidency* (New York: Basic Books, 1979), p. 17.

16. See, for example, Louis Fisher, *President and Congress: Power and Policy* (New York: Free Press, 1972); *The Politics of Shared Power: Congress and the Executive*, 2nd ed. (Washington, D.C.: Congressional Quarterly Press, 1987); and *Constitutional Conflicts between Congress and the President* (Lawrence: University Press of Kansas, 1991).

17. Robert Spitzer, *The Presidential Veto : Touchstone of the American Presidency* (Albany: SUNY Press, 1988); "The Constitutionality of Presidential Line-Item Veto," *Political Science Quarterly* 112 (Summer 1997): 261–83.

18. Kenneth Mayer, *With the Stroke of a Pen: Executive Orders and Presidential Power* (Princeton, N.J.: Princeton University Press, 2001).

19 Phillip J. Cooper, *By Order of the President: The Use and Abuse of Executive Direct Action* (Lawrence: University Press of Kansas, 2002).

20. William Howell, *Power without Permission* (Princeton, N.J.: Princeton University Press, 2003). Howell's approach, however, is premised not on a public law approach but rather a rational choice approach. For an excellent review, see Robert Spitzer's review in the June 2004 issue of *Perspectives on Politics*, pp. 374–75.

21. Richard Rose, *The Postmodern President: The White House Meets the World* (Chatham, N.J.: Chatham House, 1988).

ONE

Public Law and the "Executive" Constitution

Richard M. Pious

This chapter discusses the public law approach to the study of politics and describes its central concerns when dealing with executive power. Supplementing traditional approaches legal scholars practice (analyzing the constitutionality of a claim of prerogative, its relationship to private rights, and the likelihood that the courts will uphold the claim), the public law approach political scientists use concerns the development of "prerogative governance" as a political style, the effectiveness of claims of prerogative in advancing the president's agenda or in blocking the priorities of opponents, the use of prerogative power to defend the administration in the courts or against congressional checks, the relationship of prerogative governance to "political time," and the long-term effects that the claims of prerogative have on the development of an "executive" Constitution.

PUBLIC LAW AND POLITICAL ANALYSIS

Why should political scientists, armed with advanced theoretical insights and models, and equipped with sophisticated number-crunching capabilities, concern themselves with issues of public law? And what can political scientists do to supplement the work of legal scholars?[1] Political scientists interested in questions of war and peace, diplomacy and intelligence operations, or the development of the administrative state and the national security state will find that the materials of public law and its methods of analysis enable them to come to grips with the main issues of state power.

To begin with, politics is a form of decision making about "who gets what, when, and how," and it involves a substitution for marketplace, bureaucratic command, theocratic or technocratic decision making.[2] In systems of what nineteenth-century scholars referred to as "popular government" (which is a somewhat better descriptive phrase than "democratic government"), leaders must maintain legitimacy and authority with followers.[3] Politics involves these leaders using one or more power bases (such as wealth, knowledge, force, divinity) to command or persuade through either transforming or transactional politics.[4]

Political scientists look at constitutional law, framework laws, statutory delegations, and executive actions (agreements, ordinances, orders, proclamations, memoranda, regulations) and ask political rather than legal questions: in what way are legal resources a power base? How does the strategic use of public law determine the "rules of the game"?[5] How does the substitution of legal decision making in the courts in place of other venues affect strategies and tactics of politicians, as well as the outcomes of political conflict?[6] How do the uses of constitutional and legal prerogatives transform the political time in which institutions function?[7] And how does political time influence officialdom's use of prerogative power?

The political scientist starts with the idea that to rely on the Constitution, statute law, and judicial precedents for warrant to act unilaterally is a political decision. Politicians make substitutions and engineer transformations of state power to control events, and they have never, throughout U.S. history, taken preexisting public law as a framework to which they felt themselves bound to adhere in all circumstances. The Constitution itself was established through a highly creative side-stepping of the preexisting amendment procedures of the Articles of Confederation (procedures that would have prevented the Framers from making radical changes.)[8] Washington's Neutrality Proclamation was issued without explicit sanction in the Constitution for a presidential declaration of neutrality, setting forth a fierce debate between Hamilton and Madison as to its legality.[9] During the John Adams administration the federal courts recognized that an "imperfect war" not declared by Congress could occur.[10] Jefferson purchased the Louisiana Territory and highlighted "the need to shut the country up for awhile" because nothing in the Constitution mentioned acquisition of territory.[11] Jackson fired a cabinet secretary although the Constitution makes no mention of a removal power, and he vetoed the bank bill on policy rather than on constitutional grounds, all to control financial policy and bolster his new party.[12] Lincoln used force against the secessionist states without a congressional declaration, raised forces without congressional authorization, spent funds to win over West Virginia without a congressional appropriation, suspended the writ of habeas corpus although the suspension clause appears in the article dealing with legislative powers, and eventually emancipated slaves, relying on an expanded interpretation of his powers as commander in chief rather than asking Congress for an emancipation statute.[13] Theodore Roosevelt implemented an "executive agreement" with Santo Domingo, and when some suggested he had usurped the Senate treaty powers, he responded that he would be happy to implement it as a treaty if the Senate would only consent.[14] In the aftermath of World War II presidents made war without congressional declarations, abrogated treaties without a congressional role, and claimed a reinterpretation power to redefine treaty obligations; in the aftermath of the September 11 terror attacks, the president also instituted tribunals by military order.[15]

One might offer several generalizations about the American experience with executive power and its relationship to public law: first, in making the most important decisions, officials will almost always have to go beyond preexisting boundaries and understandings about their constitutional or statutory powers; second, the irreducible core of governmental power rests not with public opinion or electoral mandates, but rather with executive officials' substitution of contestable constitutional prerogatives for congressional authorization; and third, that much of the success or failure of executive power depends on whether that substitution, when it is contested by the opposition to the policy, is considered authoritative and legitimate by Congress, the courts, and above all the American people.

Studying the politics of prerogative power is not necessarily a prescriptive exercise because it does not require the public law scholar (unlike the constitutional lawyer) to determine whether officials have "gotten it right" when they exercise and expand their formal powers. Rather, public law analysis can be an empirical and (in the broadest sense) behavioral approach that tries to understand how actors use their claims of prerogative power as institutional resources to accomplish their goals. It may rely on case studies and single *n* hypotheses, it may rely on advanced quantitative approaches (and aggregate a vast number of discrete actions, such as vetoes or executive orders), or it may even employ the formal modeling methods of game theory and rational choice). The method used is less important than the kind of question posed in the study of public law: the doctrinal issues of constitutional law or the strategic questions of political science.

PRESIDENTIAL STUDIES: PREROGATIVE GOVERNANCE AND POLITICAL POWER

Political scientists have long understood that Article II of the Constitution does not clearly define presidential powers and that its provisions remain underdefined and ambiguous or even silent at key points.[16] So presidents can wrest power from the Constitution by defining constitutional powers to gain control of the executive establishment (the appointment and removal powers); to make policy (the use of executive orders); to block policymaking by Congress (the veto); or to shield the president and White House staffers from judicial process and other checks and balances (executive privilege and testimonial privileges). Presidents have the opportunity to claim vast executive and legislative powers,[17] including the inherent powers of a "chief executive" based on an expansive reading of specific constitutional clauses.[18] They claim implied powers, arguing that, like Congress, they may take actions "necessary and proper" to put their executive powers into effect, having all the means at their disposal that the Constitution does not forbid, and they combine their constitutional powers with statutes Congress passed to expand their administrative powers, even asserting their own reading of implicit provisions in statutory law.[19] They issue executive orders, proclamations, and decrees in effect creating their own legislative power.[20] Their orders (as well as subsidiary memoranda and directives) may go beyond the scope of the laws Congress passed to deal with a subject, sometimes covering matters on which Congress has not legislated at all.[21] They claim the power to execute a "mass of legislation" taken in the aggregate, which may involve nonfeasance of particular provisions of law.[22] They claim a "dispensing power" to dispense with the execution of laws.[23] Sometimes they reinterpret congressional intent while signing bills into law through the use of "signing statements."[24] All of this can be summarized by saying that under certain circumstances the White House can institute a form of prerogative governance.[25] Rather than a constitution of separated powers, the U.S. Constitution provided, as Madison originally indicated and Richard Neustadt subsequently observed, a system of overlapping and concurrent sharing of powers among three distinct institutions.[26]

Under what circumstances are executive officials most likely to assert prerogative power? One might hypothesize that in domestic affairs they will use their powers to further policy in the aftermath of a realigning election and when they believe they have a mandate to develop new policies. The uses of prerogative to advance policy occur with greater frequency early in the term; presidents issue more executive orders early in their first term than at any other time.[27] The checks and balances on presidential prerogatives occur later in a presidential term, particularly the defeat of presidential judicial nominations.[28] Presidents use domestic prerogative power not only during times of party governance to advance the presidential agenda, but also ever since the Tyler administration they use the veto and other executive powers when public opinion runs against them, when their party majority is not cohesive, and during periods of split government to defend against policy initiatives developed by a hostile Congress.

Taking a longer perspective, one might argue that ever since the Jefferson and Jackson presidencies, we have seen a direct link between regime formation, the claims of the plebiscitary presidency, and the expansion of many other presidential prerogatives.[29] If this is correct, the likelihood is high that successful regime creation would be immediately followed by use of and validation of prerogative power to cement the regime. Regime maintenance would involve use of prerogative power, but would be complicated by weakness of successor presidents as party leaders. The dissolution of a regime would be accompanied (and perhaps preceded) by failed exercise of prerogative power, unsustainable at least in part because of the collapse of the underlying regime. In such a model the really interesting use of prerogative power comes from the winner of deviating elections—the regime outsider—playing a high-stakes game of "preemptive politics," usually in divided party government, which might well lead to an overshoot and collapse effect.[30]

For the use of high prerogatives—the diplomatic, commitment, war and peace, and covert operations—historical evidences seems to indicate that presidents are equally likely to use prerogative power when they are in a commanding political position (Franklin Roosevelt) as when they are in a precarious position (Lincoln) and at any point in the cycle of regime formation, maintenance, decay, or dissolution.[31] The shooting war in the Atlantic in 1941, the Korean police action, the escalation in Vietnam, and the second war against Iraq all occurred during periods of party government, but similar assertions of prerogative were made by Nixon in Vietnam and Cambodia, and by Clinton in Bosnia and Serbia during periods of split governance. Presidents of all stripes tend to defend and extend their claims of war-making power.[32] Neither do we find any discernible pattern for the authorization of covert operations that can be linked to exogenous political or regime factors; rather, the patterns seem to be internally generated in the national security state in ways that are not responsive to patterns of regime formation.[33]

Under what circumstance are presidents successful in their claims of prerogative power? And under what circumstances are they likely to fail? My own theory of backlash, frontlash, and oversight and collapse suggests that the key variable is the success or failure "on the ground" of the policy instituted by relying on prerogatives.[34] When the policy is successful the president gains authority and questions of legitimacy recede into the background; his party unites behind him while the opposition divides and becomes dispirited. The prerogative power is assimilated into the "living presidency" of precedent, customs, and usages. Courts, in dealing with the subsidiary issues presidential action raises (particularly questions involving property claims) will either step out of the way on procedural grounds or uphold the exercise of power. The density, repetition, consistency, and recency of such presidential actions all are likely to impress courts, as is the willingness of Congress to delegate power or acquiesce in its exercise (opinio juris). Often (although not always) political time changes as a regime solidifies itself and gains political power as a result of the success of its policy.

When a policy fails, the party system cannot accommodate the claim of prerogative. The president's party splits over the claim, whereas the opposition is most likely to unite in opposition to the claim as well as the policy. Congress may pass legislation that repudiates or overturns the policy, or framework legislation that mandates consultation and interbranch policy codetermination in the future. The assertion of power is not assimilated into the "precedential presidency," and congressional or judicial checks create a countervailing precedent. This is not to say that the president might not try to exercise the prerogative in the future, but until he does so successfully, the powers remain contestable and the constitutional issues remain undecided.

Finally, in an overshoot and collapse situation the exercise of power is considered so illegitimate that the president faces censure or impeachment. The administration collapses (with investigations and resignations of top aides), or circles the wagons with claims of testimonial and executive privileges.[35] Congressional investigations lead to initiation of impeachment proceedings with a president either going through with it or resigning. In two instances (Nixon and Reagan) the collapse of the administration meant that political power moved to secretaries of state, who along with new White House aides held the administration together. In effect a form of quasi-parliamentary governance was instituted with a "prime minister" and top White House aides functioning only because they retained the confidence of Congress. Perhaps this is one reason why secretaries of state are often left "out of the loop" in sensitive national security operations run out of the White House, such as destabilization efforts against the Allende regime in Chile and the arms for hostages deals in the Iran-Contra affair.

Finally, whether presidents are impeached, and what happens to them if they are, depends more on political than legal factors. In the case of Andrew Johnson, Republican presidential ambitions played a key role in the votes of Republican senators voting to acquit.[36] In the case of Richard Nixon, public opinion shifted away from the president and several Republicans on the House Judiciary Committee went wobbly, leading to a vote for an impeachment resolution, followed by a delegation of Republican conservatives heading to the White House to convince Nixon to offer his resignation;

in the case of Bill Clinton, public opinion shifted to the White House and the case in the Senate was doomed as Democrats held firm.[37]

Future empirical studies will eventually be able to prove or disprove the idea that policy viability is the independent variable, and the changes in legitimacy and authority relationships become the mechanisms through which the dependent variables of constitutional interpretation and sustainable prerogative governance are affected.[38]

CONGRESSIONAL STUDIES: FRAMEWORK LAWS AND COLLABORATIVE GOVERNANCE

When Congress wishes to respond to what it views as excessive claims of presidential prerogative, it passes framework statutes requiring interbranch codetermination and balanced institutional participation.[39] Propaedeutic rather than retrospective, members of Congress involved in interbranch policy codetermination consider new policies rather than investigate past performance. The laws establish action-forcing processes with deadlines, providing incentives for informal consultations between executive officials and legislators or their staffers. Other features of these laws include committee clearances and informal legislative vetoes (now that some of the formal legislative veto mechanisms have been ruled unconstitutional), statutory requirements for agency innovation and presentation of policy options to congressional committees.

Presidents have objected to (and sometimes vetoed) these framework laws, claiming they infringe on presidential prerogatives.[40] Their passage has been followed by minimal compliance: providing brief and misleading reports; offering briefings instead of engaging in real consultations; and using loopholes to evade provisions.[41] The White House is contemptuous of congressional motives and lacks confidence in legislative capabilities because of partisan cleavage in foreign policy, because of a fear of legislative leaks to the media, and ultimately, because presidents believe that their constitutional prerogatives permit them to act outside these frameworks. Much of the study of public law involves evaluation of the effectiveness of these framework laws, including those dealing with war powers, intelligence operations, arms sales, and fiscal policymaking.

In studying intelligence operations, for example, public law scholars have identified phenomena such as policy inversion enabling operatives to make policy rather than merely implement it and in ways that keep them away from congressional oversight; privatization, so that the actual operations are conducted by nongovernmental entities; and off-the-shelf, stand-alone organizations funded outside of the appropriations processes.[42] Scholars focusing on Congress have asked if legislators follow up on formal provisions embodied in law; if legislators really want to be consulted or if they are content with briefings; and whether legislators actually intend to use mechanisms such as the legislative veto or whether these are mere "covers" instituted when vast delegations of power to the executive and the abdication of a congressional role is really intended.

JUDICIAL STUDIES: POWER STAKES AND THE PREROGATIVE TO DECIDE

Political scientists study the behavior of federal judges and Supreme Court justices when they adjudicate claims of prerogative and develop the constitutional law of presidential-congressional relations. Although legal scholars (and some political scientists) are most concerned with the development of legal doctrines and practicing lawyers are most concerned with their ability to state the law so they can properly advise clients as to the likelihood of favorable or adverse decisions, the political scientist can also focus on different questions: when and to what extent will courts render a decision when prerogatives are claimed? What reasons might account for courts deciding not to rule on such claims?

Very few cases exist in which federal courts have ruled that a president has violated the Constitution.[43] More often federal courts, even if they are willing to rule against the government, will do so by ruling against a lower level official carrying out presidential orders, rather than against the president himself.[44] An adverse decision is more likely to show "respect for a coordinate branch of government" by being cast as a declaratory judgment, giving the president time to comply once the law has been stated.[45] Similarly, federal courts also treat Congress with respect for a coordinate branch when the issue involves legislative prerogatives. In *Buckley v. Valeo*, for example, the court had to deal with the question of whether Congress could appoint four of six members of the Federal Elections Commission (FEC). Rather than rule the congressional appointment power was unconstitutional, the court offered Congress the choice: its appointees could not be considered "officers of the United States," and therefore the FEC as constituted could not issue judicially enforceable regulations; however, if Congress amended the law so that the president appointed all members, the courts could enforce its regulations.[46] Congress amended the statute.

One analysis of the resolution of this issue suggests, and others going back to *Marbury v. Madison*, that the judiciary's own power base is its power to decide. In developing its own prerogative of judicial review, not explicitly provided for in the Constitution, the Supreme Court managed to fashion a self-executing decision by finding a law unconstitutional that dealt with its own jurisdiction, and thus a law that neither Congress nor the departments of government executed, meaning that the court's decision could not be disobeyed. In *Buckley v. Valeo*, similarly, the court used its own powers to enforce regulations as an incentive for Congress to relinquish its appointment powers over FEC commissioners.

Federal courts have developed many ways of avoiding decision: restrictive interpretations of the jurisdiction of the court; limiting the standing of parties; determining that the dispute is not a case or controversy; claiming it is not ripe or alternatively that the issue is moot; claiming a lack of justiciability; and using the doctrines of political questions. The Supreme Court may deny certiorari or per curium dismiss cases involving presidential power without opinion.[47] Rather than studying the phenomena in terms of the correctness or incorrectness of its application of the doctrines of "political questions" and justiciability and the law of remedial equity, political scientists can study it empirically to develop generalizations regarding the circumstances as well as the timing under which the courts will rule. The stern lecture the Supreme Court read to Lincoln about the jurisdiction of federal courts during wartime was given, one remembers, after the Civil War was over—and after Lincoln was dead.[48] The decisions upholding the internment of Japanese and Japanese Americans during World War II, but requiring that individual proceedings be instituted to allow detainees to demonstrate their loyalty, were decided once the tide of war had turned and almost three years after evacuations had been ordered.[49]

Another analysis worth political scientists' pursuing would test the hypothesis that courts are most likely to rule against presidents or Congress—rather than evade by using the doctrine of political question or other procedural hurdles—when their own prerogatives have been infringed. In the cases involving claims of immunity or testimonial privilege and executive privilege, courts have ruled against the White House to reassert the central claims of the judiciary to determine the admissibility of evidence and to render judgment.[50] Similarly, in some of the recent terrorism cases, several lower court judges seemed particularly impatient with arguments that "the extent of the emergency determines the extent of the power" and that the government, not the courts, decides on the extent of power to be exercised, what evidence is to be admitted in the proceeding, or whether news media would have access.[51] In the past Supreme Court justices have been particularly impatient with arguments presidential counsel (or even presidents themselves) occasionally put forth that they might not obey a decision of the Court.[52] Or that they would treat decisions the federal courts intend as broad guidelines to bureaucracies in handling their own administrative caseloads to be applicable only in specific cases—positions from which the Department of Justice was forced to recede during the Reagan administration.

Again, political time is a useful concept that may help us sort out issues of political behavior on the bench, although it will have its limitations. One might assume that a lengthy period in which one party controlled the White House and Congress would lead to a judiciary sympathetic to the administration claims of prerogative. Such a political time model would be sorely tested by the *Steel Seizure* decision for example.[53] One might see it affirmed, however, in *Nixon v. U.S.*, in which a preexisting New Deal judicial regime ruled against a presidency standing in opposition to that regime.[54] Even in a period of strong regime formation, studying the other factors that intervene is beneficial: internal conceptions about the judicial role, the impact of stare decisis, and above all, considerations of institutional judicial power and how to protect it.

PUBLIC LAW RESEARCH: INTERDISCIPLINARY APPROACHES

The future of public law research will involve collaborative efforts with political scientists and others using complementary approaches to studying problems of power, authority, and legitimacy. Following are a few thoughts on how these efforts might develop into fruitful lines of research.

SITUATIONAL CONSTITUTIONALISM. Public law scholars intent on doctrinal analysis will find continuing the work of "critical law" scholars, particularly those focusing on "situational constitutionalism," useful.[55] Why do impeachment crises always take a partisan turn, so that arguments from one impeachment to the next are not only recycled, but they are also appropriated by the opposition, so that the 1868 Republican arguments are used by the 1973 Democrats, and the 1973 Democratic arguments are recycled by the 1998 Republicans?[56] One could make similar arguments about the legislative veto debates: Reaganites were for the veto before 1980, particularly to be used by Congress against rulings of regulatory agencies, but turned against it once Reagan became president. Similarly one sees partisan shifts in the debates over presidential war powers: Republicans took an expansive view until Clinton came into office, then a more restrictive view in the late 1990s, then back to the expansive position when George W. Bush took office—flip-flops complemented by the Democrats' shift of positions as well, from opposition to presidential prerogative, to support for it, and then to opposition again.[57] Of course parties flip-flop on issues—one thinks of the question of reciprocal trade or foreign aid bills in the 1950s and 1960s—but why would constitutional interpretation not be more principled and be an exception to the rule of partisan positioning?

Behavioral Political Science. We need to know a great deal more about when and how prerogative powers are used and how their use correlates with election cycles, public opinion, years in office, congressional voting patterns, and other quantified phenomena that are staples of behavioral political science. Fruitful studies of the constitutional convention using roll-call analysis of states, for example, have substantially changed our understanding of compromises involving executive power.[58] Studies of the veto power, for example, have developed some generalizations about when vetoes are most likely to be used, when they are designed to further "veto bargaining," and perhaps most important, under what circumstances they are most likely to be overturned.[59] Going a bit deeper, one might also want to link certain prerogative actions (such as presidential pardons or the issuance of executive orders and memoranda) or positions about constitutional powers (such as the legislative veto) with individual and political action committee (PAC) contributions in much the way legislative activity can be correlated with patterns of campaign contributions.

Rational Choice Modeling. The use of rational choice methodologies, particularly game theory, may offer useful insights through simplified models, particularly in veto bargaining and nomination "games." But the early models may be too simplified and that provides an opening for fruitful collaboration between model builders and those working in more traditional fields of public law.

Consider the simplified models involving a president and Congress in veto bargaining. Not all vetoes can be positioned in a single liberal-conservative spatial model. Some legislation involves "value politics" with not much room for compromising spatially, such as abortion funding cutoffs, where the issue is not really the money but the morality of the activity. Other legislation involves the scope of governmental power (issues involving federalism) or presidential war powers, or the jurisdiction of the judiciary. Spatial modeling does not always capture the essence of the policy disagreements, which may be discontinuous and not subject to much movement along a continuum. Moreover, not all payoffs can be expressed in terms of spatial positioning even on issues where such positioning is valid. Consider budget, deficit, and tax politics, which are spatially defined. Even so, other payoffs that are involved in these games involve media coverage and public opinion (which translates into public approval and prestige ratings); international expectations about U.S. policies that may serve as inducements or constraints; and of course (clearly rational choice has a lot to say about this) constituency payoffs that affect elections. Veto politics often involves the calibration of the internal spatial shifts with the external payoffs. This affects White House calculations about when and how to communicate to Congress, to posture, to make offers of compromise, to walk away, and to negotiate again. Finally, the early veto bargaining models do not specify all outcomes. In addition to "sign the bill" or "veto the bill," the president has the option to pass without his signature, register objections to sections in a "signing statement" and then narrow enforcement or even refuse to implement. These involve "dispensing" powers as well as (prior to the Budget and Impoundment Act of 1974) the assertion of power to impound appropriations and other bills involving budget authority.

American Political Development. We need to continue efforts to understand the development of government offices that deal in legal matters. The development of the White House counsel and other legal counsel (Department of State, Department of Defense, Joint Chiefs of Staff, and Central Intelligence Agency [CIA]), the question of how much institutional memory exists (and would be desirable to foster), and the study of the role of counsel and the various political and ethical cross-currents facing counsel are all important issues to study, and much important work has already been undertaken.[60] Asking questions about the relationship between partisanship and situational constitutionalism on the one hand and between institutional memory and legal codes of ethics on the other will be especially important.

A range of new materials needs to be incorporated into public law analysis. Consider the parallel unilateral policy declaration (PUPD), which at times can take the place of an executive agreement or treaty and which may be only the beginning with regard to informal mechanisms to coordinate policies with other nations.[61] Or the system by which the executive order sometimes gives way or is supplemented by White House or agency memoranda.[62] Regulatory clearances and cost-benefit clearances now complement legislative and budgetary clearances.[63] The Supreme Court constrains the formal legislative veto, and then it went "underground" as other arrangements were made among congressional committees and between committees and agencies that provides for a functional substitute.[64]

Perhaps the most important fusion in public law studies in the near future will be to incorporate more international law materials. In particular, regulatory studies will need to incorporate materials from various trade and environment regimes; war powers studies will need to incorporate more materials involving the United Nations, regional organizations, and regimes such as the Geneva conventions and the new International Criminal Court. The question to answer behaviorally is not the question of the international lawyers: should the president be bound by international law?[65] Rather, the issues Richard Rose poses are particularly apt: under what circumstances might reliance on presidential prerogative power lead to "global failure" in which the president faces backlash or collapse at home and isolation within the world community?[66]

NEW INSTITUTIONALISM. "New institutionalism" is a derivative of rational choice methodology. The approach is in its infancy, but already some of its champions have discussed the importance of incorporating prerogative powers into their analyses.[67] Clearly the principal/agent issues that are involved in delegations of power by Congress or the rule making of the bureaucracy, are easily transferable to the analysis of the use of prerogative power. Neustadt's clerkship concept can be applied to the principal/agent problem: when the president relies on prerogative power, to what extent is he a principle or an agent? To what extent is he acting on his own agenda? And to what extent is this a form of clerkship for other interests?[68] To some extent a transactional model may be applicable: the president may offer up his formal powers (an appointment, a threatened veto, an executive order, or other regulation) to advance interests of others to win over members of Congress for his legislative agenda. In some ways then prerogative power is more than a vantage point; it becomes a readily transferable "gift" for others.

UNCERTAINTY, RISK, AND PREROGATIVE POWER. Related to the study of executive prerogative is the question of how presidents manage uncertainty and risk. We need to develop systematic hypotheses that can be tested about the probability of failure or success when prerogative is exercised and when it substitutes for other forms of governance. Such studies would link up with research about decision-making processes. Decision dysfunctions may involve failure of data collection, failure of theory, or failure to manage small-group decision making in applying data and theory. One important research question would involve the way the president negotiates risk with lower level officials and how these involve constitutional and legal considerations. Researchers would study a variation of the law of anticipated reactions: the president, knowing in advance that the use of controversial prerogatives will have to be legitimized sooner or later, and knowing that the authority of the president will be at stake, operationalizes policy through risk negotiation to protect his stakes, even if this lowers the odds of success. In the Bay of Pigs invasion Kennedy shifted the location of the operation and put stringent conditions on U.S. tactical support to preserve "deniability"; in assassination attempts against Castro certain organized crime figures were used; in the Watergate break-in campaign contributions were kept out of party coffers and used to hire burglars; in the Iran-Contra affair, the transfer of arms to Iran involved using commercial cutouts known as the Enterprise. The question of how political vulnerability and legal liability may affect operational planning and execution in ways that actually raise the probability of failure (even though they are designed to provide "plausible deniability") bears directly on the viability of unfettered presidential judgment and unilateral prerogative governance.

CONSTITUTIONAL TRANSFORMATIONS: THE RED LINES

One final responsibility rests on public law scholars, which is the defense of constitutional principles and value—a duty that rests on all citizens in a democracy. In periods of crisis governance this requires heightened vigilance and sensitivity about whether fundamental constitutional transformations are needed to meet external or internal threats. What follows are red flags that signal institutional innovations that would take us to the point where countervailing centers of power, particularly the media and political parties, might be intimidated, leading to a situation in which only the form but not the substance of constitutional and democratic government would remain. These are issues on which public law scholars have done much research.[69] What follows are thoughts about a research agenda in public law dealing with national security matters.

High Prerogative: The Preemption Doctrine. We need to prevent an "imperial presidency" from relying on the presidential prerogative to engage in war with a foreign nation without a congressional declaration of war, its functional equivalent, or authorization under the War Powers Resolution of 1973. Congressional hearings over the summer of 2002, skepticism by congressional leaders, insistence that Bush explain himself to them and the American people, and Congress's eventual authorization of hostilities were all signs that constitutional mechanisms were still working. However, President Bush has developed a doctrine of preemption to replace the cold war doctrines of deterrence. "A nightmare scenario would be if a terrorist organization such as al Qaeda were to link up with a barbaric regime such as Iraq and thereby, in essence, possess weapons of mass destruction," Bush warned. "We cannot allow that to happen."[70] In his 2002 State of the Union address, then in his June 1, 2002, commencement address at West Point, and finally in his September 12, 2002, address to the United Nations, Bush espoused his doctrine. Political scientists can consider the hypothesis that a unilateral approach to war making risks converting the presidency into an institution with little authority at home and no legitimacy abroad.

National Security State Power. The privatization of intelligence initiatives, such as in the Iran-Contra affair, in which unvouchered funds can be used to hire contracted operatives, leads to excesses and illegalities by operatives who remain unaccountable to political authority. It also leads to policy inversion in which the operatives themselves make their own policies (and their own rules) and can get away with more and more because those who set up the operation in the first place can no longer afford its exposure.[71] "Rogue elephant" intelligence operations that can be plausibly denied, such as the CIA assassination attempts in the 1970s, in the past led to problems of accountability and excesses on the part of the operatives, who mounted assassination attempts against foreign leaders. Whether rogue operations and plausible deniability would occur if a national counterintelligence service is created or if Pentagon Special Operations Forces are involved is worth researching. Some national security officials are already developing the legal theory that the United States is at war, and therefore executive orders banning assassination are not viable (and which the president can change in any event) and that they are a legitimate means of exercising our right of self-defense against terrorism. Certain controls on the CIA's Special Activities Division have been rescinded to allow for assassinations, and more than $1 billion in additional funding has been allocated for covert operations against terrorists, although a corresponding development of framework legislation for control of these operations has not occurred.[72]

The growing use of U.S. paramilitary organizations of trainers, logisticians, communications specialists, and special operations commandos, especially those contracted by corporations concerned with the security of their personnel and property, or unstable governments, is another area that should be researched.[73] The militarization of security forces can in the future lead to excesses of a style well known in Latin-American authoritarian regimes. Former government officials often move into private sector security and antiterrorism efforts, and they retain their contacts with government counterparts.

The armed forces may, in the near future, engage in policing activities within the United States. The Posse Comitatus Act of 1878 made it a crime for U.S. military forces to engage in civilian law enforcement on U.S. soil.[74] General Ralph Eberhart, head of Pentagon's Northern Command charged with defending the homeland, proposed to ease these restrictions. The president already can use troops where law enforcement has broken down or where the United States is under enemy attack, to put down insurrections, assist Secret Service in protective duties, and help in drug interdiction. The military already can provide equipment, training, and advice to law enforcement agencies. In 1997 Congress gave the Pentagon power to coordinate activities with the Department of Justice to respond to biological and chemical attacks. If the military is given the power to make arrests or collect evidence for law enforcement purposes, political scientists need to investigate whether political leadership orders the use of military forces to conduct surveillance on the opposition party (as it did in the 1960s when President Johnson ordered the military to spy on dissident delegates at the Democratic National Convention in 1964) or to intimidate political opponents on the basis of vague allegations of "terrorist activities."

The growing cooperation between the CIA and Federal Bureau of Investigation (FBI) is worthy of study, including the new authority that allows the CIA access to grand jury information, as well as FBI wiretaps and criminal investigations.[75] Because secret testimony can be compelled and witnesses may be required to testify, the grand jury, if used improperly, could become an instrument designed for both domestic political investigation and foreign intelligence investigations, eroding Fourth Amendment rights against search and seizure and Fifth Amendment rights against self-incrimination. These practices could convert the Foreign Intelligence Surveillance Act (FISA) into a means of obtaining broadened warrant to go after domestic political opposition, rather than remain focused on a foreign threat of terrorism.[76]

Amendments to FISA must be closely monitored.[77] The Department of Justice argues that the FBI can use searches and wiretaps "primarily for a law enforcement purpose, as long as a significant foreign intelligence purpose remains."[78] Importantly, we must determine if using CIA and National Security Council (NSC) intelligence information by the FBI and by prosecutors is adequately supervised by the federal courts, particularly the FISA court, which has approved more than 10,000 warrants and never turned a request down. Additionally, no surveillance information ever been disqualified in a court proceeding. Worrisome signs of abuses exist, however: the Foreign Intelligence Surveillance Court (FISC), in an open opinion on May 17, 2002, unanimously criticized the FBI for providing misleading information on seventy-five applications for eavesdropping warrants during the Clinton administration and for doing the same thereafter, including applications under the new USA PATRIOT Act. The court rejected Attorney General Ashcroft's proposal for new authority to allow criminal prosecutors and FBI counterintelligence agents to work together. (This would make it easier for agents who do not have "probable cause" to install a wiretap by going to the intelligence court.) The FISC referred its decision to the Senate Judiciary Committee for further oversight. The Department of Justice appealed the decision to the U.S. Foreign Intelligence Surveillance Court of Review (three semiretired appeals court judges appointed by the chief justice of the United States), which held its deliberations in secret in the Department of Justice building itself—and only heard the government's side of the issue. After some uproar the appeals court agreed to provide the Senate Judiciary Committee with an "unclassified copy" of its ruling and a transcript of the proceedings. (From there the decision could be appealed and could go to a secret session of the U.S. Supreme Court.) In its appeal, the Department of Justice argued that FISA was trying to "micromanage" Department of Justice antiterror efforts and that it "raised significant constitutional questions" that involved separation of powers and interference with the "core functions of the executive." Just as worrisome as the provisions in the law are the Department of Justice regulations to decentralize the authorization to wiretap. FBI field offices are now permitted to make decisions about preliminary investigations. Approval for Carnivore eavesdropping on e-mail and Internet surveillance runs from an assistant attorney general to field offices. This might create a rogue elephant plausible deniability system to protect upper echelons of the Department of Justice and the FBI, which are most likely to follow past practices and mishandle the paperwork to avoid a paper trail that could provide information on their own decisions to direct the surveillance.

CONCLUSION

The public law approach is not the only methodology that political scientists should use to study decision making in U.S. politics, but it enables students of politics to go for the jugular rather than for the capillaries. Indeed, all important issues in U.S. public life, particularly issues of war and peace, diplomacy and international economic relations, and internal security, have questions of constitutional law and executive prerogative at their core. Developing an understanding of how executive officials use constitutional and statutory law as a power base, how they substitute prerogative governance for collaborative decision making, how they avoid checks and balances, and how they evade statutory frameworks requiring interbranch policy collaboration seems to be a prerequisite for any serious political scientist to claim an understanding of how executive power functions in the U.S. system of government.

NOTES

1. Some political scientists work on traditional issues of constitutional law: Has a line of cases been correctly decided, and are those decisions faithful to the logic of preexisting law? Is a statute constitutional? Does (and should) the interpretation of a statute or a decision of a court adhere to original intent? Are government officials exercising their powers constitutionally and lawfully? These scholars also develop the institutional history of an office or department of government, especially the development of the presidency, and try to determine either the original intent or embedded meaning of legal doctrines. See Edward S. Corwin, *The President: Office and Powers, 1787–1948*, 3rd ed., rev. (New York: New York University Press, 1948), for a study in institutional development, and Louis Fisher, *Presidential War Power* (Lawrence: University Press of Kansas, 1995), for a doctrinal analysis.

2. Harold Lasswell, *Politics: Who Gets What, When, How* (New York: World Publishing, 1958); Charles Lindblom, *Politics and Markets* (New York: Basic Books, 1977).

3. Carl Friedrich, *Man and His Government* (New York: McGraw-Hill, 1963), pp. 216–46.

4. Harold Lasswell and Abraham Kaplan, *Power and Society* (New Haven, Conn.: Yale University Press, 1950), pp. 83–84; Richard Neustadt, *Presidential Power* (New York: Wiley, 1960), pp. 29–49.

5. David Truman, *The Governmental Process* (New York: Knopf, 1951), p. 159.

6. E. E. Schattschneider, *The Semi-Sovereign People* (New York: Holt, Rinehart and Winston, 1960), pp. 1–26.

7. Stephen Skowronek, *The Politics Presidents Make* (Cambridge, Mass.: Belknap Press, 1993), pp. 49–58.

8. The original mandate for the Constitutional Convention came from Congress and required the convention to report amendments to the Articles which would have required a unanimous vote for passage. The convention replaced this requirement with its own ratification mechanism in the text of the new Constitution, requiring only nine states' approval to go into effect. As James Madison put it, "The people were, in fact, the fountain of all power," and "by resorting to them, all difficulties were got over. They could alter constitutions as they pleased." The existing Congress, bowing to popular pressure, passed a resolution agreeing to the procedures set forth in the draft of the new Constitution. See James Madison, *Notes of Debates in the Federal Convention of 1787* (Athens: Ohio University Press, 1966), p. 564.

9. On the debates over the constitutionality of the act, see Christopher Pyle and Richard Pious, *The President, Congress and the Constitution* (New York: Free Press, 1984), pp. 54–60.

10. *Bas v. Tingy*, 4 Dallas 37 (1800).

11. On Jefferson's reasoning see his letter to John Breckenridge in *The Works of Thomas Jefferson*, Paul L. Ford, ed. [Federal Edition] (New York and London: G. P. Put-

nam and Sons, 1892–1899), pp. 244–45; also Arthur M. Schlesinger Jr., *The Imperial Presidency* (Boston: Houghton Mifflin, 1973), p. 35.

12. Leonard D. White, *The Jacksonians* (New York: Macmillan, 1954), pp. 104–42.

13. Edward Corwin, *The President: Office and Powers, 1787—1948* (New York: New York University Press, 1948), pp. 275–83; Clinton Rossiter, *Constitutional Dictatorship* (Princeton, N.J.: Princeton University Press, 1948), pp. 223–39; Herman Belz, "Lincoln and the Constitution: The 'Dictatorship Question' Reconsidered," *Congress and the Presidency* 15 (Autumn 1988): 147–64.

14. On the development of executive agreements see John B. Moore, "Treaties and Executive Agreements," *Political Science Quarterly* 20 (September 1905): 385–420; Quincy Wright, "United States and International Agreements: Treaties and Executive Agreements," *American Journal of International Law* 38 (July 1944): 341–55; Edwin M. Borchard, "Shall the Executive Agreement Replace the Treaty?" *American Journal of International Law* 38 (October 1944): 637–43; John R. Stevenson, "Constitutional Aspects of the Executive Agreement Procedure," *Department of State Bulletin* 66 (June 19, 1972): 840–51.

15. On reinterpretation powers, see Abram Chayes and Antonia Chayes, "Testing and Development of 'Exotic' Systems under the ABM Treaty: The Great Reinterpretation Caper," *Harvard Law Review* 99 (1986): 1956–71. Joseph R. Biden Jr., and John B. Ritch III, "The Treaty Power: Upholding a Constitutional Partnership," *University of Pennsylvania Law Review* 137 (May 1989): 1529–58. On treaty termination powers, see David. G. Adler, "The Framers and Treaty Termination: A Matter of Symmetry," *Arizona State Law Journal* (1981): 891–924; Raoul Berger, "The President's Unilateral Termination of the Taiwan Treaty," *Northwestern University Law Review* 75 (November 1980): 577–634; J. Terry Emerson, "The Legislative Role in Treaty Abrogation," *Journal of Legislation* 5 (1978): 46–80; Louis Henkin, "Litigating the President's Power to Terminate Treaties," *American Journal of International Law* (October 1979): 647–54; Michael J. Glennon, "Treaty Process Reform: Saving Constitutionalism without Destroying Diplomacy," *University of Cincinnati Law Review* (April 1983): 84–107.

16. See the 1838 critique of constitutional commentator (and cabinet secretary) Abel Upshur, *A Brief Inquiry into the Nature and Character of Our Federal Government* (New York: Da Capo Press Reprint Edition, 1971), p. 116.

17. James Hart, "Ordinance Making Power of the President," *North American Review* 218 (July 1923): 59–66; Joel L. Fleishman and Arthur H. Aufses, "Law and Orders: The Problem of Presidential Legislation," *Law and Contemporary Problems* 40 (Summer 1976): 1–45; Louis Fisher, "Delegating Power to the President," *Journal of Public Law* 19 (1970): 251–82; Theodore J. Lowi, "Two Roads to Serfdom: Liberalism, Conservatism and Administrative Power," *American University Law Review* 36 (1987): 295–322.

18. Edward Corwin, "The President as Administrative Chief," *Journal of Politics* 1 (February 1939): 17–61; Clinton Rossiter, "The Constitutional Significance of the Executive Office of the President," *American Political Science Review* 43 (December 1949): 1206–16.

19. *Dames and Moore v. Regan*, 453 U.S. 654 (1981).

20. John M. Carey and Matthew Soberg Shugart, *Executive Decree Authority* (New York: Cambridge University Press, 1998); Philip Cooper, *By Order of the Presi-*

dent (Lawrence: University Press of Kansas, 2002); J. Christopher Deering and Forrest Maltzman, "The Politics of Executive Orders: Legislative Constraints on Presidential Power," *Political Research Quarterly* 52 (December 1999): 767–83.

21. Phillip J. Cooper, "The Law: Presidential Memoranda and Executive Orders: Of Patchwork Quilts, Trump Cards, and Shell Games." *Presidential Studies Quarterly* 31 (March 2001): 126–41.

22. The mass of legislation argument is found in many cases: for examples, see *In re Debs*, 158 U.S. 564 (1895); *NTEU v. Nixon*, 492 F. 2d 587 (1974); and *Train v. New York*, 420 U.S. 35 (1975).

23. A. L. Weil, "Has the President of the United States the Power to Suspend the Operation of an Act of Congress?" *California Law Review* 1 (March 1913): 230–50; Arthur S. Miller and Jeffrey H. Bowman, "Presidential Attacks on the Constitutionality of Federal Statutes: A New Separation of Powers Problem," *Ohio State Law Journal* 40 (1979): 51–80; Arthur Miller, "The President and the Faithful Execution of the Laws," *Vanderbilt Law Review* 40 (March 1987): 389–406.

24. Marc N. Garber and Kurt A. Wimmer, "Presidential Signing Statements as Interpretations of Legislative Intent: An Executive Aggrandizement of Powers," *Harvard Journal of Legislation* 24 (Summer 1987): 154–64; more generally Philip Cooper, *By Order of the President: The Use and Abuse of Executive Direct Action* (Lawrence: University Press of Kansas, 2002).

25. Larry Arnhart, "The God-like Prince: John Locke, Executive Prerogative, and the American Presidency," *Presidential Studies Quarterly* 9 (Spring 1979): 121–30; Thomas Langston and Michael Lind, "John Locke and the Limits of Presidential Prerogative," *Polity* 24 (Fall 1991): 49–68; Leonard R. Sorenson, "The Federalist Papers on the Constitutionality of Executive Prerogative," *Presidential Studies Quarterly* 18 (Spring 1988): 267–83; George Winterton, "The Concept of Extra-Constitutional Executive Power in Domestic Affairs," *Hastings Constitutional Law Quarterly* 7 (1979): 1–46; Harvey Mansfield Jr., "The Modern Doctrine of Executive Power," *Presidential Studies Quarterly* 17 (Spring 1987): 237–52; Joseph Bessette and Jeffrey Tulis, *The Presidency in the Constitutional Order* (Baton Rouge: Louisiana State University Press, 1981): 3–30; Jean S. Holder, "The Sources of Presidential Power: John Adams and the Challenge to Executive Primacy," *Political Science Quarterly* 101 (1986): 601–16; Edward S. Corwin, "Some Aspects of the Presidency," *Annals of the American Academy of Political and Social Science* 218 (November 1941): 122–31; Douglas Hoekstra, "Presidential Power and Presidential Purpose," *Review of Politics* 47 (October 1985): 566–87; Robert Scigliano, "The President's 'Prerogative Power,'" in *Inventing the American Presidency*, Thomas E. Cronin, ed. (Lawrence: University Press of Kansas, 1989), pp. 236–56.

26. James Madison, *The Federalist Papers*, No. 47. Edited by Jacob E. Cooke (Middletown, Conn.: Wasleyan University Press, 1961), pp. 324–27; Richard Neustadt, *Presidential Power* (New York: Wiley, 1960), p. 26.

27. See Kenneth R. Mayer, *With the Stroke of a Pen* (Princeton, N.J.: Princeton University Press, 2001), p. 99. Clearly, we still have a great deal to understand about the timing of the use of such powers, although in the case of executive orders and vetoes, recent studies such as Mayer's have cast a great deal of light on timing and frequency of use. See also George A. Krause and Jeffrey E. Cohen, "Opportunity, Constraints, and the Development of the Institutional Presidency: The Issuance of Executive Orders, 1939–96," *The Journal of Politics* 62 (February 2000): 88–114.

28. Thomas Halper, "Senate Rejection of Supreme Court Nominees," *Drake Law Review* 102 (September 1972): 102–13.

29. Theodore Lowi, *The Personal President* (Ithaca, N.Y.: Cornell University Press, 1985).

30. Stephen Skowronek, *The Politics Presidents Make* (Cambridge, Mass.: Belknap Press, 1993), pp. 43–44.

31. An alternative "risk homeostasis" hypothesis exists, however, which stipulates that presidents with political capital to spare, irrespective of their place in "political time," are more likely to engage in risky business: Lyndon Johnson's escalation of the Vietnam War on his own prerogative and George W. Bush's military expeditions in Afghanistan and then Iraq could fit into such a model. For example, a correlation exists between high approval ratings in the polls and presidential use of the armed forces. On risk homeostasis and prerogative power, see Richard M. Pious, "Why Do Presidents Fail?" *Presidential Studies Quarterly* 32 (December 2002): 724–43; also Timothy Y. C. Cotton, "War and American Democracy: Electoral Costs of the Last Five Wars," *Journal of Conflict Resolution* 30 (December 1986): 616–35; Richard J. Stoll, "The Guns of November: Presidential Reelections and the Use of Force, 1947–1982," *Journal of Conflict Resolution* 28 (June 1984): 231–46.

32. David Gray Adler, "The Constitution and Presidential Warmaking: The Enduring Debate," *Political Science Quarterly* 103 (1988): 1–36.

33. John Prados, *The Presidents' Secret Wars: CIA and Pentagon Covert Operations from World War II through the Persian Gulf* (Chicago: Dee, 1996); also Steven R. Weissman, "CIA Covert Action in Zaire and Angola: Patterns and Consequences," *Political Science Quarterly* 94 (Summer 1979): 263–86; Emmanuel Adler, "Executive Command and Control in Foreign Policy: the CIA's Covert Activities," *Orbis* 23 (Fall 1979): 671–96; David Charters, "The Role of Intelligence Services in the Direction of Covert Paramilitary Operations," in Alfred Mauer et al., *Intelligence Policy and Process* (Boulder, Colo.: Westview, 1985), pp. 333–51.

34. Richard M. Pious, *The American Presidency* (New York: Basic Books, 1979), pp. 47–84.

35. Richard M. Pious, "The Paradox of Clinton Winning and the Presidency Losing," *Political Science Quarterly* 114 (Winter 1999–2000): 569–94.

36. Michael Les Benedict, *The Impeachment and Trial of Andrew Johnson* (New York: Norton, 1973), pp. 126–43.

37. Richard M. Pious, "Impeaching the President: The Intersection of Constitutional and Popular Law," *Saint Louis University Law Journal* 43 (Summer 1999): 859–904.

38. But one always wants to keep in mind Dean Acheson's observation about formal models and political decisions; to wit, that he never knew he was a "dependent variable" in the Korean War until reading the political scientists who analyzed it.

39. Thomas M. Franck and Edward Weisband, *Foreign Policy by Congress* (New York: Oxford University Press, 1979), pp. 61–134.

40. James Sundquist, *The Decline and Resurgence of Congress* (Washington, D.C.: Brookings Institution, 1981), pp. 238–314.

41. On the evasion of the War Powers Resolution, see Michael J. Glennon, "The War Powers Resolution: Sad Record, Dismal Promise," *Loyola of Los Angeles Law Review* 17 (1984): 657–70; Michael Rubner, "The Reagan Administration, the 1973

War Powers Resolution and the Invasion of Grenada," *Political Science Quarterly* 100 (Winter 1985/6): 627–47; Michael Rubner, "Anti-Terrorism and the Withering of the 1973 War Powers Resolution," *Political Science Quarterly* 102 (Summer 1987): 193–215; Michael Glennon, "Strengthening the War Powers Resolution," *Minnesota Law Review* 60 (November 1975): 1–38; Thomas M. Franck, "After the Fall, the New Procedural Framework for Congressional Control over the War Power," *American Journal of International Law* 71 (October 1977): 605–42; Michael J. Glennon, "The War Powers Resolution Ten Years Later: More Politics than Law," *American Journal of International Law* 78 (July 1984): 571–81; John Hart Ely, "Suppose Congress Wanted a War Powers Act that Worked?" *Columbia Law Review* 88 (November 1988): 1379–431. On the failure of intelligence controls due to presidential evasion, see Michael J. Malbin, "Legislative-Executive Lessons from the Iran-Contra Affair," in *Congress Reconsidered*, Lawrence Dodd and Bruce Oppenheimer, eds. (Washington, D.C.: Congressional Quarterly Press, 1989), pp. 375–92; Philip L. Gordon, "Undermining Congressional Oversight of Covert Intelligence Operations: The Reagan Administration Secretly Arms Iran," *New York University Review of Law and Social Change* 16 (1987–88): 229–76.

42. Frank Church, "Covert Action: Swampland of American Foreign Policy," *Bulletin of Atomic Scientists* 32 (February 1976): 7–11; Gregory Treverton, "Covert Action and Open Society," *Foreign Affairs* 65 (Summer 1987): 995–1014; Steven R. Weissman, "CIA Covert Action in Zaire and Angola: Patterns and Consequences," *Political Science Quarterly* 94 (Summer 1979): 263–86; Emmanuel Adler, "Executive Command and Control in Foreign Policy: The CIA's Covert Activities," *Orbis* 23 (Fall 1979): 671–96; David Fagelson, "The Constitution and National Security: Covert Action in the Age of Intelligence Oversight," *Journal of Law and Politics* 5 (1989): 275–347; Robert F. Turner, "The Constitution and the Iran-Contra Affair: Was Congress the Real Law Breaker?" *Houston Journal of International Law* 11 (Fall 1988): 155–88; Daniel Feldman, "Constitutional Dimensions of the Iran-Contra Affair," *International Journal of Intelligence and Counterintelligence* 2 (1988): 381–406.

43. Craig Ducat and Robert Dudley, "Federal District Judges and Presidential Power during the Postwar Era," *Journal of Politics* 51 (February 1989): 98–118.

44. The *Steel Seizure* case was not directed against Truman, but against the action of his Secretary of Commerce in following Truman's directives, *Youngstown Sheet and Tube v. Sawyer*, 343 U.S. 579 (1952); war powers cases prior to passage of the War Powers Act were directed against the Secretary of Defense and orders to send troops abroad or orders to forces to engage in combat, as in *Massachusetts v. Laird*, 451 F 2d 26 (1971); *Mitchell v. Laird*, 488 F. 2d 611 (D.C. Cir. 1973); *Holtzman v. Schlesinger*, 484 F. 2d 1307 (1973); Nixon's impoundments were characterized as a question of whether lower level officials had an obligation under law to spend appropriated funds with the court parsing the wording of *funds* versus *all funds* in *Train v. New York*, 420 U.S. 35 (1975).

45. *National Treasury Employees Union v. Nixon*, 492 F. 2d. 587 (1974).

46. *Buckley v. Valeo*, 424 U.S. 1 (1976).

47. *Goldwater v. Carter*, 481 F. Supp. 949, 617 F. 2 697, 444 U.S. 996 (1979).

48. *Ex Parte Milligan*, 71 U.S. 2 (1866).

49. *Korematsu v. U.S.*, 323 U.S. 214 (1944); *Ex Parte Endo*, 323 U.S. 283 (1944).

50. *U.S. v. Nixon*, 418 U.S. 683 (1974); *In re Sealed Case (Espy)*, 124 F. 3d. 230 (1997); *In re Bruce Lindsey*, 158 F. 3d. 1263 (1998). For a discussion of these and other cases see Richard M. Pious, "The Paradox of Clinton Winning and the Presidency Losing," *Political Science Quarterly* 114 (Winter 1999–2000): 569–94.

51. On August 26, 2002, the Sixth Circuit Court of Appeals unanimously upheld a ruling by U.S. District Judge Nancy Edmunds in Detroit, holding that the government could not prevent the news media and the general public from immigration hearings relating to the September 11 attacks. Judge Damon J. Keith wrote for the unanimous panel that "the Framers of the First Amendment . . . protected the people against secret government." The decision did not take away the authority from immigration judges to close hearings, but held that the government would have to demonstrate the necessity that they be closed and that this would have to be done on a case-by-case basis rather than through a blanket closure. See *Detroit Free Press et al. v. John Ashcroft et al.*, 195 F. Supp. 2d. 937 (E.D. Mich. 2002).

52. Maeva Marcus, *Truman and the Steel Seizure Case* (New York: Columbia University Press, 1977), pp. 176–77.

53. *Youngstown Sheet and Tube Co. v. Sawyer*, 343 U.S. 579 (1952).

54. *U.S. v. Nixon*, 418 U.S. 683 (1974).

55. On situational constitutionalism, see J. Richard Piper, "'Situational Constitutionalism' and Presidential Power," *Presidential Studies Quarterly* 24 (Summer 1994): 577–96.

56. Richard M. Pious, "The 'Hard' Case for Presidential Power: Impeachment Politics and Law," in *Presidential Power*, Shapiro et al., eds. (New York: Columbia University Press, 2000), pp. 473–88.

57. In the run-up to the first Gulf War, on January 13, 1991, 260 Democrats and 41 Republicans voted for a resolution in the House stating its sense that the president was required to go to Congress for authorization to conduct hostilities, while 126 Republicans and 5 Democrats voted against the resolution. Partisan positions then shifted during the Clinton administration, not only on policy, but also on constitutional questions. On March 23, 1999, when President Clinton was about to order the bombing of Yugoslavia on his own prerogative, the Senate passed S. Con. Res. 21, 58–41 (16 Republicans and 42 Democrats in favor, 38 Republicans and 3 Democrats opposed), authorizing the president "to conduct military air operations and missile strikes in cooperation with our NATO allies against the Federal Republic of Yugoslavia." On the Clinton position that war powers are a presidential prerogative power, see Walter Dellinger, "After the Cold War: Presidential Powers and the Use of Military Force," *University of Miami Law Review* 50 (October 1995): 107–19; also David Gray Adler, "The Clinton Theory of the War Power," *Presidential Studies Quarterly* 30 (March 2000): 155–69; William C. Banks and Jeffrey D. Straussman, "A New Imperial Presidency? Insights from U.S. Involvement in Bosnia," *Political Science Quarterly* 114 (1999): 195–217.

58. Calvin Jillson, "The Executive in Republican Government: The Case for the American Founding," *Presidential Studies Quarterly* 9 (Fall 1979): 386–401; also William H. Riker, *The Art of Political Manipulation* (New Haven, Conn.: Yale University Press, 1986), chap. 8, "Trading Votes at the Constitutional Convention," pp. 89–102.

59. Charles Cameron, *Veto Bargaining* (New York: Cambridge University Press, 2000).

60. MaryAnne Borelli, Karen Hult, and Nancy Kassop, "The White House Counsel's Office," *Presidential Studies Quarterly* 31 (December 2001): 561–84; also see Cornell Clayton, ed., *Government Lawyers: The Federal Bureaucracy and Presidential Politics* (Lawrence: University Press of Kansas, 1995); Nancy Baker, *Conflicting Loyalties: Law and Politics in the Attorney General's Office, 1789–1990* (Lawrence: University Press of Kansas, 1990); Cornell Clayton, *The Politics of Justice: The Attorney General and the Making of Legal Policy* (New York: Sharpe, 1992); Jeremy Rabkin, "At the President's Side: The Role of the White House Counsel in Constitutional Policy," *Law and Contemporary Problems* 56 (Autumn 1993): 63–98

61. Ryan J. Barilleaux, "Executive Non-Agreements and the Presidential-Congressional Struggle in Foreign Affairs, *World Affairs* 148 (Spring 1986): 217–27; Ryan J. Barilleaux, "Parallel Unilateral Policy Declarations: A New Device for Presidential Autonomy in Foreign Affairs," *Presidential Studies Quarterly* 17 (Winter 1987): 107–17.

62. Phillip J. Cooper, "The Law: Presidential Memoranda and Executive Orders: Of Patchwork Quilts, Trump Cards, and Shell Games," *Presidential Studies Quarterly* 31 (March 2001): 126–41.

63. Joseph Cooper and William West, "Presidential Power and Republican Government: The Theory and Practice of OMB Review of Agency Rules," *Journal of Politics* 50 (November 1988): 864–95.

64. Louis Fisher, "Judicial Misjudgments about the Lawmaking Process: The Legislative Veto Case," *Public Administration Review* 45 (November 1985): 705–11; Frederick Kaiser, "Congressional Control of Executive Actions in the Aftermath of Chadha," *Administrative Law Review* 36 (Summer 1984): 239–76; Robert Gilmour and Barbara Craig, "After the Congressional Veto," *Journal of Policy Analysis and Management* 3 (1984): 373–92; Michael J. Horan, "Of Train Wrecks, Time Bombs and Skinned Cats: The Congressional Response to the Fall of the Legislative Veto," *Journal of Legislation* 13 (1986): 22–47; Daniel P. Franklin, "Why the Legislative Veto Isn't Dead," *Presidential Studies Quarterly* 16 (Summer 1986): 491–502.

65. Jonathan L. Charney, "The Power of the Executive Branch of the United States Government to Violate Customary International Law; Michael J. Glennon, "Can the President Do No Wrong?"; and Louis Henkin, "The President and International Law," all contained in *American Journal of International Law* 80 (October 1986): 913–37. Also see Jordan Paust, "The President Is Bound by International Law," *American Journal of International Law* 81 (1987): 377–90.

66. Richard Rose, *The Postmodern President*, 2nd ed. (Chatham, N.J.: Chatham House, 1991), pp. 56–58.

67. Terry M. Moe and William G. Howell, "Unilateral Action and Presidential Power: A Theory," *Presidential Studies Quarterly* 29 (December 1999): 850–72.

68. Richard Neustadt, *Presidential Power* (New York: Wiley, 1960), pp. 3–9.

69. Clinton Rossiter, *Constitutional Dictatorship* (Princeton, N.J.: Princeton University Press, 1948); also Simeon E. Baldwin, "Absolute Power, an American Institution," *Yale Law Journal* 7 (October 1897): 1–19; Clinton Rossiter, "Constitutional Dictatorship in the Atomic Age," *Review of Politics* 2 (October 1949): 395–418; Donald E. Robinson, "The Routinization of Crisis Government," *Yale Review* 63 (December 1973): 161–74; Aaron Klieman, "Preparing for the Hour of Need: The National Emergencies Act," *Presidential Studies Quarterly* 9 (Winter 1979): 47–64;

Arthur S. Miller, "Reason of State and the Emergent Constitution of Control," *Minnesota Law Review* 64 (1980): 585–633.

70. Quoted by Graham Allison, "The View from Baghdad," *Washington Post National Weekly Edition*, August 5–11, 2002, p. 27.

71. On policy inversion see Harold Koh, *The National Security Constitution* (New Haven, Conn.: Yale University Press, 1990), pp. 113–16.

72. Under existing law and procedures, any lethal mission must be approved by a presidential finding, and the Intelligence Committees must be notified. The CIA is bound by Executive Order 12,333 prohibiting assassinations. But this order does not apply to the armed forces.

73. For a description, see Leslie Wayne, "A For-Profit Secret Army, Doing the Pentagon's Bidding," *New York Times*, October 13, 2002, sec. 3, pp. 10–11.

74. Posse Comitatus Act, 18 U.S.C., sec. 1385.

75. USA PATRIOT Act, Sec. 203(2).

76. Such surveillance against political opponents of incumbent officeholders has occurred. See Christopher Pyle testimony before the Subcommittee on Constitutional Rights, Senate Judiciary Committee, *Federal Data Banks, Computers and the Bill of Rights*, Hearings before the Subcommittee on Constitutional Rights, Committee on the Judiciary, U.S. Senate, 92nd Congress, 1st Session, Part I, pp. 169–83 (1971). Also see *Uncle Sam Is Watching You* (Washington, D.C.: Public Affairs Press, 1971) reprinting testimony to the Subcommittee on Constitutional Rights, Senate Judiciary Committee in February 1971; also Frank Askin, "Police Dossiers and Emerging Principles of First Amendment Adjudication," *Stanford Law Review* 22 (1970): 196–220; and "Note: Police Infiltration of Dissident Groups," *Journal of Criminal Law, Criminology, and Police Science* 61 (1970): 181–94.

77. The surveillance laws were changed by the USA PATRIOT Act to permit the use of surveillance when collecting information about foreign spies or terrorists is "a significant purpose" rather than "the purpose."

78. The USA PATRIOT Act provides that investigators must show that intelligence is a "significant purpose" of the wiretap, but they need not show that it is its only purpose because Congress intended to loosen the "wall" between intelligence gathering and the prosecution of crimes.

TWO

Venture Constitutionalism and the Enlargement of the Presidency

Ryan J. Barilleaux

A story once repeated around Washington told of a meeting that occurred at the White House after the 1980 presidential election. Representatives of the incoming Reagan team were being shown around the West Wing by outgoing Carter administration personnel, and the White House veterans were offering advice to their successors in power. According to this account, the Carter staff offered one particular recommendation to the Reagan people, reaching across partisan and ideological lines to those who could appreciate the common bond of working for the chief executive: be sure to devote time and effort to exploring the outer limits of the president's constitutional power.

The story may be apocryphal (I have been unable to confirm it), but like many apocryphal stories it reflects an underlying truth about the U.S. presidency. A common theme runs throughout the history of the office, and it is one of the most enduring issues for students of the presidency: the question of why and how presidents push or test the limits of their constitutional power, and what the consequences of such explorations have been for the U.S. constitutional system.

Every student of U.S. politics knows that presidential power is much broader today than it was in the early days of the Republic and that, although it has waxed and waned at times, it has generally increased over the course of U.S. history. This dynamic is what Rexford G. Tugwell[1] once called the "enlargement of the presidency." Our political history is replete with stories of presidents pushing back the frontiers of power and constitutional authority—Jefferson buying the Louisiana Territory, Lincoln fighting the Civil War, and many others.

These episodes have been common, but why have they been so common? Why do presidents test the limits of their constitutional authority? The answer is surprising: because the Constitution makes them do it. I am suggesting neither that the Constitution is just so limited that it cries out to be ignored, nor that is it a colossal political dare challenging chief executives to see how much they can get away with. On the contrary, I argue that what is often going on is the playing out of the presidential conundrum.

This chapter demonstrates that our system has a conundrum built into it. A conundrum is a paradoxical problem, a question that is answered with a pun or a riddle, and the situation facing the president fits this definition. Presidents seem to be stretching the meaning of the Constitution because they are trying to live up to their constitutional responsibilities.

THE PRESIDENTIAL CONUNDRUM

Presidential power might be characterized in several ways. It might be described as a mystery—it has no precise limits and at various times has been revealed to be enormous (Lincoln's conduct of the Civil War), uneven (the "two presidencies"), mostly negative (the veto and removal powers are among its greatest weapons), and even deceptive (ours is not a presidential system, as Charles Jones[2] reminds us, but a separated one). It can be described as paradoxical, and Thomas Cronin and Michael Genovese[3] have identified several paradoxes of the U.S. presidency. It can also be described as fluid because it varies with context and with the individuals who inhabit the office. In a matter of hours, George W. Bush went from being a president of limited success and uneven reputation to being a resoundingly popular commander in chief of a united country at war. But these characterizations, however apt and accurate, do not capture all important aspects of the office.

Presidential power can be distinguished from the individual powers of the office—the veto power, the commander-in-chief power, and so on—but we can conceive of "presidential power" as both the sum of powers and something greater than these parts. Overall power is built on specific powers, but the power of the chief executive includes more than just these specific abilities. For example, Richard Neustadt[4] taught scholars and others to pay attention to the president's "professional reputation," which he argued contributed to the power to persuade, but reputation, persuasion, and other attributes came together to form a larger "presidential power." My concern is with the larger presidential power, which has grown since the country's beginning, and which I argue has been nourished by the continual testing of the limits of constitutional power.

Explaining Presidential Actions

What remains at the heart of the presidency is the question I first raised: why this almost continual testing of the limits of constitutional power? It is one of the central issues of the politics of the institution, and one for which we have no good answer. One approach to providing an answer has been to focus on the specific circumstances and events that surround assertions of broader constitutional authority: to focus on Jackson's goals in attacking the Bank of the United States, to explain the personality and political variables that contributed to Andrew Johnson's showdown with the Radical Republicans, or to emphasize the ideological and electoral considerations behind Nixon's incursion into Cambodia. This approach tells rich stories, but it leaves us wondering what presidents might have had in common.

Another approach has been to construct a good guys/bad guys model that lets an analyst reward his heroes and punish his enemies. This was Arthur Schlesinger Jr.'s method in *The Imperial Presidency*.[5] Trying to explain his rationale for condemning Johnson's and Nixon's misdeeds in Vietnam and elsewhere while celebrating Franklin Roosevelt and Kennedy, Schlesinger drew a distinction between usurpations of power and abuse of power. But Schlesinger's application of this distinction depends on his own assessment of presidential motive and ideological goals: chief executives such as Roosevelt and Kennedy engaged in noble and right-minded (in Schlesinger's view) grasps at greater presidential power, so they were participating in the (good) usurpation of constitutional power. Johnson and Nixon, on the other hand, were engaged in wrong-headed and selfish activities, so they were participating in the (bad, of course) abuse of power. The problem here is not only that this approach is ideologically driven, but also that it is idiosyncratic (it relies on Schlesinger's own assessment of good and bad actions) and is based on a distinction without a difference (it does not explain why or how usurpation and abuse are different, except that Schlesinger depends on the power of the term *abuse* to make the case that the action in question goes too far).

What we need is an explanation for these actions at the constitutional margins that can help us put individual events into a larger context without relying on simplistic good guy/bad guy distinctions. We need perspective, not polemics, in our understanding of the Republic's highest office. We can achieve that perspective if we examine the fundamentals of the presidency. The essential task before us is to recognize the existence of the presidential conundrum and its consequences.

Article II and Its Consequences

The presidential conundrum—that the Constitution itself encourages presidents to test the limits of the Constitution—stems from the ambiguity of Article II. The second article of the U.S. Constitution has been characterized as the most loosely drawn component of the nation's charter, and its language is famously broad and vague. It opens with a sweeping statement, "The executive Power shall be vested in a President of the United States of America" (Article II, Section 1). It goes on to describe the president's oath of office (the only one specified in the document), which includes the charge to "preserve, protect, and defend" the Constitution (Article II, Section 1). It also designates the chief executive as commander in chief of the armed forces, grants the power to recommend "Measures" to Congress and have a limited veto over legislation; gives the power to make treaties and appoint ambassadors, judges, and other high officials with the consent of the Senate; and charges the president to "take Care that the Laws be faithfully executed" (Article II, Section 3).

From this article emanates an office that is as much about roles and responsibilities as it is about specific powers. From the opening sentence of Article II the president is identified as chief executive (both head of government and head of state), a role sweeping in its potential. The office of commander in chief is, as William Rehnquist once put it (before he ascended to the Supreme Court), "something more than just a seat of honor in a reviewing stand."[6] Indeed, as President George W. Bush continually reminded journalists, members of Congress, and the public after September 11, 2001, his role as commander in chief represents to the incumbent president a broad and awesome responsibility.[7] Likewise, to use the famous "hats metaphor" for describing the office, the Constitution also makes the president the nation's chief diplomat, chief legislator, and protector of the peace. (This leaves out the extraconstitutional roles that go along with this metaphor—leader of public opinion, manager of the economy, party leader, and world leader.)

As Richard Neustadt famously observed, the president wears all hats at once, and the cumulative effect of these roles and duties is an almost overpowering sense of responsibility. Bruce Buchanan identifies the feeling of responsibility as the "common central predisposition of presidents in office."[8] As he explains:

> Presidential biographies concur that the euphoria of election triumph soon gives way to a sober appreciation for the enormity of the task at hand and for the inexorable accountability of the president for all that

> transpires thereafter. Responsibility is certainly the burden most frequently mentioned in the writings of former presidents, and apparently it has been seen as the sensation most joyfully dispensed with at the close of numerous presidential terms.[9]

Accordingly, the chief sensation of leaving the office for an outgoing president is that of having weight removed from one's shoulders (look at Jimmy Carter today versus the final hours of his presidency as he awaited release of the U.S. hostages in Tehran). U.S. presidents feel responsible for the fate of the nation, even if they are part of a separated (and not a truly presidential) system.

Tugwell articulated one of the best summaries of the cumulative effect of presidential roles and responsibilities.[10] A member of Roosevelt's "Brains Trust" (whose career included service as the presidentially appointed governor of Puerto Rico), Tugwell wrote an idiosyncratic but insightful survey of the evolution of the office. One of his observations was that the unique responsibility of the presidency in the U.S. system is to deal with tough, unexpected situations for which no prearranged solutions exist. In other words, the president is charged with dealing with the new and different, and this responsibility combines with existing obligations to focus each chief executive's attention. Regardless of whether we can question an individual incumbent's judgment in a particular case, and even if we question the president's motives, we cannot ignore the importance of responsibility.

In short, the roles and responsibilities of the presidency lead incumbents to do things that may leave outside observers wondering, "Why would he do that?" Even if the president in question was trying to protect his own political standing (such as Nixon in Watergate and Clinton in the Jones/Lewinsky/impeachment affair) an institutional motive still exists: protect the office and protect oneself.

The roles and responsibilities of the office shape the president's conception of his job. In *Federalist 51*, right after asserting, "Ambition must be made to counteract ambition," James Madison argued, "The interest of the man must be connected with the constitutional rights of the place."[11] The Constitution connects the interests of the president with the interests of the presidency.

This interest in living up to the roles and responsibilities of the presidency put incumbents on an almost inevitable collision course with the limits on the office other parts of the Constitution impose. The ensuing conflict creates the presidential conundrum at the center of the institution.

So what do presidents do to resolve this conundrum? They engage in forays to the outer reaches of constitutional authority. They take risks, sometimes very large risks: in the president's analysis, if successful, he will have expanded his authority and moved closer to meeting his responsibilities (and interests); if unsuccessful, then he can blame others for interfering with his attempts to serve the public interest, protect the institution, or whatever. In short, presidents engage in venture constitutionalism.

VENTURE CONSTITUTIONALISM

I define *venture constitutionalism* as an assertion of constitutional legitimacy for presidential actions that do not conform to settled understandings of the president's constitutional authority. It is, as mentioned earlier, a form of constitutional risk taking. The president gambles that other key actors in the political system will accept, or at least acquiesce to, his action.

Venture constitutionalism usually occurs when the president takes an action (including negative actions, such as claims of executive privilege or immunity, impoundment, and so forth) that "stake out" a claim to authority not already accepted as within the chief executive's constitutional orbit. It has occurred throughout U.S. history and in a wide range of cases, but it has been especially common in foreign affairs, and it has been responsible for much of the expansion of presidential power. It is has been a series of exercises in "pushing back the frontiers" of presidential constitutional authority, just as the Carter staff recommended that the Reagan staff attempt to do.

Because venture constitutionalism involves claims to constitutional legitimacy, it often creates conflicts that become Supreme Court cases. But it also includes events that do not reach the Court, but that are debated in Congress and occasionally in the court of public opinion (especially, nowadays, among the chattering class inside the Beltway).

The history of venture constitutionalism has been one of many successes: the Louisiana Purchase, the Civil War, the acceptance of the removal power (after a long struggle), and executive agreements. But it also includes many failures: the *Steel Seizure* case, Clinton's three defeats in the Supreme Court on claims of immunity and executive privilege, and the outlawing of impoundment. And we find many ambiguous instances as well, some of which are still unresolved: presidential signing statements, for example. It is a long history that dates at least as far back as Washington's Neutrality Proclamation and is as current as the war on terrorism.

The Anatomy of Venture Constitutionalism

Venture constitutionalism is not one formless agglomeration of events. Indeed, we can discern three general types of constitutional venturing according to the general purpose for which each is undertaken

> Type 1: venture constitutionalism to protect the institutional interests of the presidency;
>
> Type 2: venture constitutionalism to promote U.S. security and advance the national interest; and
>
> Type 3: venture constitutionalism to enhance the president's influence in shaping policy.

Although these types are not necessarily exclusive, they allow us to cluster related subject areas and distinguish the purposes for which presidents engage in constitutional ventures. The following discussion is illustrative and not exhaustive.

TYPE 1: PROTECTING THE INSTITUTIONAL INTERESTS OF THE PRESIDENCY. Presidents have long claimed broad authority to do things in the interest of the office. They have invoked the doctrine of executive privilege, claimed immunity from suits, and asserted extensive power to control executive subordinates. In 1977 Richard Nixon justified many actions of his tenure in office with the ultimate expression of the presidential conundrum and constitutional venturing. He told interviewer David Frost, "When the President does it that means that it is not illegal."[12]

Presidents have invoked the doctrine of executive privilege since the early years of the Republic. George Washington relied on this notion to refuse Congress access to information on a failed 1791 military expedition General Arthur St. Clair led, and again in 1794 to keep confidential his instructions to John Jay in the matter of Jay's treaty with Great Britain. Thomas Jefferson invoked executive privilege to withhold information in the treason trial of Aaron Burr, and Richard Nixon made a similar claim in attempting to withhold the Watergate tapes from the Special Prosecutor. Bill Clinton made two unsuccessful claims of executive privilege to hold off Independent Counsel Kenneth Starr, a "protective function privilege" to keep Secret Service agents from testifying about the president's actions, and a government attorney–official client privilege to keep his legal staff from testifying about discussions they had with the President and Mrs. Clinton, but the

Supreme Court rejected both. Mark Rozell[13] concluded that Nixon's and Clinton's claims of privilege were intended for personal protection rather than institutional interests, and he is largely correct in that judgment. But in each case the president had to justify his claim in terms of the office, and the merit of each claim had to be determined in terms of the office. Executive privilege has long been a source of venture constitutionalism.

Presidents have also sought immunity from suits, whether from private citizens or government employees. John Kennedy sought immunity for a suit involving a citizen injured by Kennedy's motorcade during the 1960 campaign, and Bill Clinton claimed immunity from Paula Jones's sexual harassment suit against him. Kennedy won and Clinton lost. Richard Nixon was successful in claiming absolute immunity for his official actions in the case of *Nixon v. Fitzgerald.*[14] Each claim of this sort involves the chief executive taking risks.

A third subject area included in this type are presidential claims of broad authority to control the executive branch. One of the most famous issues in this regard was the removal power, which was the subject of protracted conflict between the executive and legislative branches for decades. It was the proximate cause of Andrew Johnson's impeachment and the subject of polemics, congressional debates, and court cases for a long time. Another example of this area in recent years has been the White House claim to exercise administrative clearance, that is, the power to review and reject or amend administrative regulations executive agencies draft. Although some court tests occurred during the Reagan years, this mechanism for presidential control over rule making went from being highly controversial in the early 1980s to being standard procedure in the 1990s and the new century. As with other areas of venture constitutionalism, the accumulation of precedents (whether legal or political) tends to work in favor of broader presidential authority.

Constitutional venturing of this type is most likely to be adjudicated. One reason for this situation is that claims in this area are most likely to be—or to seem—self-serving by the president. Moreover, claims in this area often arise in the context of legal proceedings; claims of presidential immunity arise only in that context. This type also appears to be one in which the White House loses as much as it wins.

TYPE 2: PROMOTING U.S. SECURITY AND ADVANCING THE NATIONAL INTEREST. One of the main reasons the presidency has grown over the course of national history into a powerful force in U.S. government is the chief executive's roles as chief diplomat, commander in chief, and protector of the peace. This type of venture constitutionalism includes war powers, emergency powers, and the broad realm of foreign relations, and distinguishing one of these areas from another is not always easy.

Moe and Howell see presidents as rational actors who have an institutional interest in the expansion of their power. They characterize the Constitution as an "incomplete contract," arguing:

> Presidents, especially in modern times, are motivated to seek power. And because the Constitution does not say precisely what the proper boundaries of their power are, and because their hold on the executive functions of government gives them pivotal advantages in the political struggle, they have strong incentives to push for expanded authority by moving into grey areas of the law, asserting their rights, and exercising them—whether or not other actors, particularly in Congress, happen to agree.[15]

Venture constitutionalism is tied to the fundamental nature of the office.

War powers constitute not only one of the most fertile areas for constitutional venturing, but also the area about which controversy appears unending. Presidents have long asserted the authority to initiate military actions abroad without prior authorization by Congress and even broader authority to determine the conduct of wars already under way: Jefferson's conflict with the Barbary Pirates; Polk's war with Mexico; the Korean War; Vietnam War; interventions in the Dominican Republic, Grenada, Rwanda, Panama, and other places; Nixon's Cambodian invasion; Clinton's threatened invasion of Haiti; the *Mayaguez* incident; cruise missile attacks on Iraq; the elder Bush's declaration that he would fight the Gulf War with or without Congress, and on and on. During World War II, Franklin Roosevelt authorized the internment of thousands of U.S. citizens based on ethnicity alone. During the Korean War, Truman seized the steel mills, which led to one of the rare occasions when the Supreme Court has struck down a presidential action in the name of national security. The limits of presidential war power have been spotted on occasion, but not yet described.

The War Powers Resolution, which was passed in the hope that it could restrain constitutional venturing in military affairs, has done little to stop what presidents feel compelled to do. Indeed, Louis Fisher[16] argues that presidents have recently developed a new justification for circumventing Congress's constitutional role in initiating military action: authorization by international organizations. Recent chief executives, including George H. W. Bush in justifying the Gulf War and Bill Clinton in justifying the intervention in Kosovo, have invoked the authority of the United Nations or North Atlantic Treaty Organization (NATO) as sufficient to legitimize presidential initiations of the use of force. His point makes sense within the context of venture constitutionalism: recent presidents are staking out new territory for action, despite the efforts of Congress to circumscribe old territories.

Presidents have also asserted other sweeping emergency powers. The Civil War, as Clinton Rossiter[17] put it, resulted in a kind of "constitutional dictatorship." But other emergencies have also evoked an aggressive executive response, including detentions and other security measures following September 11, 2001. In 1992, the elder George Bush federalized the California National Guard and sent Federal Bureau of Investigation (FBI) agents and federal troops to deal with the riots that erupted in Los Angeles following the Rodney King verdict, despite the fact that the state's legislature was in session and could have requested presidential intervention as specified in Article IV, Section 4, of the Constitution.

Not all constitutional venturing has been limited to war or emergencies, but fall under the domain of pursuing the national interest as the president sees it. Early in our history, George Washington issued the Neutrality Proclamation regarding the emerging conflict between Great Britain and France, touching off the Pacificus-Helvidius debates over defining executive power. Thomas Jefferson purchased the Louisiana Territory because he thought it served the nation's long-term interests, and Congress went along with his action. Over the decades, presidents developed executive agreements as a nontreaty device for conducting diplomacy, and Jimmy Carter asserted the unilateral authority to terminate a treaty in force (upheld by the Court in *Goldwater v. Carter*[18]). In the 1970s and 1980s, Presidents Carter and Reagan developed a new diplomatic device for advancing the cause of executive autonomy in shaping arms-control policy: parallel unilateral policy declarations (PUPDs). These nonagreements were unilateral statements by the United States and the Soviet Union that had the effect of extending the SALT I treaty without congressional approval and implementing—and then extending the life of—the unratified SALT II treaty, all with Congress reduced to the role of helpless bystander. By the mid-1980s, arms control policy had been transformed into an almost unilateral presidential authority.[19]

Taken together, the subject areas in this type have been the basis for much constitutional venturing and have been an important force in the "enlargement of the presidency." Significantly, this is the type of venturing to which Congress, the courts, and the public are most likely to acquiesce.

TYPE 3: ENHANCING THE PRESIDENT'S INFLUENCE IN SHAPING POLICY. Presidents have also taken unilateral action to enhance the chief executive's ability to shape policy. We find less unity of subject areas to this type, but ventures of this type tend to be expansive assertions of the president's power to influence the implementation of policy. One area of action has been in fiscal policy. James Polk initiated the practice of insisting on a coordinated executive budget, and forced Cabinet departments to revise downward their planned expenditures, although this initiative did not continue when he left office.[20] Decades later, William Taft (not a president known for assertiveness) took up the cause of president budget authority and produced his own coordinated executive budget in 1913. Later, Richard Nixon used impoundment as a tool of fiscal policy, and several other chief executives mandated particular budget systems (Planning, Programming and Budgeting System, or PPBS; management by objective, or MBO; zero-based budgeting, or ZBB; and so forth) to control federal spending and bureaucratic independence.

A related and consistent theme has been shaping policy through direct White House action or monitoring of bureaucratic actions. Incidents in this category include the development of legislative clearance and administrative clearance in the Office of Management and Budget (also justified as exerting White House control over the executive branch), and the use of signing statements by Presidents Reagan, Clinton, and both Bushes to shape the implementation of laws Congress passed.[21]

Another area for presidential attention of this type has been the use of executive orders and proclamations to make policy. The original mandate that government contractors use affirmative action policies came in an executive order by Lyndon Johnson, whereas Bill Clinton issued an order preventing contractors doing business with the federal government from hiring permanent replacements for strikers. Clinton also employed an expansive reading of the American Antiquities Act of 1906 to justify proclamations setting aside millions of acres of wilderness—including the Grand Staircase-Escalante National Monument in Utah, parts of the Florida Everglades, and Idaho's Craters of the Moon National Monument—a move that was successfully defended in court by arguing for sweeping presidential authority to interpret the 1906 law.[22]

Not all presidential attempts to gain broader authority over policy have been successful, however. Taft's initiative on the budget came after Congress refused his proposal for legislation that would enhance White House power over the budget, and Nixon's aggressive use of impoundment stimulated a congressional backlash and the effective outlawing of the practice in the Budget and Impoundment Act of 1974. Likewise, a federal court voided Clinton's executive order on hiring permanent replacements for striking workers, and Congress and many of the president's supporters resoundingly denounced Franklin Roosevelt's Supreme Court-packing plan (aimed at smoothing the way for New Deal legislation) as an excessive power grab.

Venture constitutionalism is inherently risky, and the vicissitudes of the political process tend to influence Type 3 ventures. Perhaps the reason for this dynamic is that these presidential power assertions bring the chief executive into conflict with the powers and prerogatives of Congress, but in areas where national security are not at stake. Politics has freer reign in such circumstances.

The Practice of Venture Constitutionalism

Because it is directed at expanding the president's constitutional authority, venture constitutionalism does not include presidential actions for which established and accepted precedents exist. One precedent might be sufficient to gain acceptance for a presidential action, whereas in other cases numerous precedents may be necessary. Either way, venture constitutionalism works through an accretion of precedents.

One early case of constitutional venturing shows how a single precedent may be sufficient. Thomas Jefferson's purchase of the Louisiana Territory proposed to fill a gap in the Constitution—on the question of whether and how the United States could acquire more territory—with a presidential solution. This solution made Congress a reactive institution, responding to executive initiatives, in contrast to other similar matters (for example, admission of new states, constitutional amendments) Congress initiated. With that single precedent, however, the pattern was set: new territory has been acquired by executive initiative and legislative consent. Later acquisitions, such as that of the Alaska Territory, were discussed in terms of the wisdom of the specific case (for example, the debate over Seward's Folly) rather than the constitutionality of the president's initiative.

Other areas of venture constitutionalism, such as the assertion of unilateral presidential removal power and war powers, involved a longer and more complex accumulation of precedents. In both of these cases, movement has not always been in one direction—the White House suffered setbacks. Although the removal controversy was finally settled, at the latest by the Supreme Court's decision in *Myers v. United States*,[23] the war powers debate rages on. Even when myriad precedents are necessary, the long-term accumulation of them tends to favor the president.

Consequences of Constitutional Venturing

The chief consequences of this constitutional risk taking are fairly obvious, but some are more subtle. Venture constitutionalism has been one of the most important forces in the enlargement of the presidency and has helped to transform the U.S. political system from one in which Congress was largely dominant to one in which the president is at least competitive with the legislature and often dominant.

The record of venture constitutionalism has not been one of unlimited growth in presidential power, but it has generally been one of growth. Perhaps the most significant lesson to be gleaned from understanding the dynamics of this venturing is that the first precedent is the most important one. Consider, for example, Jimmy Carter's initial use of PUPDs in 1978 to extend the life of the expiring SALT I agreement: the president's action was initially denounced in the Senate as a usurpation of the upper chamber's constitutional authority regarding treaties, a violation of the Arms Control and Disarmament Act of 1961, and a dangerous precedent for unilateral executive control over a vital area of national security policy. But the Senate did not challenge Carter's action in part because influential members of the House were uninterested in the issue, and the precedent was set. Within a few years, PUPDs had become part of the governmental landscape: by the time Ronald Reagan took office, it was now taken as a matter of course that the president alone would decide whether the United States should abide by the (unratified, but implemented by PUPDs) SALT II agreement.[24] Successful risk taking begets further risk taking, and the overall trend of venture constitutionalism is in the direction of enlarged presidential power.

CONCLUSION

What does acknowledging the presidential conundrum or recognizing the underlying unity of venture constitutionalism mean? At least three reasons exist for employing these concepts.

First, this explanation of presidential behavior offers a way to link very different claims of presidential power. It is not limited to an issue area (for example, national security), time period (for example, the modern presidency), or forum for resolving disputes (for example, Supreme Court cases). The presidential conundrum and venture constitutionalism highlight the connection between the Louisiana Purchase, executive privilege, and signing statements. It also accounts for the continual testing of constitutional limits that is a feature of the office, especially in modern times.

Second, this explanation avoids the sort of good guy/bad guy judgments that flow from a more attitudinal approach to understanding presidential actions. Schlesinger's *Imperial Presidency* provides the clearest example of an attitudinal approach, but Richard Neustadt and Terry Eastland are two influential writers who also make judgments based on their political preferences.

In *Presidential Power*, Neustadt echoes Woodrow Wilson's dismissal of the "literary theory of the Constitution,"[25] and says that presidential actions should be judged according to whether they "run with or against the grain of history."[26] More than one commentator on Neustadt has observed that his history tends to have a liberal grain. Likewise, in *Energy in the Executive*,[27] Terry Eastland advances what he describes as a "constitutional corrective" to Neustadt's liberal analysis. But even a sympathetic reader is struck by the conservative policy preferences that inform this "corrective." For example, in arguing against the use of executive-congressional "summits" to construct final federal budgets in several years, Eastland takes the position that these summits violate the spirit of the separation-of-powers system. But his biggest complaint is that budget summits have not produced the sort of big spending cuts that Eastland favors. One is left with the distinct impression that he would have fewer constitutional concerns if only summits could drive down spending, taxes, or both.[28] What we need is an account of presidential constitutionalism not tied to partisan, attitudinal, or ideological agendas.

Terry Moe and William Howell have argued for a similar interpretation of unilateral presidential power as institutional rather than attitudinal. As they put it:

> Presidents have incentives to expand their institutional power, and they operate within a formal governance structure whose pervasive ambiguities—combined with advantages inherent in the executive nature of the presidential job—give them countless opportunities to move unilaterally into new territory, claim new powers, and make policy on their own authority. Congress has only a weak capacity for stopping them, because its collective action problems render it ineffective and subject to manipulation. The Supreme Court is capable of taking action against presidents, but is unlikely to want to most of the time and has incentives to be sympathetic.[29]

Third, this explanation conforms to what we know about how presidents think about their office and how they justify their actions. Cynically assuming that presidents do what they do strictly for short-term political or personal reasons would be easy but inaccurate. Even if these sorts of reasons are bound up in every president's actions, so is a sense of responsibility to advance the national interest, the public interest, or the institutional interests of the office.

This does not mean, however, that we must take the president's word for what is right; but neither should we become overly concerned about demonstrating the venality of the president's intentions. In the end, what really matters is whether a presidential action can be convincingly justified (in court, to Congress, and so forth) as serving the proper interest and the Constitution, not whether the president's intentions were pure.

In 1937, as controversy erupted over Roosevelt's Court-packing plan, hostile critics accused him of seeking one-man rule and friendly critics interpreted the idea as a bad one borne of frustration with the "nine old men" on the Supreme Court. But what rendered the proposal stillborn was a broad-based sense that the idea itself was a bad one because it threatened to undermine the independence of the judiciary. Instances of venture constitutionalism stand or fall on their own merits.

This is as it should be: if the president engages in some constitutional risk taking, then the action in question can and must be examined for what it does or does not do for the political system. Richard Nixon wanted to avoid embarrassment and political damage by withholding the Watergate tapes, but that does not mean that executive privilege did not exist. Likewise, one might argue that Bill Clinton had good reason for trying to withhold embarrassing information from his political enemies, but this does not mean that his claim of protective function privilege had constitutional merit. Venture constitutionalism must be evaluated on the merits of the action itself. Otherwise, someone might question the validity of the Louisiana Purchase according to whether it established Jefferson as a compulsive shopper.

The presidential conundrum and venture constitutionalism will remain with us unless we make some drastic changes in the presidency itself or in the larger Constitution. The conundrum is built into the heart of Article II, and venturing flows from the conundrum. Together, they have been central factors in fueling the enlargement of the presidency and will continue to influence presidential action in the future. Acknowledging them helps us to make sense of our own politics.

NOTES

1. Rexford G. Tugwell, *The Enlargement of the Presidency* (New York: Doubleday, 1960).

2. Charles Jones, *The Presidency in a Separated System* (Washington, D.C.: Brookings Institute Press, 1994).

3. Thomas E. Cronin and Michael A. Genovese, *The Paradoxes of the American Presidency* (Ithaca, N.Y.: Cornell University Press, 1998).

4. Richard E. Neustadt, *Presidential Power and the Modern Presidents* (New York: Free Press, 1990).

5. Arthur Schlesinger, *The Imperial Presidency* (Boston: Houghton Mifflin, 1973).

6. William H. Rehnquist, "The Constitutional Issues—Administration Position," in *The Growth of Presidential Power, vol. III*, William H. Goldsmith, ed. (New York: Chelsea House, 1974), p. 2104.

7. For example, see Bob Woodward, *Bush at War* (New York: Simon and Schuster, 2002).

8. Bruce Buchanan, *The Presidential Experience* (Englewood Cliffs, N.J.: Prentice-Hall, 1978), p. 27.

9. Buchanan, pp. 27–28.

10. Tugwell.

11. Clinton Rossiter, *The Federalist Papers* (New York: Penguin Putnam, 1999), p. 29.

12. Quoted in Stephen E. Ambrose, *Nixon, Volume Three: Ruin and Recovery, 1973–1990* (New York: Simon and Schuster, 1991), p. 508; see also David Frost, *I Gave Them a Sword: Behind the Scenes of the Nixon Interviews* (New York: Ballantine Books, 1977).

13. Mark Rozell, "Executive Privilege: From Washington to Clinton," in *The Presidency Then and Now*, Phillip G. Henderson, ed. (Lanham, Md.: Rowman and Littlefield, 2000).

14. *Nixon v. Fitzgerald*, 457 U.S. 731 (1982).

15. Terry M. Moe and William G. Howell, "Unilateral Action and Presidential Power: A Theory," *Presidential Studies Quarterly* 29 (1999): 856.

16. Louis Fisher, "Clinton's Military Actions: No Rivals in Sight," in *Rivals for Power*, James Thurber, ed. (Lanham, Md.: Rowman and Littlefield, 2002).

17. Clinton Rossiter, *Constitutional Dictatorship* (New Brunswick, N.J.: Transaction Publishers, 2002).

18. *Goldwater v. Carter*, 444 U.S. 996 (1979).

19. See Ryan Barilleaux, "Parallel Unilateral Policy Declarations: A New Device for Presidential Autonomy in Foreign Affairs," *Presidential Studies Quarterly* 18 (1987): 107–17.

20. See Sidney M. Milkis and Michael Nelson, *The American Presidency: Origins and Development, 1776–1993*, 2nd ed. (Washington, D.C.: Congressional Quarterly Press, 1994).

21. See Christopher S. Kelley, "Faithfully Executing and Taking Care: The Unitary Executive and the Presidential Signing Statement" (paper presented to the annual meeting of the American Political Science Association, Boston, Mass., 2002).

22. *Mountain States Legal Foundation v. Bush*, Civ. no. 00–2072, D.C. (November 16, 2001); see also Carol Hardy Vincent, "National Monument Issues," *CRS Report for Congress*, http://www.cnie.org/nle/crsreports/public/pub-21.pdf, December 19, 2001 (accessed January 15, 2003).

23. *Myers v. United States*, 272 U.S. 53 (1926).

24. See Ryan Barilleaux, "Executive Non-Agreements, Arms Control, and the Invitation to Struggle in Foreign Affairs," *World Affairs* 148 (1986): 217–27.

25. Neustadt, p. 37.

26. Neustadt, p. 167.

27. Terry Eastland, *Energy in the Executive: The Case for the Strong Presidency* (New York: Free Press, 1992), p. 8.

28. See Ryan Barilleaux, "Liberals, Conservatives, and the Presidency," *Congress and the Presidency* 20 (1993): 75–83.

29. Moe and Howell, p. 870.

THREE

Executive Orders from Nixon to Now

Graham G. Dodds

Executive orders are a little-known but powerful policy-making tool that can provide a unique perspective on the politics of presidential power. Strictly speaking, executive orders are written documents that the president issues to govern the actions of the executive branch. As such, they afford presidents an independent means of controlling a wide range of activities in the federal government. More controversially, executive orders may enable presidents to enact their own policy preferences by a mere stroke of a pen because they can serve to prompt congressional action, to preclude it, or to circumvent a recalcitrant Congress. Indeed, executive orders have figured in many of the most important moments in U.S. political history and have often been at the heart of interbranch struggles.

From George Washington to George W. Bush, every president has used executive orders with the sole exception of William Harrison, who died after just one month in office. Early executive orders—or their legal equivalents, proclamations—include Washington's Neutrality Proclamation, Thomas Jefferson's Louisiana Purchase, and Abraham Lincoln's Emancipation Proclamation. These noteworthy examples notwithstanding, however, executive orders before the twentieth century generally were used for purposes that were regarded at the time as mundane or uncontroversial, such as managing government lands and personnel. This changed with Theodore Roosevelt, for whom executive orders were the perfect means by which to execute his stewardship theory of presidential leadership. Roosevelt issued almost as many executive orders as all of his predecessors combined, often for policies that were highly controversial. Woodrow Wilson and Franklin Roosevelt built on Theodore Roosevelt's precedents and used executive orders with even greater frequency to fight World War I, the Great Depression, and World War II.

Presidential use of executive orders abated somewhat in the postwar era, but executive orders continued to figure in many important and controversial policies. For example, Harry Truman used the president's unilateral powers to desegregate the military, and he used an executive order to seize the nation's steel mills during the Korean War, although the Supreme Court overturned that order in *Youngstown Sheet and Tube v. Sawyer* (1952). Despite the cautionary case of *Youngstown*, subsequent presidents have continued to use executive orders for a variety of purposes, often with little explicit constitutional or legislative authority. For example, John Kennedy used an executive order to create the Peace Corps, and Lyndon Johnson used an executive order to institute affirmative action.

This chapter discusses the presidential use of executive orders from Richard Nixon to the present, briefly describing the major executive orders in that period and considering some trends and possible implications for the future presidential use of executive orders.[1] Although this period does not necessarily indicate a noticeable change in the number of executive orders a particular president issued, it does highlight one reoccurring theme through each president: using the executive order to gain control of the administrative state. This trend fits nicely with the thesis that presidents during this period were having difficulty leading Congress to fulfill popular expectations of the presidency, so they had to turn to the bureaucracy to meet popular expectations of the office.

RICHARD NIXON

Richard Nixon's five years as president made many people keenly aware of the potential dangers of a strong, assertive president. Nixon's actions in the Watergate scandal, his institutional struggles with Congress over impeachment and other matters, and his invocation of executive privilege are perhaps the most memorable ways in which he sought to deploy the full powers of the presidential office for his own ends, but like other presidents, Nixon also turned to executive orders to further his political preferences. Given Nixon's proclivity for strong executive action, that he did not make greater use of executive orders is perhaps surprising. Nixon issued 346 executive orders while in office, but his use of executive orders was in some respects less assertive than other presidents.[2]

Many of Nixon's more noteworthy executive orders were for environmental purposes.[3] In his first eighteen months in office, Nixon responded to growing public pressure for environmental protection by issuing a barrage of environmental executive orders. These included establishing the Environmental Protection Agency, or EPA (via Reorganization Order No. 3), implementing the National Environmental Policy Act (NEPA) of 1969, reducing pollution in government facilities, barring federal contracts with businesses that violated the Clean Air and Water Acts, and revising procedures under the Refuse Act of 1899 to help the government enforce water pollution controls. Environmental groups supported these measures but criticized Nixon's Executive Order 11,523, which established the Department of Commerce's National Industrial Pollution Control Council, a group comprised entirely of industry executives that had the ability to press for changes formally in proposed environmental regulations.[4]

In addition to establishing the EPA, Nixon used executive orders to restructure the executive branch in other ways. The president proposed that seven cabinet departments concerned with domestic affairs be consolidated into four, but Congress declined to act on the matter. Nixon then used executive orders effectively to implement his rejected reorganization plan by naming four cabinet members as counselors to the president and instructing them to coordinate the seven departments as if they had been formally combined into four.[5] In 1970 Congress approved the reorganization of the old Bureau of the Budget into the new Office of Management and Budget (OMB). Nixon followed this with Executive Order 11,541, which directed the OMB to monitor agency programs and budgets closely, thereby transforming the OMB "from a low-profile budget office into a powerful and controversial policy-making arm of the presidency."[6] This proved to be an important precedent on which future presidents would build considerably.

Nixon issued several other executive orders that were ostensibly administrative in nature but that actually had a significant impact on public policy, such as creating the Drug Enforcement Agency (DEA) and strengthening the Central Intelligence Agency (CIA) and the Federal Bureau of Investigation (FBI).[7] Also, by issuing Executive Order 11,605 in 1971, he created sweeping new authority for the Subversive Activities Control Board (SACB) to investigate U.S. citizens to determine whether they were threats to national security. A year later, Congress used its budget power to prohibit SACB from carrying out Nixon's order.[8]

One of Nixon's more interesting executive orders involved wage and price controls. The Economic Stabilization Act of 1970 authorized the president "to issue such orders and regulations as he may deem appropriate to stabilize prices, rents, wages, and salaries at levels not less than those prevailing on May 25, 1970."[9] Nixon was opposed to such controls, but Democrats passed the act and then continued to extend it to embarrass him politically;

Congress claimed that it was trying to improve the nation's economic situation by giving the president a powerful anti-inflation tool, yet the president stubbornly refused to use his new power. Congress was therefore quite surprised when Nixon issued Executive Order 11,615 on August 15, 1971, pursuant to the act, placing a ninety-day freeze on all prices, rents, wages, and salaries and establishing the Cost of Living Council to administer the controls. Two months later, Nixon issued another executive order, extending the freeze to May 1972 and establishing additional administrative machinery to monitor it. Critics complained that such presidential control of the economy was excessive, and Nixon's orders were challenged in federal court, but they were upheld.[10]

GERALD FORD

Gerald Ford came to office under the most difficult of circumstances. Although not popularly elected, and assuming the presidency from a president who had completely lost the trust of the American people, Ford still had to exercise the responsibilities of his office faithfully, despite the conditions of the political environment.

Gerald Ford's most famous (or infamous) unilateral executive action was his pardon of Nixon, but Ford also issued several noteworthy executive orders. Like Nixon, Ford used executive orders for economic purposes. For example, he responded to the Arab oil embargo by issuing an executive order to impose a fee on imported oil.[11] Also, Ford issued Executive Order 11,821 in 1974, requiring federal agencies to conduct an inflationary impact analysis of major proposed regulations.[12] The OMB and the Council on Wage and Price Stability were given the authority to review the inflation impact statements, but they lacked the authority to force agencies to revise their regulations, and in fact agencies faced no penalties for refusing to submit to regulatory analyses altogether.[13] While Ford's order was thus ineffective, it marked another step in the executive order–driven development of the OMB.

One of Ford's more noteworthy orders repealed an earlier executive order, namely Franklin Roosevelt's infamous World War II internment order. In 1942 Roosevelt issued Executive Order 9,066, calling for the internment of all Japanese Americans on the West Coast. Some 120,000 Americans of Japanese ancestry were interned for two years in concentration camps located in remote, desert areas. Asian immigrants were barred from becoming citizens until 1952, but two-thirds of those interned were U.S. citizens by birth, and many of the others had lived in the United States for decades. Most had to sell homes and businesses at significant losses, many had their education disrupted, and all had to endure bleak conditions at the camps. Roosevelt's internment order was still technically operational in 1976, when Ford issued Proclamation 4,417, formally terminating the prior order. The main impact of Ford's order was of course symbolic, but it was a crucial step in a long process that later culminated in an official governmental apology and reparations for those interned.

Also in 1976 Ford issued an executive order to reorganize intelligence agencies and make them more directly accountable to the president.[14] Ford's most famous executive order in intelligence and military matters was Executive Order 11,905, which prohibited assassination. Ford issued this directive after the Church Committee documented various CIA abuses, and its impact was as sweeping as its language was brief. The order stated: "No person employed by or acting on behalf of the United States shall engage in, or conspire to engage in, assassination." Subsequent presidents have sought to circumvent Ford's assassination ban, but it remains the law of the land.[15]

Ford's executive orders are remarkable in that they show the sorts of political problems that the administration faced. Executive Order 11,905 was largely in response to the constraints Congress, which was looking to unpeel all remaining vestiges of the imperial presidency, placed on the administration. Executive Order 11,821 ran contrary to his promises on taking office to govern in the open and not attempt the sorts of administrative actions President Nixon made famous.

JIMMY CARTER

Although Jimmy Carter's administration ended in political frustration, he was able to use executive orders to enact his policy preferences successfully in several important areas. Despite his differences with the Ford administration, and in particular with the Nixon administration, President Carter also looked to the executive order as a means to gain a presidential foothold into the administrative state.

One of Carter's more important executive orders concerned regulatory reform. In March 1978 Carter issued Executive Order 12,044, replacing Ford's Executive Order 11,821 with a more demanding requirement for economic analysis. Carter's executive order required that in submitting proposed regulations with an economic impact in excess of $100 million, federal agencies had to file brief statements that described the problem being addressed, the ways in which the problem might be handled, the reason for deciding on the particular regulation desired, and the economic impact of the proposed regulation.[16] Thus, Carter's order shifted the terms of debate from inflationary impact to whether a proposed regulation was worth its cost.[17] Carter also created two organizations to monitor compliance with Executive Order 12,044: the Regulatory Analysis Review Group and the Regulatory Council. Carter wanted to include a third change, namely the extension of regulatory review to independent regulatory agencies, such as the Nuclear Regulatory Commission (NRC), but he was advised that such an action would be an unlawful extension of executive authority.[18] Evaluations of Carter's success with deregulation are mixed, but scholars attribute Executive Order 12,044 with having "substantially broadened both the scope and the impact of central regulatory clearance on behalf of the President."[19]

Beyond regulatory reform, Carter sought to change federal procurement policy via executive order. Specifically, his Executive Order 12,092 required government contractors to follow the Council on Wage and Price Stability's wage and price guidelines or be barred from receiving federal contracts. The order was challenged, but a federal appellate court upheld the order on the grounds that it was based on a statutory requirement that procurement decisions consider "economy and efficiency."[20]

In terms of environmental policy, Carter issued Executive Order 11,911 in 1977 to authorize the Council on Environmental Quality (CEQ) to issue binding regulations. The Supreme Court upheld Carter's order in *Andrus v. Sierra Club* (1979), but many agencies were slow to comply with CEQ's new regulations.[21] Carter also issued executive orders protecting wetlands and floodplains, and in 1979 he issued Executive Order 12,114 to stipulate how agencies should review the environmental impact of their actions in foreign countries. The order sought to strike a compromise between the Department of State and the CEQ about the reach of NEPA beyond U.S. territory.[22] Carter's most dramatic use of unilateral presidential powers for environmental purposes was in December 1978, when he issued a series of proclamations to turn 55 million acres of public land in Alaska into national monuments. Carter proclaimed fifteen new national monuments in Alaska after Congress adjourned without passing a major Alaska lands bill that was strongly opposed in that state. Congress passed a revised version of the bill in 1980, incorporating most of the new national monuments into national parks and preserves, but it also curtailed the president's ability to establish additional national monuments in Alaska.[23]

Carter also used executive orders to impose a fee on imported oil just as Ford did to expand Ford's restrictions on actions by the intelligence community, to reduce secrecy and enhance governmental openness, to maintain unofficial relations with the people of Taiwan, to create the Federal Emergency Management Agency (FEMA), and to call for consistent and effective implementation of various laws prohibiting discrimination on the basis of race, color, national origin, gender, disability, or religion. And Carter issued Proclamation 4,771 in 1980 to reinstate draft registration for men at age eighteen.[24]

The Iranian hostage crisis dominated the end of Carter's term, and Carter issued numerous executive orders that addressed the situation in Iran. For example, shortly after the hostages were taken in November 1979, Carter issued an executive order to block the removal or transfer of Iranian assets in the United States. When the United States and Iran finally reached an agreement according to which Iran would release the hostages and the United States would suspend claims against Iran, Carter implemented the agreement via executive orders. In fact, all ten of the executive orders that Carter issued on his last day in office concerned the agreement with Iran, and Ronald Reagan issued his own order when he became president to ratify Carter's orders. The Court upheld these orders in 1981 in *Dames and Moore v. Reagan*.[25]

Notably, Carter instituted an important shift in presidential control of the bureaucracy. Whereas the Ford administration constrained rulemaking in terms of the impact a rule might have on inflation, Carter insisted that the regulatory agencies justify the costs of a rule to the benefits of society. This would be an important foundation for the Reagan administration, which would push the Carter administration changes even further toward presidential control of the administrative state.

RONALD REAGAN

Ronald Reagan's most famous executive directive may have been his secret order authorizing arms shipments to Iran despite an embargo, but he also issued several important and controversial executive orders.[26] For example, in 1981 Reagan's Executive Order 12,333 changed intelligence policies that Carter had established by executive order, shifting the emphasis from restricting to authorizing the activities of the twelve agencies comprising the intelligence community.[27] In 1982 Reagan followed this with an executive order that reversed another Carter era intelligence policy by loosening the requirements for openness in classifying information.[28]

Although these executive orders addressed policy differences with the previous administration, Reagan also turned to executive orders because of policy differences with Congress. In 1985 Congress was becoming increasingly critical of the South African government's policy of apartheid and appeared to be moving toward imposing stringent economic sanctions on the country. Reagan opposed such a move and turned to an executive order to thwart Congress. Reagan's executive order imposed limited sanctions in the hope that such preemptive action would deflate the growing congressional consensus for stronger sanctions. Congress later passed tougher sanctions, which Reagan vetoed, but Congress then overrode the veto and imposed its own sanctions, effectively nullifying Reagan's executive order some thirteen months after it was issued.[29]

That same year, Reagan again used an executive order to try to preempt possible congressional action, this time concerning government employees and drug testing. Reagan's Executive Order 12,564 required all executive branch agencies to establish drug-testing programs, effectively mandating a drug-free federal workplace.

Reagan also used an executive order to further his states' rights agenda by changing the balance of federalism in favor of the states over the federal government. Executive order 12612 established guidelines for government agencies when dealing with states. The order referenced the Tenth Amendment and "instituted a presumption of state sovereignty to be observed by federal agencies."[30]

Reagan's most effective and far-reaching use of executive orders was arguably for regulatory reform. A few weeks after he was inaugurated, Reagan issued Executive Order 12,291 in an effort to curtail governmental regulation. The order sought to shift the control of federal regulations from the various executive agencies to the White House; it centralized Carter's system of management and regulation in a newly strengthened OMB.[31] Executive Order 12,291 created the Office of Information and Regulatory Affairs (OIRA) in OMB and mandated that all executive branch agencies submit all their proposed regulations to it for review, along with a regulatory impact statement. The OMB would then subject the regulations to a cost-benefit analysis to ensure that the potential benefits of a proposed regulation would outweigh its costs. The OMB could then pose objections to proposed regulations that failed the test and could stop publication of the regulations until such time as the relevant agency formally responded to OMB's concerns.[32] OMB objected to roughly one-fifth of the nearly 12,000 regulations that it reviewed between 1981 and 1986, and most of those were later revised to meet OMB's objections.[33]

Several years later, Reagan issued Executive Order 12,498, which extended the review process that had been enacted by Executive Order 12,291. The new order increased the reach of OMB's regulatory review to virtually any agency activity that could conceivably ever lead to the consideration of the need for regulation.[34] It also required agencies to publish an annual list of regulations that they anticipated in the new fiscal year, which OMB would then review to ensure conformity with administration priorities.[35]

Reagan clearly used executive orders to protect the prerogatives of his office as well as to advance clear preferences of his administration despite congressional or popular opposition. Not only was he able to build on the administrative oversight attempts of his predecessors, but also he used the executive order to deflect Congress's attempts to meddle in foreign policy decisions of the administration—executive orders that would ultimately become problematic for his presidency.

GEORGE H. W. BUSH

George H. W. Bush issued 166 executive orders during his four years as president. One of these modified Reagan's regulatory review system, transferring OIRA's review power to the Council on Competitiveness, which Vice President Dan Quayle chaired.[36] Bush also used executive orders to establish a human fetal tissue bank for research projects, to stop the U.S. Navy from bombing the Hawaiian Island of Kahoolawe for target practice, and to prohibit logging within 1,000 feet of a sequoia grove.[37]

Some of Bush's most notable executive orders concerned organized labor. For example, Bush's Executive Order 12,800 required government contractors to advise their union employees of their rights not to join the union and to object to the use of their dues for purposes not directly related to collective bargaining and union administration. In addition, Bush's Executive Order 12,818 barred union-only labor agreements for federal and federally funded construction work.

One of Bush's most intriguing executive orders was one which was never fully issued. Shortly after the controversial and racially charged 1991 Senate confirmation hearings on Supreme Court Justice Clarence Thomas, Congress and the White House agreed on a compromise civil rights bill. The day before Bush signed the legislation, however, he issued an order to all federal agencies to end programs involving quotas, preferences, or set-asides. The order was reportedly just a draft and was intended to be included in Bush's signing statement for the civil rights bill, but when critics charged that Bush effectively using an executive order to repudiate the same legislation that he was signing, the president withdrew the order and modified his signing statement.[38]

For the Bush administration, the executive order (much like the signing statement) was used to signal support to key administration constituencies, such as the business community, as well as to deflect public attention away from the manipulation of a civil rights bill that the administration opposed.

BILL CLINTON

As the first Democratic president in twelve years, Bill Clinton issued a lot of executive orders early in his first term to reverse policies that his predecessors had enacted by executive orders. For example, "within two days of taking office in January 1993 he issued no fewer than five separate orders or directives to departments, overturning restrictive abortion-related policies from the Reagan and first Bush administrations," such as the "Mexico City gag rule" and the ban on importation of RU–486.[39] Similarly, in his second week in office, Clinton issued Executive Order 12,836 to assist organized labor, reversing Bush's Executive Order 12,800.[40]

Also in 1993 Clinton issued an executive order to end the ban against homosexuals serving in the military. As Lyn Ragsdale and Jerrold Rusk explain, "He did this rather than sending legislation to Congress. The White House was correct in assuming that they did not have the political capital necessary to win a fight on Capitol Hill over the issue; they were incorrect in assuming that there would be no fight if they issued an executive order. Congress and military officials forced Clinton to rescind, revise, and reissue the order."[41] The result was the awkward compromise policy known as "don't ask, don't tell." Several years later, Clinton issued Executive Order 13,087, prohibiting federal agencies from discriminating based on sexual orientation.[42] Congress tried but failed to overturn this order in 1998.[43]

In another early-term executive order, Clinton sought to change the system of OMB-centered regulatory review Reagan established. He abolished Quayle's Council on Competitiveness and revoked Reagan's two regulatory executive orders, replacing them with Executive Order 12,866. In many respects, Clinton's regulatory scheme was substantively and administratively similar to Reagan's.[44] However, it had a less stringent efficiency test: whereas Reagan's order required that the benefits outweigh the costs, Clinton's order required that the benefits merely justify the costs. Clinton's order also stipulated that not all regulatory benefits could be monetized and that nonmonetary consequences should nevertheless factor into regulatory analysis.[45] And significantly, the order extended regulatory planning to independent regulatory agencies and commissions, something about which the Reagan administration could only dream.

Several years later, Congress sought to reverse Clinton's modifications to the Reagan-Bush system of regulatory review. The eighth item of the Contract with America was the Job Creation and Wage Enhancement Act of 1995, which would have made Reagan's Executive Order 12,291 statutory, superceding Clinton's executive order and requiring that the benefits of regulations outweigh the costs. However, this measure did not make it out of Congress.[46]

Many of Clinton's more noteworthy executive orders came after the 1994 midterm elections delivered the Congress to Republican control for the first time in a half century. Facing a hostile and assertive House of Representatives under Speaker Newt Gingrich, Clinton often turned to executive orders to further his policy aims; two years after the 1994 elections, Clinton remarked, "One of the things that I have learned in the last two years is that the President can do an awful lot of things by executive orders."[47] Clinton's post-1994 executive orders often provoked strong criticisms from his partisan detractors. Congress held hearings on the supposed presidential abuse of executive orders, and several bills were introduced to restrain the practice, but none made it out of committee.[48]

Clinton's controversial executive orders in this period included a 1995 order authorizing $20 billion in loan guarantees from the Exchange Stabilization Fund to stabilize the Mexico peso. Members of Congress complained that this action went far beyond the intent of the fund, and it may well have. Congress held hearings to investigate the matter but took no other action.[49]

In addition to using executive orders to circumvent Congress, Kenneth Mayer suggests that Clinton also used executive orders to appeal to key electoral constituencies before the 1996 election. For example, Executive Order 13,017 created the Advisory Commission on Consumer Protection and Quality in Health Care, Executive Order 13,019 implemented procedures to collect delinquent child support payments, and Executive Order 13,021 provided funds and administrative support for Native American colleges and universities.[50]

Several years after his failed health-care reform initiative, Clinton issued an executive order in 1998 to enact a patients' bill of rights, when Congress failed to do so. Clinton's order granted various protections to all 75 million Medicare and Medicaid recipients and to 9 million federal employees and family members covered by other governmental health plans.[51]

Clinton often turned to executive orders for environmental purposes. In 1994 he issued Executive Order 12,898 to fight "environmental racism." The order instructed federal agencies to conduct their programs to achieve environmental justice and promote nondiscrimination against minorities and people with low incomes.[52] Many of Clinton's environmental executive orders consciously emulated Theodore Roosevelt's uses of executive orders for environmental conservation and stewardship some ninety years earlier. Acting pursuant to the American Antiquities Act of 1906, Clinton issued presidential directives to create nineteen national monuments, unilaterally conferring protected status on millions of acres of land.[53] For example, when Congress failed to pass legislation to protect some 1.8 million acres of southern Utah, Clinton unilaterally ordered the creation of the Grand Staircase-Escalante National Monument.[54] Similarly, Clinton preempted pending congressional legislation on protecting rivers in 1997 by issuing Executive Order 13,061, the American Heritage Rivers initiative. The order directed agencies to "coordinate their functions, programs, and resources to preserve, protect, and restore rivers and their associated resources important to our history, culture, and natural heritage."[55] Members of Congress went to court to block implementation of the rivers order, but their case was dismissed for lack of standing.[56]

Another of Clinton's executive orders fared less well in court. Clinton wanted to reverse a 1938 Supreme Court interpretation of the National Labor Relations Act, in which the Court accepted employers' right to permanently replace striking workers.[57] In 1993 Clinton asked Congress to pass legislation prohibiting employers from permanently replacing striking workers, but Congress did not do so. When Republicans gained congressional control after the 1994 elections, Clinton despaired of a legislative solution and instead turned to unilateral executive action, issuing Executive Order 12,954 to prohibit employers under federal contracts from permanently replacing striking workers.

Congress considered legislation to overturn Clinton's order, but the judiciary acted before the legislature.[58] In *Chamber of Commerce v. Reich* (1996), the U.S. Court of Appeals for the District of Columbia Circuit unanimously overturned the executive order and the implementing regulations the Secretary of Labor issued.[59] The court said Clinton's order contradicted both a previous Supreme Court ruling (that is, the 1938 precedent) and legislation on the subject (that is, the National Labor Relations Act).[60] The case marked the first time since the Court's 1952 rejection of Harry Truman's executive order seizing the steel industry that the judiciary overturned an executive order in its entirety.[61]

Two years after the judiciary overturned his striker-replacement ban, Clinton faced opposition to another executive order. In 1998 Clinton issued Executive Order 13,083, revoking Reagan's 1987 executive order on federalism. Clinton sought to shift the federalism balance in favor of the federal government; in lieu of Reagan's presumption of state sovereignty, Clinton's order outlined nine circumstances in which an agency could intervene and override state-level decisions.[62] Reaction from Congress and the states was strongly negative. When the House voted to withhold funds for implementing the executive order, Clinton suspended the order that same day. A year later, Clinton issued another executive order on federalism that maintained much of Reagan's policy.[63]

Clinton was similar to Reagan in his use of the executive order. He certainly benefitted from the groundwork both the Reagan and Bush administrations laid in the area of bureaucratic control. But more important, when the political environment turned openly hostile, in Clinton's case after the 1994 midterm elections, Clinton found that the executive order was a useful instrumental to bypass the stalemate and policy conflicts he had with Congress.

GEORGE W. BUSH

After the disputed 2000 presidential election was decided but before he took office, George W. Bush signaled that he intended to reverse many of Clinton's executive orders. His administration even threatened to reverse systematically all of Clinton's so-called last-minute executive orders, but ultimately Bush adopted a more piecemeal approach.[64] For example, in his first week in office, on the anniversary of *Roe v. Wade*, Bush (like his father) issued an order to block funding for international family planning groups that provided abortion-counseling services, effectively reversing Clinton's reversal of the Reagan-Bush policy.[65] In early May 2001 the House International Relations Committee voted 26 to 22 to overturn Bush's ban, but two weeks later the entire House narrowly voted to retain Bush's Mexico City policy.[66]

Similarly, on February 17, 2001, Bush issued several executive orders concerning organized labor to reverse policies that Clinton had established by executive order. Bush issued two executive orders to rescind Clinton's establishment of labor-management councils in unionized federal workplaces. He also issued an executive order banning "project labor agreements," which can require contractors in federally funded projects to follow union standards. And he reinstated his father's requirement that federal contractors post notices of workers' right to a refund of union fees used for political purposes. A federal judge overturned this last order, but an appeals court later upheld it.[67]

In his first week in office, Bush issued two executive orders to launch his faith-based service initiative by establishing the White House Office of Faith-Based and Community Initiatives and directing agencies to investigate how faith-based groups could participate in federal programs. He initially sought congressional approval, but when the legislation stalled in the Senate, he acted unilaterally. In 2002 Bush followed these orders with an executive order requiring that the federal government not discriminate against religious organizations in awarding money to groups that help people in need.

In November 2001 Bush issued Executive Order 13,233, making private many presidential records that previously had been publicly accessible, including some of his father's records. Bush's order revoked Reagan's Executive Order 12,667 and altered policies the Presidential Records Act of 1978 established, greatly angering presidency scholars who rely on archival research.

Since September 11, 2001, many of Bush's more noteworthy executive orders have concerned the war on terror. Bush's controversial order authorizing secret military tribunals for suspected terrorists was a military order rather than an executive order per se, but other directives took the form of an executive order. For example, Executive Order 13,224 froze terrorist assets, and Executive Order 13,228 broadened the scope of airline security and established the Office of Homeland Security. When a political battle erupted regarding staffing the new agency, the White House and House Republicans tried unsuccessfully to block the federalization of airport security workers by threatening that Bush would use an executive order.[68] And an executive order figured into the administration's controversial policy of "rendition," in which terrorist suspects are seized by the CIA and sent to foreign countries for interrogation. As Bush's war on terror continues, executive orders will continue to play an important role in it.

In many respects, President George W. Bush was much like his father in the use of the executive order. In three high-profile instances, President Bush has used the executive order to show his support to important political constituencies (antiabortion groups, the business community, and religious groups). He also found that the executive order was important in helping the president act "with energy" to respond to an emergency, as his executive orders in the aftermath of September 11 have clearly shown.

CONCLUSION

Although the forgoing chronology notes most of the more important executive orders issued over the last thirty-plus years, several points deserve further comment here. First, the preceding discussion suggests several trends in executive order usage. For instance, many of the executive orders mentioned here address the same policy areas: executive orders for general regulation, intelligence, labor, abortion, and environmental uses are common in this period. A trend also exists of presidents using executive orders to reverse or rescind policies their predecessors enacted by executive orders. This is certainly the case with abortion, labor, and federalism, and these reversal orders often occur early in a new administration.[69]

Second, presidents over the last three decades have clearly used executive orders for a variety of important and controversial purposes, and there may well be an increasing awareness—among politicians, scholars, and journalists—of the fact that executive orders can be a very potent and effective policy-making tool. However, whether executive orders during the period considered here differ markedly from earlier executive orders is not clear. Indeed, although some recent critics have decried executive orders as excessive and as even marking a return to the Imperial Presidency, earlier presidents often issued far more executive orders than more recent presidents. For example, Franklin Roosevelt averaged 286 executive orders a year, whereas Reagan averaged only 51.[70] However, even though total executive order usage has declined since Roosevelt, we have reason to think that the proportion of significant executive orders is increasing. According to William Howell, of the executive orders issued between 1900 and 1945, only about 2 percent were significant, but of the executive orders issued since then, about 15 percent have been significant.[71] In short, although executive orders since Nixon are not altogether unprecedented in either number or type, executive orders are perhaps becoming an increasingly important part of presidential power and politics.

Third, executive orders are only one type of unilateral presidential power; one scholar has identified twenty-three other types of presidential directives.[72] Perhaps presidents are increasingly choosing to use other executive directives in addition to or even instead of executive orders (or even choosing to call an executive order by another name to escape publication in the *Federal Register*).[73] For example, presidents can use executive memoranda to implement many decisions, but memoranda need not be made public and are not much regulated in terms of their issuance or codification. Reagan supplemented his second OMB-regulation executive order with an executive memorandum, as did Clinton with his executive order on environmental racism.[74] Furthermore, George H. W. Bush's Executive Order 12,807 was supposedly intended to direct the Coast Guard to return Haitian refugees to Haiti. However, the order did not mention Haitian refugees. That specification was contained in a news release that stated, "President Bush has issued an executive order which will permit the U.S. Coast Guard to begin returning Haitians picked up at sea directly to Haiti." In *Sale v. Haitian Centers Council* (1993), the Supreme Court ruled that the news release was a sufficient articulation of the policy.[75] In short, despite their significance for a variety of policies over the past three decades, executive orders are only part of a much larger story about presidential power. Nevertheless, the history of executive order usage over the past three decades suggests that executive orders will continue to play an important role in presidential power, policymaking, and politics.

NOTES

1. My determination of which executive orders qualify as major or significant is subjective and is based on my reading of the relevant scholarly literature and news coverage. Mayer and Price employ several means of identifying significant executive orders and find that roughly one in seven executive orders issued between 1944 and 1999 was significant. Kenneth Mayer and Kevin Price, "Unilateral Presidential Powers: Significant Executive Orders, 1949–99," *Presidential Studies Quarterly* 32 (June 2002): 375.

2. Melissa K. Matthews, "Restoring The Imperial Presidency: An Examination of President Bush's New Emergency Powers," *Hamline Journal of Public Law and Policy* 23 (Spring 2002): 471.

3. Although he was the first Republican president in eight years, Nixon continued the use of executive orders for affirmative action policies that Presidents Kennedy and Johnson had started. In particular, Secretary of Labor George Schultz issued "Revised Order #4," which effectively revised LBJ's Executive Order 11,246 by extending the "Philadelphia Plan" to all contractors with the federal government.

4. Robert Shanley, "Presidential Executive Orders and Environmental Policy," *Presidential Studies Quarterly* 13 (1983): 405–16, 406.

5. James L. Sundquist, *The Decline and Resurgence of Congress* (Washington, D.C.: Brookings, 1981), pp. 1–2.

6. Michael Nelson, ed., *Congressional Quarterly's Guide to the Presidency* (Washington, D.C.: Congressional Quarterly Press, 1989), p. 483.

7. Nelson, p. 1234.

8. Norman C. Thomas, Joseph A. Pika, and Richard A. Watson, *The Politics of the Presidency*, 3rd ed. (Washington, D.C.: Congressional Quarterly Press, 1994), p. 261; Nelson, p. 484.

9. Louis Fisher, *Constitutional Conflicts between Congress and the President*, 4th ed. (Lawrence: University Press of Kansas, 1997), p. 114.

10. Phillip J. Cooper, *By Order of the President* (Lawrence: University Press of Kansas, 2002), p. 28; Nelson, p. 1234; Thomas et al., p. 260.

11. Alexis Simendinger, "The Paper Wars," *National Journal* 30 (July 25, 1998): 1732.

12. Kenneth R. Mayer and Thomas J. Weko, "The Institutionalization of Power," in *Presidential Power*, Robert Y. Shapiro, Martha Joynt Kumar, and Lawrence R. Jacobs, eds. (New York: Columbia University Press, 2000), p. 199.

13. Kenneth R Mayer, *With the Stroke of a Pen: Executive Orders and Presidential Power* (Princeton, N.J.: Princeton University Press, 2001), p. 124–25.

14. Thomas et al., p. 261.

15. According to Mayer, Reagan's 1986 bombing of Muammar Qadhafi's home may have violated Ford's assassination ban (Mayer, *With the Stroke of a Pen*, p. 180). Clinton's missile strike against Osama bin Laden and George W. Bush's attempt to bomb Saddam Hussein also raise questions about the efficacy of Ford's ban.

16. Shanley, p. 412.

17. Mayer, pp. 125–26.

18. Mayer, *With the Stroke of a Pen*, pp. 125–26. Clinton's Executive Order 12,866 changed this.

19. James G. Benze Jr., *Presidential Power and Management Techniques* (Westport, Conn.: Greenwood Press, 1987), pp. 85–86.

20. Mayer, *With the Stroke of a Pen*, p. 47; Louis Fisher, *Constitutional Conflicts between Congress and the President* (Princeton, N.J.: Princeton University Press, 1985), p. 117; *American Federation of Labor, Etc. v. Kahn*, 618 F.2d 784, 794 n. 51 (D.C. Cir. 1979).

21. Shanley, p. 408.

22. Mayer, *With the Stroke of a Pen*, p. 64.

23. Shanley, p. 410; Mayer, *With the Stroke of a Pen*, p. 76.

24. Mayer, *With the Stroke of a Pen*, pp. 172–73; some scholars trace the origin of FEMA to President Kennedy's Executive Order 11,051 or Nixon's Executive Order 11,490.

25. Cooper, p. 24.

26. Nelson, p. 484.

27. Mayer, *With the Stroke of a Pen*, p. 173.

28. Mayer, *With the Stroke of a Pen*, p. 147.

29. William G. Howell, *Power without Persuasion* (Princeton, N.J.: Princeton University Press, 2003), pp. 58–59.

30. Tara L. Branum, "President or King? The Use and Abuse of Executive Orders in Modern-Day America," *Journal of Legislation* 28 (2002): 41.

31. Mayer, *With the Stroke of a Pen*, p. 6; Nelson, pp. 479, 483.

32. Benze, p. 86.

33. Terry Eastland, *Energy in the Executive* (New York: Free Press, 1992), p. 163.

34. Nelson, p. 483.

35. Nelson, p. 954; Mayer, *With the Stroke of a Pen*, p. 129.

36. Mayer, *With the Stroke of a Pen*, p. 131.

37. John Contrubis, "Executive Orders and Proclamations," *CRS Report for Congress* (July 3, 1995): 17; John M. Broder, "Agreeing to Protect Giant Treasures, but How?" *New York Times*, June 11, 2003, p. 18.

38. Mayer, *With the Stroke of a Pen*, p. 209.

39. Nancy Kassop, "Expansion and Contraction: Clinton's Impact on the Scope of Presidential Power," in *The Presidency and the Law: The Clinton Legacy*, David Gray Adler and Michael A. Genovese, eds. (Lawrence: University Press of Kansas, 2002), p. 7.

40. Mayer, *With the Stroke of a Pen*, p. 89.

41. Lyn Ragsdale and Jerrold G. Rusk, "Elections and Presidential Policymaking," in *Presidential Policymaking*, Steven A. Shull, ed. (Armonk, N.Y.: Sharpe, 1999), pp. 105–6.

42. Mayer, p. 214.

43. Mayer, *With the Stroke of a Pen*, pp. 214–15.

44. Robert W. Hahn and Cass R. Sunstein, "A New Executive Order for Improving Federal Regulation?" *University of Pennsylvania Law Review* 150 (May 2002): 1489–90; Contrubis, p. 16; Mayer, *With the Stroke of a Pen*, p. 132.

45. Robert W. Hahn, Sheila M. Olmstead, and Robert N. Stavins, "Environmental Regulation in the 1990s: A Retrospective Analysis," *Harvard Environmental Law Review* 27 (2003): 382.

46. Hahn et al.

47. Quoted in Ragsdale and Rusk, p. 126. Clinton actually issued more executive orders when Democrats controlled Congress, but his later executive orders were more controversial (Mayer, *With the Stroke of a Pen*, pp. 99, 101).

48. Legislation during this time to curtail the presidential use of executive orders in general included the Separation of Powers Act and the Executive Order Limitation Act. Of course, Congress has also attempted to reverse particular executive orders. According to Moe and Howell, Congress attempted to overturn an executive order thirty-seven times from 1973 through 1997, and eleven of those attempts were between 1995 and 1997, but only three of the thirty-seven attempts were successful. Terry Moe and William G. Howell, "The Presidential Power of Unilateral Action," *Journal of Law, Economics, and Organization* 15 (1999): 132–79, 165–67.

49. Kassop, p. 7.

50. Mayer, *With the Stroke of a Pen*, p. 91.

51. George C. Edwards III and Stephen J. Wayne, *Presidential Leadership: Politics and Policy Making*, 6th ed. (New York: St. Martin's, 2003), p. 301.

52. The same day that Clinton issued Executive Order 12,898, he also issued a presidential memorandum on environmental justice, which sharpened the executive order by requiring federal agencies to use civil rights laws, especially Title VI of the Civil Rights Act of 1964, in ensuring the government does not engage in or support environmental racism. Phillip J. Cooper, "The Law: Presidential Memoranda and Executive Orders: Of Patchwork Quilts, Trump Cards, and Shell Games," *Presidential Studies Quarterly* 31 (March 2001): 131.

53. Edwards and Wayne, p. 301.

54. Branum, pp. 39–40.

55. Bryan A. Liang, "'A Zone of Twilight': Executive Orders in the Modern Policy State," *Briefly: Perspectives on Legislation, Regulation, and Litigation* 3 (March 1999): 39.

56. Branum, p. 41.

57. Branum, p. 40.

58. Kassop, p. 8.

59. Todd F. Gaziano, "The Use and Abuse of Executive Orders and Other Presidential Directive," legal memorandum, Heritage Foundation, January 21, 2001, p. 8.

60. Branum, p. 63.

61. Branum, p. 63.

62. Branum, p. 41.

63. Branum, p. 41.

64. Mayer and Price, p. 370.

65. Branum, p. 44.

66. Marc Lacey, "House Votes to Keep Bush's Family Planning Rule," *New York Times*, May 17, 2001, p. A4.

67. Sean Paige, "A Union Divorce without Remorse," *Insight on the News* 17 (March 26, 2001): 47; Branum, p. 47.

68. Branum, p. 55.

69. Mayer, pp. 88–89. For quantitative analyses of other trends in recent executive order usage, see Christopher J. Deering and Forrest Maltzman, "The Politics of Executive Orders: Legislative Constraints on Presidential Power," *Political Research Quarterly* 52 (December 1999): 767; George A. Krause and David B. Cohen, "Presi-

dential Use of Executive Orders, 1953–1994," *American Politics Quarterly* 25 (October 1997): 458; Kenneth R. Mayer, "Executive Orders and Presidential Power," *Journal of Politics* 61 (May 1999): 462.

70. Bass, p. 87.

71. Howell, p. 83. Compare to Mayer and Price's finding that one in seven executive orders issued between 1944 and 1999 were significant (p. 375).

72. Harold C. Relyea, cited in Gaziano, p. 10.

73. See Cooper, "The Law."

74. Cooper, "The Law," p. 131.

75. Page, 509, U.S. 155.

FOUR

The Significance of the Presidential Signing Statement

Christopher S. Kelley

INTRODUCTION[1]

The 21st Century Department of Justice Appropriations Authorization Act[2] contained a provision[3] that dealt with the nonenforcement of sections of law that the president determines to be unconstitutional. The section prohibits the president from declining to enforce those provisions or to advise any of his subordinates not to enforce sections of law the president has determined to be unconstitutional.

When President George W. Bush signed the bill into law, he noted in his signing statement that he would construe this section so that it conforms to the president's constitutional responsibility to supervise the unitary executive branch. In other words, the president commented on the constitutionality of the section and decided how he—independent of Congress—would decide to enforce it if at all.

This defies our understanding of the political process of lawmaking. The Congress presents the president with a bill and the president then determines whether to sign it or veto it. If he signs it, then he has a constitutional obligation to enforce it. If a dispute arises over its constitutionality, then the courts should be left to determine what the law is. However, with the presidential signing statement, the Congress seems to be addressing a systematic pattern of the executive determining what sections of law he will or will not enforce.

This chapter examines the significance and importance of the presidential signing statement: what the signing statement is, how it has been used over time, and exactly how it enhances presidential power.

THE SIGNING STATEMENT DEFINED

Little has been written about the presidential signing statement. It has been overshadowed by the executive order, the proclamation, and other contentious unilateral actions the president has taken for himself. Furthermore, when the signing statement has been discussed, it has often been portrayed inaccurately[4] or the discussion has been incomplete.[5] Additionally, little is known about the origins of the signing statement and how many have been issued.

Signing statements generally fall into three distinct categories: the constitutional signing statement, the political signing statement, and the rhetorical signing statement. Most of the signing statements are simply written and added as part of the legislative history of the bill, whereas some are both written and presented formally in a bill signing ceremony. Usually when this occurs, the two statements differ with the written portion containing most of the president's objections to the bill and the formal statement casting a conciliatory tone to the audience. Finally, a single bill may contain one, two, or all three types of statements.

A constitutional signing statement is one that addresses a constitutional defect in a bill, ranging from an infringement on presidential prerogatives to violations of the principles of federalism to an infringement on the rights of the individual. The president will cite the section as erroneous and may urge Congress to pass corrective legislation or may more drastically refuse to execute the law or to defend it if it is challenged. From Washington through Clinton, 397 constitutional signing statements have been issued, with most (367) occurring since the Nixon administration.

A political signing statement is one that may appear similar to the constitutional signing statement, but its focus has a political rather than a legal intent. A political signing statement is usually meant as a directive to an executive branch agency to carry out the intent of the president. More often than not, the political signing statement exploits an ambiguity in a section of the legislation that will allow the executive branch to breathe life, albeit with the president's interpretation, into the defective section of law. In the course of the legislative process, contentious provisions of a bill may be left intact while in conference, but the meaning of specific terms are stripped to meet with the approval of both houses of Congress. The president can then exploit this dispute in a way that moves the bill closer to the president's preferred position. From Washington through Clinton, 106 political signing statements have been issued, with most (82) occurring since the Nixon administration.

A rhetorical signing statement is one that generally does not make either a constitutional or a political interpretation of a section of bill, but one that is generally aimed at a larger audience, such as the media. The rhetorical signing statement is the most common type of statement and involves a president either commending or criticizing members of Congress for their work on the bill or for adding language that recognizes an important constituency to the president. From Washington through Clinton, 1,594 rhetorical signing statements have been issued with the greater proportion (41 percent) found in the period between Nixon through Clinton.

HISTORICAL DEVELOPMENT OF THE SIGNING STATEMENT

The signing statement has enjoyed a rich and illustrative history. President James Monroe issued the first signing statements. In one instance, he issued a statement that interpreted a law that he had previously signed. The law had directed the president to reduce the size of the army, and it outlined how he would select officers. Monroe argued that the law infringed on his prerogatives as commander in chief and took the directions from Congress as advisory.[6]

During the Jackson administration, President Jackson incurred the ire of the Congress when he refused to extend a federal road project through the Michigan Territory into Illinois. Even though he signed the internal improvements bill, he deemed it unconstitutional to extend federal authority into an area that is the sole responsibility of the states.[7] After issuing his signing statement, some members of Congress complained that Jackson had in effect issued an ironclad item veto of the bill.[8]

President Tyler bore the full brunt of a rebuke from the Congress for issuing what was a rather timid signing statement. President Tyler disagreed with a portion of a bill dealing with the apportionment of congressional districts. Tyler wrote:

> In approving this bill I feel it due to myself to say, as well that my motives for signing it may be rightly understood as that my opinions may not be liable to be misconstrued or quoted hereafter erroneously as a precedent, that I have not proceeded so much upon a clear and decided opinion of my own respecting the constitutionality or policy of the entire act as from respect to the declared will of the two Houses of Congress.[9]

The House of Representatives would have none of it. In a sharp and lengthy protest (John Quincy Adams which authored[10]), a House Select Committee wondered why the president would add this extraneous document to the public record. The committee argued:

> The private and personal interest of the president in the organization of the House of Representatives of the next Congress suggests motives on his part for desiring to influence that organization in the direction of his individual interest. . . .[11]

The House concluded that President Tyler's signing statement should "be regarded in no other light than a defacement of the public records and archives."[12]

In 1899 the Supreme Court recognized the signing statement as a legitimate presidential practice noting, "it has properly been the practice of the President to inform Congress by message of his approval of bills, so that the fact may be recorded."[13] That said, the practice of using the signing statement nearly ceased. Not until Franklin Roosevelt's administration did the practice of using the signing statement become political and constitutional reasons returned. For example, President Roosevelt issued an objection to a bill[14] he signed that helped stabilize the economy during the height of World War II. His objection centered on "protectionist measures for farmers" in the United States, and if the Congress refused to remedy the flawed provision he would treat it as a nullity.[15]

In a separate bill,[16] President Roosevelt was forced to sign the legislation even though it singled out three federal bureaucrats for punishment. Roosevelt was forced into this position because the bill funded nearly all government agencies, and in his signing statement he noted that the punishment directed toward the federal bureaucrats amounted to an unconstitutional bill of attainder and was not "binding upon them."[17] When the bureaucrats sued and the case reached the Supreme Court, the Roosevelt administration sided with them and against the Congress, forcing the Congress to hire a special counsel to write an amicus brief defending the statute. In the end, the Supreme Court sided with the plaintiffs and with Roosevelt's interpretation of the bill.[18]

THE SIGNING STATEMENT AND THE ENHANCEMENT OF PRESIDENTIAL POWER

In the contemporary context as noted herein, the use of the signing statement escalated between the Nixon administration and the Clinton administration. What follows is an explanation of why the signing statement became instrumental during this period.

The two most significant events of the era—the Vietnam War and Watergate—factor into why the executive turned toward the signing statement, as well as other unique "power tools," to navigate the difficult political conditions left in the wake of those two events. With the revelations of the abuses of Watergate and the horror of an Imperial Presidency, Congress, the media, and the public sought to harness executive power within the confines of the Constitution. Yet during this same period, the expectations that the president will be a leader and will govern remained. Those presidents needed to figure out how to rectify two contradictory expectations.

The president would now aggressively interpret the oath clause and the take care clause of Article II to mean that the president could both refuse to enforce legislation that he determines to be unconstitutional and to mean that the president, as the only nationally elected individual in the United States, could interpret for the executive branch agencies the meaning of law.

During both the Ford administration and the Carter administration, the Department of Justice was aggressively defending executive branch prerogatives from congressional encroachment. For example, during the Ford administration, his Department of Justice interpreted the Federal Advisory Committee Act[19] to exclude the American Bar Association from the open meeting provision. The attorney general opined that this requirement violated the separation-of-powers doctrine, an opinion that ultimately the Supreme Court upheld in 1988.[20] Furthermore, both Ford and Carter systematically refused to enforce the legislative veto amounting to seventeen signing statements that dealt with the unconstitutionality of the provision. For example, in 1980 when the Secretary of Education was faced a forty-five-day wait and report provision in the General Education Provisions Act,[21] Attorney General Benjamin Civiletti instructed the secretary to ignore it because it was unconstitutional. According to Civiletti:

> [O]nce a function has been delegated to the executive branch, it must be performed there, and cannot be subjected to continuing congressional control except through the constitutional process of enacting new legislation.[22]

Finally, Nixon, Ford, and Carter administrations also sought greater administrative control over the decision-making process in the executive branch agencies. Long sought to be a source of great consternation for an ambitious president seeking to challenge the status quo, these three administrations instituted myriad initiatives, such as politicizing the Office of Management and Budget (OMB) in an effort to exert control over administrative discretion and to centralize the policymaking process within the White House. Furthermore, a couple of key Supreme Court decisions[23] gave the various agencies final say over the interpretation of law.

All of this proved valuable for the Reagan administration, which had outlined a plan prior to taking office to protect executive branch prerogatives aggressively while asserting centralized control over the policymaking process, both of which would include the use of the signing statement.

The administration was given an early boost from the Supreme Court when it picked up the challenge to the legislative veto, something that contradicted the campaign promise of candidate Reagan. Nonetheless, when the challenge[24] to the legislative veto reached the Supreme Court, the Supreme Court sided with the president that it violated the presentment clause of the U.S. Constitution. Furthermore, the Supreme Court noted the value of the presidential signing statement in placing the president on a consistent stance to the dubious constitutionality of the legislative veto.[25]

The Reagan administration enjoyed a second victory in the Supreme Court over its use of the constitutional signing statement when it disagreed with the comptroller general provisions of the Balanced Budget and Emergency Deficit Reduction Act,[26] or better known as Gramm-Rudman-Hollings. When President Reagan signed the bill[27] into law, he issued two constitutional objections to the bill. First, in a separation-of-powers objection, he noted that both the directors of the Congressional Budget Office (CBO) and the comptroller general in the budget process were given executive powers, and as such, were not appointed by the president. Second, he argued that the responsibilities given to the comptroller general to terminate or modify defense contracts for deficit reduction purposes violated *INS v. Chadha*.

President Reagan was not alone in this assessment. Within hours of signing the bill into law, Rep. Mike Synar (D-OK), along with eleven other members of Congress as well as the National Treasury Employees Union, filed a suit in federal district court for the District of Columbia challenging the constitutionality of the authority vested in the Government Accounting Office (GAO) to make automatic cuts.[28] On July 7, 1986, the Supreme Court issued its decision in which it upheld the district court's ruling that the deficit reduction procedure was unconstitutional.

In the decision, *Bowsher v. Synar* (1986),[29] the Court, in footnote one, relied on President Reagan's signing statement issued when he signed Gramm-Rudman-Hollings into law. The Court validated both objections President Reagan raised. It held that the powers given to the comptroller general violated the separation-of-powers doctrine in so far it does not give the president the right to remove officers involved in executive powers. Furthermore, the deficit reduction provisions violate the separation-of-powers doctrine by giving executive powers to an agent of Congress.

The Department of Justice in the Reagan administration under Attorney General Edwin Meese also was very public in its defense of the prerogative of the president to independently interpret the constitutionality of law, a principle often referred to as "coordinancy," or "departmentalism," which is the basis of Madison's argument in *Federalist* 49. In a 1986 speech at Tulane, Ed Meese argued that "constitutional interpretation is not the business of the Court only, but also properly the business of all branches of government."[30] Attorney General Meese seemed to have found a sympathetic ear in the Supreme Court because Justice Scalia, in a concurring opinion, noted that:

> . . . it was not enough simply to repose the power to execute the laws (or to appoint) in the President; it was also necessary to provide him with the means to resist legislative encroachment upon that power. The means selected were various, including a separate political constituency, to which he alone was responsible, and the power to veto encroaching laws . . . or even to disregard them when they are unconstitutional.[31]

To centralize control over the policymaking process, the Reagan administration also issued two important executive orders[32] that gave to OMB's Office of Information and Regulatory Affairs a central role in enforcing the administration's wishes on policy decisions within the executive branch agencies. Taken together, these two executive orders have allowed the White House to impact the regulatory process at an early stage and often against the policy wishes of the agency head and allowed the OMB to monitor informally and to communicate directly with the agencies.

The administration also received a great boost in its effort to centralize control over the administrative agencies from the Supreme Court. In 1984 the Supreme Court issued an opinion[33] that placed interpretation of unclear legislation into the hands of the executive branch administrator, as long as the legislative history of the bill is not clear on the intent of the legislation. This gave the administration the chance to test whether the executive orders giving them oversight of the executive branch were really working.

In February 1986 Ed Meese explained at a gathering at the National Press Club that the administration had worked out an agreement with the West Publishing Company to have the president's signing statement added to the Legislative History section of the *United States Code Congressional and Administrative News (USCCAN)*. This was done, according to Meese, to:

> . . . make sure that the President's own understanding of what's in a bill is the same . . . or is given consideration at the time of statutory construction later on by a court.[34]

Because the courts had earlier recognized the signing statement, placing it beside the other pieces of the legislative history that the courts consider when they come across ambiguous or undefined sections of legislation being disputed seemed prudent. But even more important, the administration wanted to make sure that because bureaucratic agency heads would now be free to interpret undefined or unclear pieces of legislation (as long as the intent of Congress was not clear), the decision that would be made would have the administration's preferences in mind.

The Reagan administration used the political signing statement to take advantage of contentious debates within the Congress. The administration used this to skew legislation in a way that either advantaged the administration or advantaged key administration constituents. This could not have been clearer than in the case of the Immigration Reform and Control Act, 1986" (IRCA).[35]

The IRCA took several years to make it through the Congress, and it sought to address the problem of illegal and undocumented foreign-born people coming to the United States every year. When President Reagan signed the bill, he issued eight separate statements, three of which dealt with constitutional objections and five that made political interpretations.

One of the interpretations that President Reagan made dealt with the "Frank" amendment to the bill, named for Congressman Barney Frank (D-MA). Congressman Frank had worked diligently for several years to ensure legal protections for those who may be dismissed from their place of employment for discriminatory reasons rather than for performance-based reasons. He feared the IRCA would allow some businesses to discriminate against some employees by firing them for fear of violating federal law. Thus his amendment built into the law protections from discrimination by placing the burden of proof on the employer to show that the firing had to do with poor job performance rather than the person's race or ethnicity.

When the IRCA went to conference, Congressman Frank's amendment was left intact, but because some participants objected to the burden-of-proof provision, the definition of what amounted to discrimination was deleted. When President Reagan issued his signing statement of IRCA, he took advantage of the vulnerable Frank provision by defining discrimination in a way that shifted the burden of proof onto the fired employee and not the employer, something that clearly contradicted the intent of the author. In fact, after President Reagan issued the signing statement, Congressman Frank charged that the shift in the burden of proof "tells the bigots how to be smart and evade the law."[36] However, when the final rule was published, the interpretation of the Reagan administration prevailed.

The Reagan administration had now given to subsequent presidents a real power that had not been of much use prior to the Reagan administration. The courts recognized the signing statement as a legitimate device to put in effect the executive's coordinate power and the administrative agencies used the signing statement as a playbook when making determinations on undefined or vague portions of law.

The Bush administration took advantage of the addition of the signing statement to the USCCAN by the Reagan administration. In two very high-profile incidents, the Bush administration sought to resolve a political problem by working with fellow partisans in the Congress to create an alternative legislative history of a bill that the president could then point to in his signing statement.

In the first instance, President Bush attempted to take control of a political problem stemming from the Iran-Contra controversy during the Reagan administration. The Iran-Contra controversy, which had implicated Vice President Bush, involved officials within the Reagan administration who circumvented the will of the Congress by trading arms with Iran and then using that money to aid the Contra rebel force fighting the Sandinista government in Nicaragua. By selling arms to the Iranians, the Reagan administration broke a public pledge to not deal with terrorists. By using that money to aid the Contras, the Reagan administration violated public law, which prohibited any "funds available to the Central Intelligence Agency, the Department of Defense, or any other agency or entity of the United States"[37] from supporting "directly or indirectly" the Nicaraguan Contras. The 1989 trial of Colonel Oliver North renewed public attention both to the controversy and to President Bush's role in the sordid affair.

Congress used this renewed interest to assert a more active role in foreign policy. During congressional debate on the Foreign Operations, Export Financing, and Related Programs Appropriations Act,[38] Rep. David Obey (D-WI) added an amendment to the bill that "prohibited the sales of arms or aid to any foreign government to further U.S. foreign policy objectives if the U.S. would be prohibited for the same kind of influence."[39]

President Bush[40] vetoed an earlier attempt to insert this amendment as unconstitutional violations of the president's power over foreign policy and to control internal deliberations within the executive branch. In addition to these objections, President Bush also objected to a provision of the bill that mandated international family planning policies that included contraceptives and abortion funding. A subsequent bill, the one the president signed, had removed the family planning provisions but retained the provisions contained in the Obey amendment in "a classic case of veto bargaining."[41]

President Bush's signing statement of the bill noted his "serious misgivings as to the constitutionality" of many of its provisions and his intent to "construe any constitutionally doubtful provisions in accordance with the requirements of the Constitution."[42] One of the doubtful provisions was the Obey amendment. President Bush argued that his intent is to construe this narrowly in accordance with the view expressed on the House and Senate floor that the provision only applies to quid pro quo transactions—"transactions in which U.S. funds are provided to a foreign nation on the express condition that the foreign nation provide specific assistance to a third country, which assistance U.S. officials are expressly prohibited from providing by U.S. law."[43] Bush finds his interpretation of this section in an "explanatory colloquy" between Senators Robert Kasten and Warren Rudman.[44] According to this "colloquy," a quid pro quo arrangement is one that:

> . . . requires that both countries understand and agree that the U.S. aid will not be provided if the foreign government does not provide the specific assistance. The Senate record also makes clear that neither the criminal conspiracy statue, nor any other criminal penalty, will apply to any violation of this section. My decision to sign this bill is predicated on these understandings of Section 582.[45]

According to Charles Tiefer, this was done for the sole purpose of manipulating the legislative history.[46] Tiefer claims that this was a strategy worked out between the White House and Senator Bob Dole, then-Senate Minority Leader. The Republicans in Congress planted an alternative legislative history that would give an "alternative account of what Congress was doing in passing the bill without the changes in the bill that Congress would make."[47] The purpose was to supplant "congressional legislating on a central and hotly contested issue."[48]

Indeed, an examination of section 582 shows that the Congress took care to point out that it excluded any "funds to governing governments 'in exchange' for taking actions prohibited to the U.S. government," and not just the those with a quid pro quo agreement.[49]

In 1991 President Bush was forced to sign a civil rights bill that contained language his administration found particularly disagreeable, particularly sections that dealt with quotas. The president vetoed the Civil Rights Act of 1990, an earlier bill, because it had contained the very same language as the 1991 bill.[50] However, in 1991 the political climate had changed substantially for the president. First, in the period between the two bills, the president had emerged from a bitterly fought confirmation process for

Clarence Thomas in which a great deal of Bush's political capital was spent in the Senate. Second, the campaign of white supremacist David Duke in Louisiana adopted language that the Bush administration had used when it publicly campaigned against the Civil Rights Act of 1990. The Bush administration was sensitive to claims that it was hostile toward minorities and thus worked with the Congress to pass the 1991 legislation.

At the heart of the 1991 act was the push by the Congress to reverse a Supreme Court decision[51] in 1989 that changed the meaning of "disparate impact" that controlled the hiring practices within the private sector. Prior to this decision, some businesses were required to hire by quota to alleviate certain disparities among those businesses that competed for government contracts. The new meaning shifted the burden of proof to the plaintiff to prove that hiring practices were discriminatory.

During the course of the legislative process, the Congress (with Senator John Danforth serving as the administration's point man in the debate) and the administration agreed to explicit wording inserted into the *Congressional Record* that read:

> The terms "business necessity" and "job related" are intended to reflect the concepts enunciated by the Supreme Court in *Griggs v. Duke Power Co.*, 401 U.S. 424 (1971), and in other Supreme Court decisions prior to *Wards Cove Packing v. Antonio*, 490 U.S. 642 (1989).

However, when President Bush signed the bill, he issued a signing statement that was meant to neutralize the portions he did not agree with and to give him advantages not won during the legislative debate. At the start of the signing statement, he noted that the bill "codifies" rather "overrules" the Supreme Court decision in *Wards Cove*.[52] Furthermore, even though he had worked with the Congress through his liaison Senator Danforth to construct the language noted previously, in the president's signing statement he pointed to the *Congressional Record* entries of Senator Bob Dole (R-KA) and others as the authoritative guidance—the legislative history—of the act. Executive branch agencies were then instructed to follow the Dole interpretation and not the Danforth interpretation when interpreting the meaning of disparate impact.

The Bush administration was able to capitalize on the work the Reagan administration did to develop the power of the signing statement and to have it added as judicial and executive branch guidance.

The Clinton administration seized on the efforts of the Reagan and Bush administrations and used the signing statement along with a variety of unilateral actions to deal with a hostile Congress and hostile political environment following the 1994 midterm election.

Not long after Clinton took office, White House Counsel Bernard Nussbaum requested that the Office of Legal Counsel (OLC) advise the administration as to the constitutionality of the signing statement. The response came from Walter Dellinger, assistant attorney general in the OLC who argued that a president may use the signing statement to "declare that the legislation (or relevant provisions) would be unconstitutional in certain applications; statements that purport to construe the legislation in a manner that would 'save' it from unconstitutionality; and statements that state flatly that the legislation is unconstitutional on its face."[53]

A year later, Dellinger followed up with a memorandum to White House Counselor Abner Mikva that a president has "enhanced responsibility to resist unconstitutional provisions that encroach upon the constitutional powers of the Presidency."[54] A president should predict whether the piece of legislation would be something that the courts would strike down if enforced. However, even if he cannot make that determination, the president's responsibility is to the Constitution first—"the obligation is reflect in the Take Care Clause and in the President's oath of office."[55]

President Clinton also used the signing statement strategically to help him politically. For example, one of the president's most influential constituents was the homosexual community. In an effort to create a wedge issue for the 1996 presidential election, an amendment was added to the National Defense Authorization Act for Fiscal Year 1996[56] that sought to discharge members of the military who were HIV-positive. President Clinton vetoed an earlier version of the bill for containing the amendment among other things.[57] Rep. Robert Dornan (R-CA), who at the time was about to become a presidential candidate, offered the amendment to both bills.

In President Clinton's signing statement, he argued that neither the secretary of defense nor the Joint Chiefs of Staff found this policy to be a wise one—that it would waste government resources spent on training and would do nothing to improve the defense of the United States. President Clinton instructed the Department of Justice not to defend this amendment if it were challenged, and he instructed the executive branch agencies that would be affected by the amendment to give those service members and their families affected the "full benefits to which they are entitled. . . ."[58] Additionally, White House lawyer Jack Quinn and Assistant Attorney General Dellinger held a joint news conference in which they argued the administration was willing to use whatever measure necessary to ensure the amendment would not be enforced.

Representative Dornan, however, argued that this was more of the Clinton administration ignoring "the needs and requirements of the military while deferring to the wishes of a vocal minority who donate heavily to his presidential campaign."[59] Dornan also suggested that the section had a "snowball's chance in hell" of being repealed and that he "welcomed the court challenge."

The act would not take effect until six months after it was signed. The Clinton administration, however, was able to work for its repeal[60] just two months after he had signed it into law, thus never giving the administration the chance to test its resolve. We have little reason to think that the administration would not have followed through on the threat laid out in the signing statement and in the public appearances of administration officials, and considering the lack of support in Congress for the Dornan amendment, little evidence exists to suggest that Congress as an institution would have defended against the Clinton action.

The Clinton administration was equally aggressive in its use of the signing statement to protect executive branch prerogatives. In early 1999 a political firestorm errupted when the public learned that our nation's nuclear laboratories were not secure. A presidential advisory board recommended the creation of an independent oversight agency within the Department of Energy that would not be pressured by the secretary of energy. Five bills were introduced that sought to put the recommendation of an independent agency into practice. Only one, the National Defense Authorization Act for Fiscal Year 2000,[61] made it out of Congress with the new agency intact.

While the act was in conference committee, members stuck into it the agency that the administration bitterly opposed. This new agency, the National Nuclear Security Administration (NNSA), would have a semi-autonomous director responsible for "the safety, reliability, and effectiveness of the U.S. nuclear weapons stockpile, nuclear non-proliferation, and naval nuclear reactors."[62]

When President Clinton signed the bill, he noted his disapproval with this last-minute action and that the creation of this new agency would significantly hurt the ability of the secretary of energy to supervise those under him.[63] President Clinton then bluntly stated that he did not recognize the authority of this new agency or its director and would instruct the secretary of energy to carry out the duties assigned to the new director.[64]

The administration's action outraged members of Congress, who called Secretary of Energy Bill Richardson to appear before the House Armed Services Committee to explain the administration's action. When Secretary Richardson was directed toward testimony by the GAO that the administration's action undermined U.S. national security, Secretary Richardson flippantly responded,

"I have yet to find the GAO to say something positive about anything."[65] Furthermore, Secretary Richardson told the committee that he did not feel obligated to follow the intent of the law because the version the Clinton administration told Congress they supported was stripped out in secret and this new agency was put in its place.

In the end, the Clinton administration did appoint a director for the NNSA, but never did accept the independence Congress envisioned for this officer. When Congress passed two laws[66] outlining the conditions under which the director could be removed, one of which was "neglect of duty," President Clinton noted in his signing statements for each law that "neglect of duty" was to mean "among other things, a failure to comply with the lawful directives of policies of the President."[67]

President Clinton would leave office before this issue could be resolved. Importantly, however, while he remained in office, up to the very end, he used the signing statement in a fit of presidential power at the very moment when many presidential scholars suggest the president's power should be at its weakest.

CONCLUSIONS

This chapter discussed what the signing statement is, how it developed, and most important, it illustrated the importance of the presidential signing statement from the Reagan administration through the Clinton administration. It showed that over the last thirty years the political division between the White House and the Congress has been such that a president's employing many of the traditional resources equated with bargaining and persuasion to push his preferred policies has been difficult. Furthermore, the period following Watergate saw an assault on the prerogatives of the presidency as the Congress and the public attempted to reign in the imperial presidency.

The presidential signing statement, in all of its forms, will continue to play a role in future presidencies because it enables the president to win battles that he may not be able to win in the normal course of the legislative process. The strategic use of the signing statement also demonstrates the importance of the executive's aggressive constitutional interpretation when the tools of the modern presidency break down.

NOTES

1. Portions of this chapter are taken from Christopher S. Kelley, *The Unitary Executive and the Presidential Signing Statement* (Ph.D. dissertation, Miami University, 2003).

2.Public Law No. 107–273, 21st Century Department of Justice Appropriations Act, November 2, 2002.

3. Ibid., Section 202.

4. Chris Cookson, in a 1997 *Southeastern Political Review* article both greatly overstates the power of the signing statement and falsely charges popular hostility to the use of the signing statement in the Reagan and Bush administrations. Chris E. Cookson, "Formal Executive Power: The Contemporary Presidency," *Southeastern Political Review* 25 (September 1997).

5. Phillip J. Cooper's recent book, *By Order of the President: The Use and Abuse of Executive Direct Action* (Lawrence: University Press of Kansas, 2002), does a good job discussing what a signing statement is, but does not provide an adequate picture of how they affect the political process.

6. Christopher N. May, *Presidential Defiance of "Unconstitutional" Laws: Reviving the Royal Prerogative* (Westport, Conn.: Greenwood Press, 1998), p. 116.

7. Bradley Waites, "Let Me Tell You What You Mean: An Analysis of Presidential Signing Statements," *Georgia Law Review* 21 (Winter 1987): 777.

8. Louis Fisher, *Constitutional Conflicts between Congress and the President* (Lawrence: University Press of Kansas, 1991), p. 128.

9. James D. Richardson, *Messages and Papers of the Presidents*, vol. 2 (Washington, D.C.: Bureau of Natural Literature and Art, 1903), p. 159.

10. Paul E. McGreal, "Unconstitutional Politics," *Notre Dame Law Review* 76 (January 2001): 519–637.

11. HR. Resp., no. 909 (apportionment bill can act for an apportionment of representatives), 27th Congress, 2nd sess. (1842).

12. Ibid.

13. *La Abra Silver Mining Co. v. United States*, 175 U.S. 423 (1899).

14. *Emergency Price Control Act of 1942*, 56 Stat. 26, PL77–421 (January 30, 1942).

15. See Franklin D. Roosevelt, "Statement on Signing the *Emergency Price Control Act* (New York: Harpers Brothers Publishing, January 30, 1942), p. 69.

16. See the Urgent Deficiency Appropriation Act of 1943. 57 Stat. 431, 450. 1943.

17. Franklin D. Roosevelt, "Statement on Signing the *Urgent Deficiency Appropriation Act*, 1943," *The Public Papers and Addresses of Franklin Delano Roosevelt* (New York: Harper, 1943), p. 385–86.

18. *U.S. v. Lovett*, 328 U.S. 303 (1946).

19. Public Law 92–463, Federal Advisory Committee Act (1972).

20. *Washington Legal Foundation v. U.S. Department of Justice*, 88–494 (1988); *Public Citizen v. Justice Department*, 88–429 (1988).

21. 20 U.S.C. 31, General Education Provisions Act (1980).

22. Benjamin Civiletti, "Constitutionality of Congress' Disapproval of Agency Regulations by Resolutions not Presented to the President," 4A OP. O.L.C. 21, 27 (Washington, D.C.: U.S. GPO, 1980).

23. See *Mathews v. Eldridge*, 424 U.S. 319 (1976); *Vermont Yankee Nuclear v. Natural Resources Defense Council, Inc. et al.*, 435 U.S. 519 (1978).

24. See *INS v. Chadha*, 462 U.S. 919 (1983).

25. See *INS v. Chadha*, 462 U.S. 919 (1983), footnote 13.

26. Public Law 99–177 (1985).

27. Ronald Reagan, "Statement on Signing H.J. Res. 372 into Law," *Weekly Compilation of Presidential Documents* 21 (December 12, 1985): 1490–91.

28. "Constitutionality of Automatic Cuts Challenged," *CQ Almanac* (1985): 461.

29. *Bowsher v. Synar*, 478 U.S. 714 (1986)

30. Edwin Meese III, "Perspectives on the Authoritativeness of Supreme Court Decision: The Law of the Constitution," *Tulane Law Review* 61 (April 1987): 986.

31. *Freytag v. Commissioner*, 501 U.S. 868 (1991).

32. Executive Order no. 12,291, *Federal Register* 46 (February 1981); Executive Order no. 12,498, *Federal Register* 50 (January 1985).

33. *Chevron v. Natural Resources Defense Council*, 467 U.S. 837 (1984).

34. Quoted in Marc N. Garber and Kurt A. Wimmer, "Presidential Signing Statements as Interpretations of Legislative Intent: An Executive Aggrandizement of Power," *Harvard Journal on Legislation* 24 (1987): 367.

35. Public Law 99–603, Immigration Reform and Control Act, November 1986.

36. Mark R. Killenbeck, "A Matter of Mere Approval? The Role of the President in the Creation of Legislative History," *Arkansas Law Review* 48 (1995): 272.

37. Louis Fisher, *Constitutional Conflicts between Congress and the President* (Lawrence: University Press of Kansas, 1991), p. 211.

38. Public Law 101–67 (1989).

39. Charles Tiefer, *The Semi-Sovereign Presidency: The Bush Administration's Strategy for Governing without Congress* (Boulder, Colo.: Westview, 1994), p. 38.

40. George H. W. Bush, "Message Returning to the House of Representatives without Approval the Foreign Relations Authorization Act, Fiscal Years 1990 and 1991," *Weekly Compilation of Presidential Documents* 25 (November 21, 1989): 1806–7.

41. Tiefer, p. 38.

42. George H. W. Bush, "Statement on Signing the Foreign Operations, Export Financing, and Related Programs Appropriations Act, 1990," *Weekly Compilation of Presidential Documents* 25 (November 21, 1989): 1811.

43. Bush, "Statement," p. 1811.

44. Bush, "Statement," p. 1811.

45. Bush, "Statement," p. 1811.

46. Tiefer, p. 40.

47. Tiefer, p. 40.

48. Tiefer, p. 40.

49. Tiefer, p. 38.

50. See George H. W. Bush, "Veto Message on S. 2104 entitled *Civil Rights Act of 1990*," *Congressional Record* 136 (October 24, 1990): S16562.

51. *Wards Cove Packing Co. v. Atonio*, 490 U.S. 642 (1989).

52. Tiefer, p. 57. "The Civil Rights Act of 1991," *The Congressional Record* 137 (October 25, 1991): S15273

53. Walter Dellinger, "The Legal Significance of Presidential Signing Statements," Memorandum, Office of Legal Counsel (November 3, 1993). http://www.usdoj.gov/olc/signing.htm.

54. Walter Dellinger, "Presidential Authority to Decline to Execute Unconstitutional Statutes," Memorandum for the Honorable Abner J. Mikva, Counsel to the President, November 2, 1994. http://www.usdoj.gov/olc/nonexecut.htm.

55. Dellinger, "Presidential."

56. Public Law 104–106 (1996).

57. See William J. Clinton, "Message to the House of Representatives Returning without Approval the *National Defense Authorization Act for Fiscal Year 1996*," *Weekly Compilation of Presidential Documents* 31 (December 28, 1995): 2233–35.

58. Clinton, "Message."

59. Kathy Lewis, "Clinton Blasts HIV Provision; But He Says He Will Sign Military Bill," *The Dallas Morning News*, February 10, 1996, p. 1A.

60. See section 2702, *Making Appropriations for Fiscal Year 1996 to Make a Further Down Payment toward a Balanced Budget, and for Other Purposes*, Public Law 104–34 (April 26, 1996).

61. Public Law No. 106–65 (October 5, 1999).

62. Floyd D. Spence, "Statement of Chairman Floyd Spence, Full Committee Hearing on National Nuclear Security Administration" (Washington, D.C.: USGPO, March 2, 2000).

63. William J. Clinton, "Statement on Signing the *National Defense Authorization Act for Fiscal Year 2000*," *Weekly Compilation of Presidential Documents* 35 (October 5, 1999): 1928.

64. Clinton, "Statement on Signing the National Defense," p. 1928.

65. "NNSA Starts Up as Richardson and Congress Clash," *Science and Technology in Congress*, http://www.aaas.org/spp/cstc/bulletin/articles/3–00/nnsa.htm (accessed March 17, 2002).

66. "Making Appropriations for the Departments of Veterans Affairs and Housing and Urban Development and for Sundry Independent Agencies, Boards, Commissions, Corporations, and Offices for the Fiscal Year Ending September 27, 2000, and for Other Purposes," Public Law 106–377 (October 27, 2000); "Floyd D. Spence National Defense Authorization Act for Fiscal Year 2001—HR 4205," Public Law 106–398 (October 30, 2000).

67. William J. Clinton, "Statement on Signing the Fiscal Year 2001 Appropriations Legislation," *Weekly Compilation of Presidential Documents* 36 (November 6, 2000); William J. Clinton, "Statement on Signing the Floyd D. Spence National Defense Authorization Act for Fiscal Year 2001," *Weekly Compilation of Presidential Documents* 36 (October 30, 2000): 2651–760.

FIVE

Executive Privilege in an Era of Polarized Politics

Mark J. Rozell

Executive privilege is the right of presidents to withhold information from those entities that have compulsory power, particularly Congress and the judicial branch. It is thus also a power that enables presidents to keep information secret from the media and the public. The Constitution makes no mention of this presidential power; it is an implied power. Because democratic society has a strong presumption of openness, executive privilege is a controversial power.

Reasonable people agree that presidents have secrecy needs. But how far do these needs extend? When is exercising executive privilege appropriate and how are disputes over access to information properly resolved? Until the Nixon years, most disputes over executive privilege were largely muted and few in the public had ever heard of this presidential power. The Watergate scandal marked a turning point in the exercise of executive privilege because President Richard Nixon tried to use this power to conceal the wrongdoing that eventually brought down his administration. Nixon's actions ignited a national debate over executive privilege and eventually gave this presidential power a bad name.

Nonetheless, despite the taint of Watergate, executive privilege has made something of a comeback, especially in the Clinton and Bush eras of highly polarized politics. This chapter focuses on the evolution of executive privilege in the modern presidency with a special emphasis on the most recent controversies over this power during the George W. Bush administration. Executive privilege, despite the Watergate taint and then the added taint of the Clinton scandal in 1998 and 1999, remains an important tool of modern presidential power. As long as presidents believe that they have secrecy needs, and all of them do at some point, conflicts over executive privilege will arise.

THE EVOLUTION OF EXECUTIVE PRIVILEGE IN THE MODERN PRESIDENCY

President Dwight Eisenhower's administration originated the use of the phrase executive privilege and expanded the actual practice of that power. Members of Congress rightfully concerned about the expanded practice sought to limit Eisenhower's successors by articulating standards for the use of executive privilege. Rep. John Moss (D-CA), the chairman of the House Subcommittee on Government Information, led the effort. Beginning with President John Kennedy's administration, Moss sent letters to successive presidents requesting written clarification of policy toward the use of executive privilege. President Kennedy replied that executive privilege "can be invoked only by the president and will not be used without specific presidential approval."[1] President Johnson similarly responded, "the claim of 'executive privilege' will continue to be made only by the president."[2]

Ironically, President Nixon responded most forthrightly to Moss's inquiry when he wrote, "the scope of executive privilege must be very narrowly construed. Under this Administration, executive privilege will not be asserted without specific presidential approval. . . . I want open government to be a reality in every way possible."[3] Nixon issued the first detailed presidential memorandum specifically on the proper use of executive privilege.

> The policy of this Administration is to comply to the fullest extent possible with Congressional requests for information. While the Executive branch has the responsibility of withholding certain information the disclosure of which would be incompatible with the public interest, this Administration will invoke this authority only in the most compelling circumstances and after a rigorous inquiry into the actual need for its exercise. For those reasons Executive privilege will not be used without specific Presidential approval.[4]

The memorandum outlined the procedure to be used whenever a question of executive privilege was raised. If a department head believed that a congressional request for information might concern privileged information, he or she would consult with the attorney general. The two of them would then decide whether to release the information to Congress or to submit the matter to the president through the counsel to the president. At that stage, the president either would instruct the department head to claim executive privilege with presidential approval or request that Congress give some time to the president to make a decision.

Nixon's response to Moss and the executive privilege memorandum were important to the development of standard procedures on the scope and application of that power. Unfortunately Nixon's practices gave executive privilege a bad name and had a chilling effect on the ability of his immediate successors either to clarify procedures or properly exercise that power. President Gerald Ford began avoiding executive privilege inquiries and used other constitutional or statutory powers to justify withholding information. Within a week of Ford's inauguration, Rep. Moss sent an inquiry to the president requesting a statement on executive privilege policy.[5] Unlike presidents Kennedy, Johnson, and Nixon, Ford ignored the letter. Other members of Congress weighed in with their own requests and Ford ignored their letters too. Numerous discussions took place within the White House over the need for the president either to reaffirm or to modify Nixon's official executive privilege procedures. Ford took no action on the recommendations.

The associate counsel to the president summed up the dilemma when he suggested three options: (1) cite exemptions from the Freedom of Information Act (FOIA) as the basis for withholding information "rather than executive privilege"; (2) use executive privilege only as a last resort—even avoid the use of the phrase in favor of "presidential privilege" or "constitutional privilege"; (3) issue formal guidelines on executive privilege.[6] Ford chose to handle executive privilege controversies on a case-by-case basis rather than to issue general guidelines. He understood that for many people "executive privilege" and "Watergate" had become joined.

President Jimmy Carter similarly did not respond to congressional requests for clarification of administration policy on executive privilege. Not until the week before the 1980 election did the Carter administration established some official executive privilege procedures. On October 31, 1980, White House Counsel Lloyd Cutler issued an executive privilege memorandum to White House staff and heads of units within the Executive Office of the President. The memorandum established that those considering the use of executive privilege must first seek the concurrence of the Office of Counsel to the President. The memorandum also emphasized that only the president had the authority to waive executive privilege.[7] Cutler later would become counsel to the president in the Clinton administration and would write new procedures on the use of executive privilege in 1994.

On November 4, 1982, President Ronald Reagan issued an executive privilege memorandum to heads of executive departments and agencies. The

Reagan procedures dovetailed closely with the 1969 Nixon memorandum. For example, Reagan's guidelines affirmed the administration policy "to comply with congressional requests for information to the fullest extent consistent with the constitutional and statutory obligations of the executive branch."[8] The memorandum reaffirmed the need for "confidentiality of some communications"[9] and added that executive privilege would be used "only in the most compelling circumstances, and only after careful review demonstrates that assertion of the privilege is necessary."[10] Finally, "executive privilege shall not be invoked without specific presidential authorization."[11]

The Reagan memorandum developed greater clarity of procedures than before. All congressional requests must be accommodated unless "compliance raises a substantial question of executive privilege."[12] Such a question arises if the information "might significantly impair the national security (including the conduct of foreign relations), the deliberative process of the executive branch or other aspects of the performance of the executive branch's constitutional duties."[13] Under these procedures, if a department head believed that a congressional request for information might include privileged information, he or she would notify and consult with both the attorney general and the counsel to the president. Those three individuals would then decide whether to release the information to Congress or have the matter submitted to the president for a decision if any one of them believes invoking executive privilege necessary. At that point, the department head would ask Congress to await a presidential decision. If the president chose executive privilege, he would instruct the department head to inform Congress "that the claim of executive privilege is being made with the specific approval of the president." The Reagan memorandum allowed for the use of executive privilege even if the information originated from staff levels far removed from the Oval Office.

By avoiding executive privilege, presidents Ford and Carter actually succeeded more than Reagan did at protecting secrecy. Ford and Carter understood the negative connotations of executive privilege. President Reagan tried to reestablish the legitimacy of executive privilege only to have the opposition party–led Congress harshly criticize and fight him every step of the way. Reagan ultimately backed down from his several claims of executive privilege and did more to weaken this power as a result.

President George H. W. Bush did not initiate any new executive privilege procedures. The 1982 Reagan memorandum remained in effect as official executive privilege policy during the Bush years. Bush frequently withheld information without invoking executive privilege. Like Ford and Carter, he avoided the negative taint of executive privilege and generally used other bases of authority for withholding information. When the Bush administration wanted to withhold information from the Congress, it used a variety of names other than executive privilege to justify that action. Among them were "internal departmental deliberations," "deliberations of another agency," and the "secret opinions policy."[14] The chief investigator to the House Committee on the Judiciary during the Bush years said that Bush "avoided formally claiming executive privilege and instead called it other things. In reality, executive privilege was in full force and effect during the Bush years, probably more so than under Reagan."[15]

President Bill Clinton used executive privilege elaborately. Unlike Bush, he did not conceal executive privilege. Like Nixon, he concealed wrongdoing—or tried to—by resorting to executive privilege. Like Nixon, Clinton gave executive privilege a bad name and made reestablishing the legitimacy of this constitutional power difficult once again for future presidents.

In 1994 the Clinton administration issued its own executive privilege procedures. The memorandum from the special counsel to the president Lloyd Cutler stated:

> The policy of this Administration is to comply with congressional requests for information to the fullest extent consistent with the constitutional and statutory obligations of the Executive Branch. . . . [E]xecutive privilege will be asserted only after careful review demonstrates that assertion of the privilege is necessary to protect Executive Branch prerogatives.

The memorandum further stated, "Executive privilege belongs to the President, not individual departments or agencies."[16]

The Cutler memorandum described formal procedures for the use of executive privilege and these were not significantly different from those outlined in the Reagan memorandum. In light of Clinton's aggressive use of executive privilege during the presidential scandal of 1998 and 1999, one sentence stands out: "In circumstances involving communications relating to investigations of personal wrongdoing by government officials, it is our practice not to assert executive privilege, either in judicial proceedings or in congressional investigations and hearings."[17]

The Clinton administration also adopted the very broad view that all White House communications are presumptively privileged and that Congress has a less valid claim to executive branch information when conducting oversight than when considering legislation.[18] On several occasions the administration used executive privilege to thwart congressional investigations of alleged White House wrongdoing.

GEORGE W. BUSH: EXECUTIVE PRIVILEGE REVIVED?

In the early stages of the second Bush presidency, the administration was involved in three policy disputes that either had implications for the development of executive privilege or involved the president's direct claim of privilege. It became clear early in Bush's term that the president was committed to regaining lost ground on executive privilege. Nonetheless, Bush chose some very untraditional cases for reestablishing executive privilege. Also clear was that Bush not only wanted to revitalize executive privilege, but he also tried to expand the scope of that power substantially.

The Presidential Records Act of 1978 and Executive Order 13,223

In 1978 Congress passed the Presidential Records Act to establish procedures for the public release of the papers of presidential administrations twelve years after an administration left office. The principle behind the law was that these presidential records ultimately belong to the public and should be made available for inspection within a reasonable period of time. Section 2206 gave responsibility for implementing this principle to the National Archives and Records Administration (NARA). The 1978 act retained the public disclosure exemptions of the FOIA so that certain materials involving national security or state secrets could be withheld from public view for longer than twelve years.

On January 18, 1989, President Reagan issued an Executive Order 12,267, which expanded certain implementation regulations of NARA. Reagan's executive order identified three areas in which records could be withheld: national security, law enforcement, and the deliberative process privilege of the executive branch (section 1g). Reagan's executive order gave a sitting president primary authority to assert privilege over the records of a former president. Executive Order 12,267 recognized that although a former president has the right to claim executive privilege over his administration's papers, the archivist of the United States did not have to abide by his claim. The incumbent president could override the archivist with a claim of executive privilege, but only during a thirty-day review period. After that period, absent a formal claim of executive privilege, the documents were to be automatically released unless FOIA exemptions applied.

On November 1, 2001, President George W. Bush issued Executive Order 13,223 to supercede Reagan's executive order and to expand vastly the scope of privileges available to current and former presidents. Bush's executive order dropped the law enforcement category and added two others: the presidential communications privilege and the attorney-client or attorney–work-product privileges. Under the new executive order, former presidents may assert executive privilege over their own papers even if the incumbent president disagrees. Bush's executive order also gives a sitting president the power to assert executive privilege over a past administration's papers even if the former president disagrees. The Bush standard therefore allows any claim of privilege over old documents by an incumbent or past president to stand.[19] Furthermore, the Bush executive order requires anyone seeking to overcome constitutionally based privileges to have a "demonstrated, specific need" for presidential records (section 2c). The Presidential Records Act of 1978 did not contain such a high obstacle for those seeking access to presidential documents to overcome. Thus, under the Bush executive order, the presumption always is in favor of secrecy, whereas previously the general presumption was in favor of openness.

The Bush executive order set off challenges by public advocacy groups, academic professional organizations, the media, and some members of Congress. All were concerned that the executive order vastly expanded the scope of government secrecy in a way that was damaging to democratic institutions. Several groups, including the American Historical Association, the Organization of American Historians, and Public Citizen, initiated a lawsuit to have the executive order overturned. Congress held hearings that were highly critical of the executive order.[20] Although this controversy remained unresolved in 2004, Bush's executive order clearly improperly supercedes an act of Congress and attempts to expand executive privilege far beyond the traditional standards for the exercise of that power.

First, the handling of presidential papers is a matter that should be regulated by statute and not by executive order. Presidential papers are ultimately public documents—a part of our national records—and they are paid for with public funds. They should not be treated merely as private papers.

Second, legal precedent exists for allowing a former president to assert executive privilege, but the standard for allowing such a claim is very high. Executive privilege cannot stand merely because a former president has some personal or political interest in preserving secrecy. A former president's legitimacy in maintaining confidentiality erodes substantially once he leaves office, and it continues to erode even further over time. The Bush executive order does not acknowledge any such limitation on a former president's interest in confidentiality.

Third, the executive order makes it easy for such claims by former presidents to stand and makes it almost impossible for those challenging the claims to get information in a timely way. The legal constraints could effectively delay requests for information for years as these matters are fought out in the courts. These obstacles alone will settle the issue in favor of former presidents because many with an interest in access to information will conclude that they do not have the ability or the resources to stake a viable challenge. The burden will shift from those who must justify withholding information to those who have made a claim for access to information.

Fourth, executive privilege may actually be frivolous in this case because other secrecy protections are already in place for national security purposes. Basically the administration is trying to expand executive privilege substantially to cover what existing statutes and regulations already cover. Furthermore, a general interest in confidentiality is not enough to sustain a claim of executive privilege over old documents that may go back as far as twenty years.

Cheney Energy Task Force

Bush appointed Vice President Richard Cheney to direct an energy policy task force to develop the administration's energy policy. In April 2001 two Democratic members of Congress, Representatives Henry Waxman and John Dingell, requested from Cheney information about the composition and activities of the task force. Their request was in response to media reports that the task force had been meeting in secret with representatives of various groups that had a direct interest in the development of a national energy policy. The lawmakers asked the General Accounting Office (GAO) to investigate the activities of the task force. The GAO responded with a broad-based request for information about the task force meetings, including the identities of individuals present at task force meetings, the identities of persons the task force consulted about the development of energy policy, and the cost of the meetings. The vice president's counsel refused this request. After several months of wrangling over access to the information, on August 2, 2001, the vice president wrote to Congress that the GAO lacked authority to seek access to the task force information. According to Cheney, the GAO has the authority only to review the results of programs, not to seek information from a task force involved in program development.

U.S. Comptroller General David M. Walker objected to this description of the GAO's scope of authority. Nonetheless, the GAO narrowed the scope of its information request and sought only the names of task force members and the dates and locations of the meetings. The GAO and the members of Congress had thus dropped their insistence that Cheney disclose substantive details about the meetings.

The conflict between the GAO and the vice president's office appeared headed to a courtroom until the September 11, 2001 terrorist attacks on the United States. Walker issued a statement in late September that the dispute remained unresolved, but "given our current national focus on combating terrorism and enhancing homeland security, this matter is not a current priority."[21] On January 27, 2002, Cheney declared that the administration was steadfast in its refusal to provide even the most basic information about the meetings because of an important principle involved: doing so would contribute to a further eroding of traditional presidential prerogatives. The conservative group Judicial Watch filed a lawsuit against the Cheney task force to try to compel public disclosure of information about the names of persons who had met with the task force. The liberal National Resources Defense Council also initiated a lawsuit to get access to administration information on the development of energy policy. On January 30, 2002, the GAO announced its intention to initiate a lawsuit to force Cheney to reveal the names of task force members.

In his August 2, 2002 letter to the Congress, Cheney asserted that to provide the information requested by GAO would interfere with the constitutional duties of the executive branch by undermining the confidentiality of internal deliberations. Walker correctly pointed out that Cheney had thereby introduced "the same language and reasoning as assertions of Executive Privilege." Walker also noted that the GAO had merely requested factual information such as the names of persons who attended meetings and the costs of meetings, not deliberative information.[22]

Because of this narrow scope of inquiry, any claim of executive privilege in this controversy, whether made explicit by the president or implicit by the vice president, lacked credibility. The vice president was on stronger ground in his refusal to cooperate with the initial request for information because that inquiry was overly broad. The definition of "records" the GAO sought initially went on for half a page, reaching to e-mails, voice mail messages, drawings, plans, checks and canceled checks, bank statements, ledgers, books, diaries, logs, video recordings, telexes, notes, invoices, and drafts. Because of that initial broad request, Cheney may have perceived the later narrow request as merely the GAO's first effort to drag him into a multistep process of getting increasingly detailed information over time. Cheney may also be concerned that releasing the names of those who met with the task force would result in those individuals being called in the future to testify to Congress. Nonetheless, these concerns are not sufficient to sustain a claim of executive privilege because the narrow scope of the GAO request for information involves neither direct presidential decision making nor even deliberative matters in any sense. Thus, the administration pursued a two-pronged strategy of (1) making the traditional arguments for executive privilege without making a formal claim of that principle, and (2) claiming that the GAO lacks statutory authority to access executive branch information about task force matters. Walker lost this battle with Cheney in federal court. Rather than appeal, Walker allowed the decision to stand. Predictably, the court ruled that GAO had overstepped its authority and that ultimately Congress had not exhausted all of its powers to get access to the task force information.

Yet in 2004, private groups continued their legal challenges. The U.S. District Court and the Court of Appeals both ruled Cheney either must invoke executive privilege as the basis for withholding this information and then submit the matter to the courts for review or he must produce the information for the plaintiffs. In a controversial decision, the Supreme Court overruled this judgment of the lower courts and accepted the administration's argument that no claim of executive privilege was necessary, that the president or vice president could merely assert a more generalized "executive power" as the basis for withholding information.

Department of Justice Documents and Congressional Oversight

President Bush made his first formal claim of executive privilege on December 12, 2001, in response to a congressional subpoena for prosecutorial records from the Department of Justice (DOJ). The House Government Reform Committee, chaired by Rep. Dan Burton, was investigating two separate matters that concerned DOJ decision making. First, the committee was examining former Attorney General Janet Reno's decision to refuse to appoint an independent counsel to investigate allegations of campaign finance abuses in the 1996 Clinton-Gore campaign. Second, the committee was examining allegations of Federal Bureau of Investigation (FBI) corruption in its Boston office handing of organized crime in the 1960s and 1970s. The committee made clear that it was not requesting DOJ documents or other materials pertaining to any ongoing criminal investigations.

Bush instructed Attorney General John Ashcroft not to comply with the congressional request for any deliberative documents from the DOJ, and Ashcroft clashed with committee chair Burton over the administration's refusal to cooperate with the legislative investigations. At the core of this battle was a dispute over whether an administration can withhold any and all documents that involve prosecutorial matters, even if those matters are officially closed. Burton and members of the committee were upset that the Bush administration was trying to expand the scope of its authority to withhold information from Congress by refusing documents from terminated DOJ investigations. They were also upset that the Bush DOJ had closed the unfinished investigation of the 1996 campaign finance controversy. Burton and his colleagues clearly believed that former Attorney General Reno had hampered legitimate investigations and that Bush's desire to have certain Clinton-era controversies ended had the effect of denying full public disclosure of government misconduct. Burton penned a strongly worded letter to Ashcroft protesting the administration's "inflexible adherence to the position" that all deliberative materials from the DOJ be routinely withheld from Congress. Burton pointed out that the administration had not made a valid claim of executive privilege and therefore had no right to withhold the documents his committee requested.[23]

White House Counsel Alberto Gonzales recommended that the president assert executive privilege in response to any congressional subpoena for the documents or if Ashcroft was called to appear before the committee. The committee subpoenaed the documents and called Ashcroft to appear at a hearing on September 13, 2001. Because of the terrorist attacks two days before the scheduled hearing, Ashcroft's appearance was rescheduled for December 13, 2001. Bush wrote a memorandum to Ashcroft asserting executive privilege.

At the hearing (Ashcroft was not present), Burton fumed, "This is not a monarchy. . . . The legislative branch has oversight responsibility to make sure there is no corruption in the executive branch."[24] In place of Ashcroft, DOJ Criminal Division Chief of Staff Michael Horowitz issued the administration's statement before the committee. The statement claimed that revealing information about DOJ investigations would have a "chilling effect" on department deliberations in the future. Nonetheless, during the hearing Horowitz allowed that although the administration had adopted the policy that Congress should never receive access to deliberative documents, in the future the DOJ could conduct a case-by-case analysis of the validity of congressional requests for such documents.[25] This statement indicated for the first time that the administration had some flexibility with regard to the principle of withholding deliberative materials.

Bush's executive privilege memorandum to Ashcroft emphasized the deliberative nature of some of the prosecutorial materials the committee requested. The president also expressed concern that releasing materials regarding confidential recommendations to an attorney general "would inhibit the candor necessary to the effectiveness of the deliberative processes by which the Department makes prosecutorial decisions." More vaguely, the president asserted the separation-of-powers doctrine, the need "to protect individual liberty," and he stated that "congressional access to these documents would be contrary to the national interest."[26]

The DOJ followed with a letter to Burton emphasizing the president's assertion of executive privilege over the subpoenaed documents and expressing a desire to reach some accommodation. Assistant Attorney General Daniel Bryant expressed DOJ's unwillingness to release certain memoranda pertaining to former Attorney General Janet Reno's decision not to appoint a special counsel to investigate allegations of campaign improprieties in the 1996 Clinton-Gore campaign. Regarding the investigation of allegations of FBI corruption, he expressed at some length the DOJ's willingness to "work together" with the committee to provide "additional information without compromising the principles maintained by the executive branch."[27] Burton responded that the offer of accommodation was meaningless because, ultimately, the administration remained unwilling to allow the committee to review the most crucial documents for the purposes of an investigation.[28] White House Counsel Alberto Gonzales followed with the assurance that the administration did not have a "bright-line policy" of withholding all deliberative documents from Congress, yet he stated with regard to such memoranda, "the Executive Branch has traditionally protected those highly sensitive deliberative documents against public and congressional disclosure," a characterization that Burton strongly rejected.[29]

That Bush took his first official executive privilege stand over materials concerning closed DOJ investigations is truly puzzling. The Bush administration made clear that regaining the lost ground of executive privilege after the years of Clinton scandals and misuses of that power was necessary. Yet it chose a circumstance in which little justification appeared for the exercise of that power. The legislative investigation had no national security implications. No clear public interest was at stake in protecting old investigative documents and other materials. This claim of privilege did not even fall into the category of protecting the integrity of ongoing criminal investigations.

The dispute over DOJ documents became especially heated when news stories reported that the FBI had abused its authority when it investigated organized crime in the 1960s and 1970s. Credible evidence was found that the FBI had caused the wrongful imprisonment of at least one person, whereas it protected a government witness who committed multiple murders even while he was in protection. Burton demanded access to ten key DOJ documents to investigate the allegations of FBI wrongful conduct. The documents that Burton requested were on average twenty-two years old.[30] The administration refused to turn over DOJ documents and Burton threatened to take this controversy to the courts.

Burton had the complete support of the committee, as evidenced by a February 6, 2002, hearing at which all the members, Republican and Democrat alike, joined in lambasting the administration's actions and declared their intention to carry the fight for the documents as far as necessary.[31] The complete unanimity of the committee was remarkable, especially given that the administration—during a period of war and with an extraordinary high level of public approval—had made direct appeals for support to Republican Party committee members on the eve of the hearing. At the opening of the hearing several Republican Party members openly declared their disdain for this tactic and said regardless of party affiliation or a president's popularity, they were ready to defend Congress's prerogatives. Some members used colorful language to describe their anger at the administration's refusal to cooperate with the committee.

The administration witness at the hearing was Daniel Bryant, an assistant attorney general in the DOJ Office of Legislative Affairs. He asserted the position that all prosecutorial documents are "presumptively privileged" and never available for congressional inspection. This claim ran counter to a long history of congressional access to DOJ prosecutorial documents, especially in cases of closed investigations where the need for secrecy has disappeared. It also appeared to run counter to earlier administration policy clarifications that no blanket policy of withholding such materials from Congress existed. Bryant stated that the administration was willing to give an oral presentation about the general contents of the disputed documents to members of the committee, but not to allow the members actually to see the documents. This offer only brought more comments of disdain from committee members.

On March 1, 2002, the two sides reached an accommodation in which the committee would be permitted to view openly six of the ten disputed documents. This agreement allowed both sides to declare victory. The committee claimed that it had won the right to access to the most important documents that were necessary for its investigation of the Boston FBI office scandal. The administration took the view that it had allowed access only to a narrow category of documents—in this case, those that concerned an indicted FBI agent and were considered necessary to Congress's oversight function. The administration continued to insist that it did not have to give Congress access to deliberative documents. Ultimately, the committee accepted this agreement because of a lack of a consensus that members should instead continue to push for all ten documents.

The administration also prevailed in withholding three key documents pertaining to former Attorney General Reno's decision not to appoint a special counsel to investigate 1996 Clinton-Gore campaign finance abuses. The committee's inability to achieve a total victory indeed reflected the unwillingness of certain Democratic members to push for these three documents.

Because of Clinton's and Bush's controversial uses of executive privilege, many argue that the time has come for some greater clarification of the meaning and application of that power. Because executive privilege is a discretionary power—but one subject to limits—used in the service of the public interest, legalistic precision is not possible or desirable. Executive privilege should be used properly within the normal constraints built into the system of separation of powers.

SEPARATION OF POWERS: RESOLVING EXECUTIVE PRIVILEGE DISPUTES

Executive privilege clearly is a constitutional power. Since the Nixon years, presidents have not made effective use of that power. Some have devised means of concealing executive privilege and some have used that power improperly. Congress has shown little deference toward presidential secrecy. The reality is that presidents have secrecy needs and Congress has investigative powers. Executive privilege inevitably leads to interbranch clashes.

In light of events during the Clinton and George W. Bush administrations, why some would find a statutory definition of executive privilege or a judicial clarification of the limits of that power appealing is understandable. Yet over the course of presidential history an understanding of executive privilege has evolved that has been established through precedent, court decisions, and presidential declarations. Executive privilege is legitimate when it applies to protecting (1) certain national security needs; (2) the privacy of official White House deliberations when it is in the public interest to do so; or (3) the secrecy of ongoing investigations. In our democratic system, the presumption must be in favor of openness. The burden is on presidents to prove that they have a compelling need for secrecy, not on those who have legitimate compulsory powers to prove that they need information.

Resolving such disputes cannot occur through statutory guidelines or court-directed definitions. The proper resolution to conflict over presidential secrecy is rooted in the separation of powers. Congress and the courts already have the institutional means to challenge executive privilege. The proper solution to the potential abuse of executive privilege is not legalistic precision, but rather for the other branches to use fully the powers that they already possess.

If members of Congress are not satisfied with the president's response to their requests for information or testimony, they have numerous options.

Congress can issue a subpoena and perhaps ultimately a contempt of Congress resolution, retaliate by withholding support for the president's agenda or for one or more of his nominees, or simply withhold funding for presidential favored programs. These actions give the president the option of weighing the importance of secrecy against such interbranch conflict and the problems it may cause for him. If executive privilege can be exercised only for the most compelling reasons—a real threat to the national security or compromising internal discussions in a way that will clearly harm the public—then forcing the president's hand in this fashion is not unreasonable. Presumably, information being withheld for such vital purposes would take precedence over pending legislation or a presidential appointment.

In most cases in which presidents have withheld information or testimony and Congress has retaliated in some form, presidents ultimately have either ceded to Congress's demands or worked out some form of agreement to accommodate both sides in the dispute. In my studies of the history of executive privilege I have not come across a single incident in which a president gave in to Congress's demands and thereby committed a substantial harm to the national security or created a precedent that undermined the right of confidential deliberations for his successors.

Presidents simply are not powerless in these disputes. They have the ability to rally opinion against members of Congress for bottling up the agenda, program spending, or nominations. They can shift the burden to Congress to decide how important the information they seek is and how much political heat they should withstand. Presidents also have the powers of their office to help or to frustrate the needs of individual members of Congress.

The history of executive privilege shows that the president and Congress resolve these disputes and that the lack of precise legal guidelines on the use of that power has not resulted in constitutional crises. Someone gives in or there is an agreed-on accommodation. The extreme case would of course involve Congress using its power of impeachment against the president who refused to cooperate with demands for information. President Theodore Roosevelt in one case personally seized government papers and dared Congress to impeach him for doing so. But Congress could have tried to get the documents by retaliating in less dramatic ways. The key point is that in legislative-executive disputes over information, Congress possesses the ultimate weapon of impeachment should no action short of that step resolve the situation.

Rarely does either side benefit from disputes over information access that result in retaliatory measures. Both branches have powerful incentives to reach some accommodation. One approach has been for the executive to allow a few members of Congress—for example, the chair and ranking minority member of the committee seeking the information—to review privately confidential documents. During World War II President Franklin Roosevelt personally shared sensitive national security information with a few trusted and highly respected members of Congress, and they respected the sanctity of that information. Having the executive limit access to secret information to some members of Congress who can attest to the validity of the need for secrecy is not improper at all.

The judicial branch sometimes is a party to an interbranch dispute over access to information. President Clinton tried to shield White House information and testimony from the Office of Independent Counsel (OIC) in 1998, but a federal judge ultimately decided that the constitutional balancing test weighed in favor of the OIC's need for information. The process of accommodation is obviously more difficult between the president and a judicial entity than between a president and Congress. But the same principle applies: each side should use the powers already at its disposal as fully as possible.

When a dispute over information rises to the level of a constitutional crisis, the courts may get involved, which happened in the Watergate episode. The unanimous court in *U.S. v. Nixon* declared the privilege "constitutionally based" and that on matters of national security or foreign policy deliberations, such a power is difficult for another branch to overcome. Yet the court made clear that the privilege may, at times, have to defer to the constitutionally based powers of the coordinate branches of the government. In that case, the need for information in a criminal trial had to outweigh any presidential claim to secrecy. The Supreme Court in that case upheld the legitimacy of the judicial branch to pose as a viable check on the abuse of executive privilege.

Considerable legal precedent also exists for the courts' in camera review of sensitive information. Rather than compelling disclosure of information for open court review, the executive may satisfy the court in secret chambers of the need for nondisclosure. The courts have repeatedly affirmed their right to decide in particular cases whether the necessity of protecting sensitive information does indeed outweigh the need for evidence in criminal justice matters.

Disputes over executive privilege cannot be resolved with constitutional or statutory exactitude. Such disputes can best be resolved through the normal political flunctuations as provided for by the system of separation of powers. Through our presidential history, the doctrine of executive privilege has evolved with only one constitutional crisis peaceably resolved. No credible evidence is found that without additional legalistic precision regarding executive privilege we will someday experience an intractable constitutional crisis.

NOTES

1. Clark Mollenhoff, *Washington Cover-Up* (Garden City, N.Y.: Doubleday, 1962), p. 239.

2. Senate Subcommittee on Separation of Powers of the Committee of the Judiciary, *Executive Privilege: Hearings before the Subcommittee on Separation of Powers of the Committee on the Judiciary*, 92nd Congress, 1st sess., 1971, p. 35.

3. Rep. John E. Moss to President Gerald R. Ford, August 15, 1974, folder: "Executive Privilege (2)," Box 13, Edward Schmults Files, Gerald R. Ford Library, Ann Arbor, Michigan.

4. Memorandum by President Richard M. Nixon, March 24, 1969, folder: "Executive Privilege [1973]," White House Staff Files, Ronald Ziegler Files, Nixon Presidential Materials Project, Alexandra, Va.

5. Rep. John E. Moss to President Gerald R. Ford, August 15, 1974, folder: "Executive Privilege (2)," Box 13, Philip W. Buchen Files, Gerald R. Ford Library, Ann Arbor, Michigan.

6. Memorandum by Dudley Chapman, November 5, 1974, folder: "Executive Privilege—General (1)," Box 13, Edward Schmults Files, Gerald R. Ford Library, Ann Arbor, Michigan.

7. Memorandum by Lloyd Cutler, September 28, 1994, copy obtained by author.

8. Memorandum from President Reagan to Heads of Executive Departments and Agencies, "Procedures Governing Responses to Congressional Requests for Information," November 4, 1982.

9. Reagan, "Procedures Governing."

10. Reagan, "Procedures Governing."

11. Reagan, "Procedures Governing."

12. Reagan, "Procedures Governing."

13. Reagan, "Procedures Governing."

14. Mark J. Rozell, *Executive Privilege: Presidential Power, Secrecy and Accountability* (Lawrence: University Press of Kansas, 2002), chap. 5.

15. James Lewin, author interview, November 19, 1992.

16. Memorandum from Lloyd Cutler.

17. Ibid.

18. Letter from Attorney General Janet Reno to President Clinton, September 20, 1996, copy obtained by author. The administration derived its view that Congress lacks a compelling need for executive branch information in cases of oversight from a dubious interpretation of the District of Columbia Circuit Court's 1974 ruling in *Senate Select Committee on Presidential Campaign Activities v. Nixon* (498 F. 2d 725). Although the court did not explicitly acknowledge Congress's need for information in cases of oversight, that is not the same as saying that the court overruled the well-established investigative powers of legislative committees. The Reagan and Bush administrations made similarly too-broad claims in this regard.

19. Alberto Gonzales to Rep. Stephen Horn, November 2, 2001, on file with the author.

20. U.S. Congress, Subcommittee on Government Efficiency, Financial Management, and Intergovernmental Relations of the House Committee on Government

Reform and Oversight, *Hearings on the Presidential Records Act*, 107th Cong., 1st sess., November 6, 2001 (hearing attended by author as expert witness).

21. Statement of Comptroller General David M. Walker, September 28, 2001, on file with the author.

22. Comptroller General David M. Walker to Speaker of the House Dennis Hastert, August 17, 2001, on file with the author.

23. Rep. Dan Burton to Attorney General John Ashcroft, August 29, 2001.

24. Ellen Nakashima, "Bush Invokes Executive Privilege on Hill," *Washington Post*, December 14, 2001, p. A43.

25. Statement of Michael Horowitz, chief of staff, Criminal Division, Department of Justice, before the Committee on Government Reform and Oversight of the United States House of Representatives, December 13, 2001, on file with author.

26. Memorandum by President George W. Bush to Attorney General John Ashcroft, December 12, 2001, on file with the author.

27. Daniel J. Bryant to Rep. Dan Burton, December 19, 2001, on file with author.

28. Rep. Dan Burton to Attorney General John Ashcroft, January 3, 2002.

29. Letter from Counsel to the President Alberto Gonzales to Rep. Dan Burton, January 10–11, 2002, on file with author.

30. Letter from Rep. Dan Burton to Attorney General John Ashcroft, February 4, 2002.

31. U.S. Congress, House Committee on Government Reform and Oversight, *The History of Congressional Access to Deliberative Justice Department Documents*, 107th Cong., 2nd sess., February 6, 2002 hearing attended by author as expert witness.

SIX

The "Protective Return" Pocket Veto: Presidential Aggrandizement of Constitutional Power

Robert J. Spitzer

In recent decades,[1] students of the presidency have debated with no little fervor the extent to which the institution has become more imperial, especially and most important, in the realm of constitutional authority. Many have argued that presidents have accumulated power beyond constitutional bounds in areas such as war powers,[2] executive privilege,[3] budgeting and impoundment,[4] executive orders,[5] the use of signing statements,[6] and other areas.[7] Whereas disputes over presidential use or abuse of constitutionally claimed powers are well known in areas such as war powers, other such executive aggrandizements are little known.

For example, Phillip Cooper describes the relatively unknown yet burgeoning practice of recent presidents using memoranda in tandem with executive orders to mask actual policy initiatives. Cooper discusses several instances where the first Bush and Clinton administrations issued executive orders stating one goal or objective, but then issued executive memoranda to initiate a very different, more controversial, and often covert action. Cooper's important work is fascinating in the way it reveals the complexity of White House subterfuge that "is deliberately attempting to hide its intentions."[8] The constitutional and policy consequences of this constitutional aggrandizement are considerable, a fact that takes on greater importance when compared with the extent to which this effort has proceeded nearly unimpeded and unnoticed.

This chapter clarifies another area where presidential aggrandizement of a constitutionally based power has steadily progressed below scholarly and political radar screens: so-called protective return pocket vetoes. This chapter discusses the basis for the pocket veto and its relationship with the regular veto. It then discusses pertinent case law, recent presidential experiments with the pocket veto, and the constitutional problems with that experimentation as they pertain to so-called protective return vetoes, a term and process so little known that this modest research apparently represents its first appearance in print.[9] The analysis concludes with an assessment of the merits and consequences of this idea.

THE REGULAR AND POCKET VETO POWERS

The Constitution provides the president with two kinds of vetoes in Article I, Section 7. The regular or return (sometimes also called qualified) veto is exercised when the president withholds executive signature and then returns the bill "with his Objections to that House in which it shall have originated. . . ." The bill is then subject to congressional override. The pocket veto, by contrast, not only observes different and more circumscribed procedures, but also has a different and more emphatic effect because it is absolute—that is, the exercise of a pocket veto kills the legislation in question because there is no bill return and therefore no possibility of override. Congress's only alternatives to dealing with a pocket veto are either to stay in session for at least ten days after the passage of a bill that may be subject to pocket veto so that the bill can be returned to Congress, or to start from the beginning and repass the bill when Congress reconvenes. As the Constitution states, "If any Bill shall not be returned by the President within ten Days (Sundays excepted) after it shall have been presented to him, the Same shall be a Law, in like manner as if he had signed it, unless the Congress by their Adjournment prevent its Return, in which Case it shall not be a Law." The first part of this sentence states that if the president takes no action on bills Congress presents, they become law automatically after ten days. The necessity of this provision is evident because presidents could halt bills by simply withholding their signature. This circumstance is then modified by the phrase, "unless the Congress by their Adjournment prevent[s] its Return," in which case any bill not signed by the president is vetoed by pocket veto, even though it is not returned to Congress.

The very existence of the pocket veto seems to contradict the sentiments of most of the Constitution's Framers concerning the executive veto because the pocket veto is, in its effect, an absolute veto, a power squarely opposed by most at the Constitutional Convention of 1787. James Madison, Roger Sherman, Pierce Butler, and Benjamin Franklin among others all spoke against an absolute veto for the president, fearing that it would gather too much power into the hands of the executive. The country's experience with the absolute veto was immediate and painful (British monarchs and colonial governors had used it for decades to thwart colonial legislation and to leverage political concessions as a condition for approval of colonial legislation).[10] To be sure, the absolute veto had several articulate champions, including Alexander Hamilton, James Wilson, George Read, and Gouverneur Morris. Yet in votes at the Constitutional Convention on June 4 and August 4, the proposal was emphatically rejected: 0–10 and 1–9 (votes were cast by state delegations).[11] Thus, the verdict of the convention was decisively against an absolute veto. How, then, is its presence in the Constitution in the form of the pocket veto explained?

The convention entertained no debate on what later came to be called the pocket veto,[12] yet the motive for its inclusion is clear. Quite simply, the pocket veto power was inserted to guard against the possibility that Congress could pass a bill and then quickly adjourn as a way of avoiding a veto before the president had a chance to return the bill because the regular veto can be executed only if Congress receives the returned bill along with the president's objections to it. Such quick adjournment practices had indeed occurred in some state legislatures before the 1780s. Joseph Story[13] noted in 1833 that the pocket veto was necessary precisely because it prevented Congress from circumventing a regular veto. After quoting from the constitutional provision describing the regular veto process, Story observed, "if this clause stood alone, congress might, in like manner, defeat the due exercise of his qualified negative by a termination of the session, which would render it impossible for the president to return the bill. It is therefore added, 'unless the congress, by its adjournment, prevents its return, in which case it shall not be a law.'"[14] Thus, the pocket veto was inserted to prevent the prospect of a bill automatically becoming law despite the president's objections but without the president's signature after ten days (remembering that signatureless bills automatically become law after ten days when Congress is in session).

One additional insight concerning the pocket veto case can be culled from the constitutional debates. In Document VIII of the Committee of Detail (a committee of five convened to hammer out constitutional language at the Constitutional Convention), the first language of what became the pocket veto clause called for no pocket veto at all; rather, it called for legislation that could not be vetoed and returned to the house of origin in circumstances where "their adjournment, prevent its Return" to instead "be returned on the first Day of the next Meeting of the Legislature."[15] This procedure was the one provided for in the New York Constitution of 1777, from which this and other elements of the federal Constitution were most likely borrowed.[16] In the committee's subsequent Document IX, and in the version presented to the convention on August 6, the postadjournment return language was dropped, giving the president the pocket veto.[17] The initial wording underscores the Founders' devotion to the principle of bill return. Edward Kennedy argues that the earlier language was dropped to avoid long delay and uncertainty over the fate of vetoed bills. Illumination of this issue can be gleaned from debate at the convention over language requiring Congress to meet at least once a year (Article I, Section 4). It detailed the expectation that Congress would meet for sessions lasting only a few months out of the year, owing to factors such as travel problems related to weather, the need for members to conduct "private business" during the summer, and the desirability of holding congressional elections at the same time as elections for state offices.[18] Because the Founders knew that many months would elapse between sessions and were keenly aware of obvious travel and communication problems, they would know also that bills the president had not signed at the end of a session would simply languish absent a pocket veto.

Four critically important conclusions about the relationship between the regular veto and the pocket flow from this analysis. First, the president was given the pocket veto to defend against any congressional effort to duck, and therefore thwart, the regular veto. Unlike the regular veto, the use of which the Constitution does not circumscribe, pocket veto use is carefully circumscribed by the fact that it may be used only when congressional adjournment prevents a bill's return. Second, the Constitution establishes a clear preference for regular veto over pocket veto use. That is, given any choice, ambiguity, or overlap between possible regular and pocket veto exercise, the Constitution is biased in favor of the exercise of the former rather than the latter. Not only did the clear majority of Founders disdain an absolute veto, but they also placed great emphasis on the value to be derived from granting Congress an additional opportunity to consider once more legislation before it is either enacted into law or killed. Contrary to contemporary impression, the veto was viewed in the eighteenth century as more than a simple negative or block. In referring to the veto as the "revisionary" power, the Founders referenced the veto's more positive and constructive quality, especially as a way to provide a final check against legislation that might be hastily or incompletely conceived, or that would benefit from a final round of revision through the process of a veto override.[19] Third, the Founders were concerned about the uncertainty that might arise from legislation passed by both houses at the end of a session that was followed by a lengthy break and about which presidents had reservations. This concern about uncertainty was sufficiently great to overcome the Founders' objections to an absolute veto power for the president. It is also reflected in a little-known fact about the early operation of Congress: Owing to the lapse of many months between sessions of early congresses, the institution ended all business at the end of each session as if each were an entirely new Congress. In other words, unfinished legislative matters were considered dead at the end of each session within a two-year congress. The House ended this practice in 1818 and the Senate in 1848.[20] Fourth, the pocket veto wording that defines the power as available when adjournment prevents bill return also means that adjournments happen when a bill return is possible; that is, not all adjournments invite or allow a pocket veto.

EVOLVING INTERPRETATION AND USE

Presidents exercise pocket vetoes in three circumstances: at the end of a two-year congress, during intersession adjournments, and during intrasession adjournments. The mere fact of this precedent would seem to buttress the idea that modern presidents are free to use the pocket veto during any adjournment lasting more than ten days or even during briefer adjournments when the tenth day falls during the break. Yet intersession pocket vetoes made sense in the country's early years because, as just mentioned, Congress operated as though the end of a session were the practical equivalent of the end of a congress. And intrasession pocket vetoes were the product of historical accident. The first intrasession pocket veto occurred in 1867 when Congress completed work on a joint resolution, HRJ Res. 6, pertaining to Civil War troop benefits, just before a spring recess. The senator who chaired the committee on enrolled bills placed the bill on his desk, but then absentmindedly left it there for eight days. When the bill was found, it was hurriedly presented to President Andrew Johnson, who refused to sign it—not because he wanted to veto the bill, but because he believed that he could only sign it when Congress was in session.[21] Thus was the first intrasession pocket veto exercised (all previous twenty-six pocket vetoes eight presidents used were exercised after sine die[22] adjournments at the conclusion of the first, second, or third sessions of congresses). As has so often occurred with the presidency, a precedent-setting action became the basis for repeating and routinizing the action.

Even setting aside these historical circumstances, practice alone does not define constitutional right or power, a fact that the Supreme Court has noted on many occasions.[23] For example, another little-known feature of the presidential-congressional relationship is that for the first 140 years of the country's history, presidents traveled in person to the Capitol on the last day of a congressional session to sign those bills that were not to be vetoed, based on the belief that presidents could not approve legislation after Congress had adjourned.[24] The Supreme Court swept this notion aside for congressional recesses in *La Abra Silver Mining Co. v. U.S.* (175 U.S. 423, 1899) and for sine die adjournments in *Edwards v. U.S.* (286 U.S. 482, 1932).

Evolving congressional practices and court rulings have helped resolve other ambiguities concerning the pocket veto. In *The Pocket Veto Case* (279 U.S. 644, 1929), the Supreme Court ruled on a challenge to a pocket veto by President Calvin Coolidge that occurred between sessions at the start of a six-month congressional break in 1926. In its ruling, the court upheld the intersession veto. Yet this decision, plus subsequent rulings and evolving practices, ultimately undercut the legitimacy and necessity of both inter- and intrasession pocket vetoes, paving the way for a growing consensus that pocket vetoes should only be used after sine die adjournments at the end of a two-year congress.[25] The court first noted that the specific matter before it was whether the congressional adjournment in question had prevented the president from returning the bill. In addressing the pertinence of adjournment, the court noted, "the determinative question . . . is not whether it is a final adjournment of Congress or an interim adjournment . . . but whether it is one that 'prevents' the President from returning the bill to the House in which it originated within the time allowed." The court rejected the argument of those challenging the veto that a bill could be returned to a duly designated agent when Congress was not in session because Congress had never actually done this and because the court feared that bills might hang in limbo for many months.

In *Wright v. U.S.* (302 U.S. 583, 1938) the court considered a challenge to a regular veto of a bill returned to the secretary of the Senate during a three-day Senate recess. In upholding the veto, the court said that it did not consider the three-day period an adjournment, but it also contradicted its previous conclusion in the *Pocket Veto* case by saying that Congress could indeed designate agents on its behalf, rejecting what it now considered "artificial formality" by saying, "The Constitution does not define what shall constitute a return of a bill or deny the use of appropriate agencies in effecting the return." The court also dismissed the potential delay problem mentioned in the *Pocket Veto* case as "illusory." Even though the *Wright* case pertained to three-day recess of one house and did not actually overturn the *Pocket Veto* case, it rejected the impediments to bill return cited in the earlier case.

In 1974 the U.S. Court of Appeals upheld a lower court ruling that struck down a 1970 pocket veto by President Richard Nixon that occurred during a six-day Christmas recess (*Kennedy v. Sampson*, 511 F 2d 430 [D.C. Cir. 1974]); that is, the tenth day lapsed during the six-day break. The court noted that bill return could have been effected, consistent with *Wright*, and the court also cast doubt on pocket vetoes applied during any intra- or intersession adjournment as long as appropriate arrangements were made for bill receipt, suggesting that a pocket veto was now only necessary after Congress adjourned sine die at the end of a two-year congress. The court also noted that congressional practices had changed dramatically since the 1920s because Congress was now in session nearly year-round. In addition, there was no longer any meaningful difference between intrasession and intersession breaks. The Nixon administration declined to appeal the ruling to the Supreme Court. During the 1970s, presidents Gerald Ford and Jimmy Carter abided by the principle of avoiding pocket vetoes during intra- and intersession adjournments, and Congress formalized procedures for receiving presidential messages during adjournments, just as presidents have long delegated agents to receive enrolled bills on their behalf, a practice considered acceptable even when the president is out of the country.[26]

WIDENING THE CONTRACTED POCKET

President Ronald Reagan backtracked on this arrangement when he pocket vetoed an obscure bill that provided relief for a Florida company in December 1981 between the first and second sessions of the 97th Congress. The affected company took the matter to court, but nothing came of the action. A significant challenge emerged from Reagan's pocket veto of HR 4042, a bill designed to prod human rights advances in El Salvador, between the first and second sessions of the 98th Congress in 1983. Members of Congress took the president to court, but the Supreme Court refused to hear the case on its merits, vacating it as moot in 1987 (*Burke v. Barnes*, 479 U.S. 361). Although Reagan exercised no other intersession (nor any intrasession) pocket vetoes, he did continue to argue for the constitutionality of intersession pocket vetoes.

The first Bush administration significantly escalated the pocket veto debate by arguing for intrasession, as well as intersession, pocket vetoes. Beginning with a little-noticed action, President Bush claimed to apply a pocket veto to a bill during a thirty-one-day intrasession adjournment of Congress in August 1989. The bill in question, HJRes. 390, dealt with a minor, technical matter concerning the waiving of certain printing requirements for enrolled bills. This pocket veto attempt (flagged by Bush's issuance of a memorandum of disapproval, the message accompanying pocket vetoes, rather than issuing a veto message, which accompanies regular or return vetoes) seemed trivial and insignificant, and in fact was considered to have been enacted into law and not vetoed because of Bush's failure to return the bill to Congress. The action was paradoxical because the pocket veto was entirely unnecessary as both houses of Congress had designated legal agents to receive vetoed bills during such breaks and had successfully received such vetoes on numerous previous occasions. Thus, Bush could have easily used a return veto. Furthermore, the bill was completely uncontroversial, and congressional leaders evinced no desire to challenge the president on the substance of the decision. Why, then, apply a pocket veto?

Similar questions arose with three other pocket veto Bush attempted. In December 1991, Bush claimed to issue a pocket veto through a memorandum of disapproval of a bill, S 1176, to establish the Morris K. Udall Scholarship and Environmental Policy Act. In an explanatory letter, Bush claimed that he favored the bill, but considered some technical elements of the bill to be unconstitutional.

Despite Bush's claim to having pocket vetoed both HJRes. 390 and S 1176 (neither of which he returned to Congress), Congress considered both to have been enacted into law without the president's signature because (1) Bush had withheld his signature from both bills, (2) the bills could have been returned to Congress via legally designated agents, and (3) legislation automatically becomes law after ten days if the president does not sign. In neither instance did Bush mount a legal challenge to Congress's assertion that these bills in fact became law (neither is today considered pocket vetoed, and both are omitted from Bush's veto totals as tabulated by the authoritative source on vetoes, the U.S. Senate Library [1992]).

In November 1989 Bush vetoed a Chinese immigration bill, HR 2712, which he similarly treated as a pocket veto, in that he issued a memorandum of disapproval, saying that a congressional adjournment prevented the bill's return. Yet in this instance, Bush in fact returned the bill to Congress, which in turn treated the veto as a regular veto (override votes were held in both houses; the veto was overridden in the House, but sustained in the Senate). Bush made the same claim for an appropriations bill for the District of Columbia, HR 2699, vetoed in August 1991 (Congress took no override votes). Even though Bush called these two actions pocket vetoes by saying that bill return was impossible based on the meaning of the Article I, Section 7, veto paragraph, he nevertheless did the impossible and returned the two bills to Congress.

The explanation for these actions was revealed in part in testimony Bush's Assistant Attorney General William P. Barr gave during hearings held by a subcommittee of the House Rules Committee in July 1989. Barr testified to speak against HR 849, a bill to define the president's pocket veto powers. If enacted, the bill would have limited pocket vetoes to final, sine die adjournments at the end of a congress. Speaking for the administration, Barr asserted that "the Constitution implies that any adjournment by the Congress—that is, any adjournment of either house for longer than three days—gives occasion for a pocket veto."[27] So, for example, a congressional weekend or holiday of four days would open the door to a pocket veto if a bill were presented to the president ten days before the break. Barr also challenged Congress's right to define the term *adjournment* by legislative means. The rationale for the three-day rule arises from Article I, Section 5, which says that neither house of Congress shall adjourn for more than three days without the consent of the other house. Because Congress consists of two houses, it may be considered as adjourned if one house is not in session. To the Bush White House, the fact that Congress delegates agents to receive veto messages was irrelevant.[28]

ENTER THE "PROTECTIVE RETURN"

The Bush administration's treatment of the four bills discussed previously is matched by other administration claims concerning unilateral assertions of presidential powers that would seem to have little or no constitutional justification.[29] But our interest here is with two of these four "vetoes": the 1989 Chinese immigration bill and the 1991 District of Columbia appropriations bill. In both of these cases, Bush not only returned the vetoed bill to Congress, but also claimed simultaneously to have used a pocket veto against them. This is the action that has come to be known as a "protective return."[30] These actions, it turned out, were presaged by little-noticed actions during the Ford administration.

Prior to the time that Ford had agreed to use his pocket veto only at the end of a two-year congress, he did on five occasions shortly after the start of his presidency engage in the same game as Bush—returning bills to Congress while claiming that he had also pocket vetoed them. Ford took these actions during a congressional adjournment from October 4 to November 18, 1974. As with Bush, Congress treated the bills as return vetoes. Senator Edward Kennedy (D-MA) folded a challenge to this procedure into his litigation against a Nixon pocket veto, yielding the case of *Kennedy v. Jones* (412 F.Supp. 353 [D.D.C. 1976]), in which the appeals court ruled that pocket vetoes could be used only after sine die adjournments, unless Congress failed to designate an agent to receive veto messages (the administration decided against an appeal). This result prompted Ford to accept a sine die–only pocket veto arrangement.[31] Whereas the Bush administration did not cite Ford's actions as precedent, one might speculate that Ford's actions provided some impetus for those of Bush. Unlike Ford's suspect vetoes, none of those of the Bush administration resulted in litigation.

There the matter remained until 2000, when President Bill Clinton resurrected the same dual veto procedure. In three instances, Clinton claimed to exercise both a regular veto and a return veto simultaneously against HR 4810, the Marriage Tax Relief Reconciliation Act of 2000 on August 5; HR 8, the Death Tax Elimination Act of 2000 on August 31; and HR 4392, the Intelligence Authorization Act for Fiscal Year 2001 on November 4. In all three instances, his veto message concluded with the same wording:

> Since the adjournment of the Congress has prevented my return of ——— within the meaning of Article I, section 7, clause 2 of the Constitution [the clause describing the regular and pocket veto], my withholding of approval from the bill precludes its becoming law. *The Pocket Veto Case*, 279 U.S. 655 (1929). In addition to withholding my signature and thereby invoking my constitutional power to "pocket veto" bills during an adjournment of the Congress, to avoid litigation, I am also sending ——— to the House of Representatives with my objections, to leave no doubt that I have vetoed the measure.[32]

Although not identical, this wording parallels that used in Ford's five double-veto messages from 1974 and that of Bush in 1989 and 1991.

In response to Clinton's actions, Speaker of the House Dennis Hastert (R-IL) and Minority Leader Richard Gephardt (D-MO) sent correspondence to the White House objecting to the procedure, noting prior congressional objections to Bush's comparable actions and making clear that they would treat these dual vetoes as return vetoes (*Congressional Record* 2000, H 11853).[33] No legal challenges ensued.

CONCLUSION: THE FLAWS AND DANGERS OF "PROTECTIVE RETURN" VETOES

One may be tempted to dismiss all this as inconsequential constitutional trivia. After all, Bush's and Clinton's dual vetoes failed to spawn court challenges or disrupt the usual lawmaking process, why be concerned? We should be concerned for two reasons: first, the procedure is flagrantly, even outrageously, extraconstitutional, and second, it may ultimately have profound institutional and policy implications.

Bearing in mind the earlier discussion about the bases of the regular and pocket vetoes, and the extant case law, several conclusions arise from this presidential gamesmanship over pocket veto use:

1. Presidential claims of simultaneous pocket veto and regular veto use—the so-called protective veto—are utterly incompatible with each other because:
   a. the regular veto and the pocket are, by constitutional definition and design, mutually exclusive and different acts;
   b. the Constitution treats the regular veto as the preferred means for vetoing a bill, meaning that if any doubt or ambiguity exists concerning whether to use the regular or pocket veto, constitutional design favors the former over the latter; and
   c. the fact that Ford, Bush, and Clinton all succeeded in returning the ten vetoed bills in question to Congress while claiming that they were also pocket vetoing the bills obliterates their pocket veto claims. Congress's successful receipt of return veto messages in these cases vindicates its assertion that no pocket veto actually occurred, thereby undercutting any justification for a pocket veto. In each case, the presidents' own deeds superseded their contradictory words.

2. The executive branch argument on which these suspect vetoes rest—that a pocket veto may be properly exercised during any adjournment of longer than three days—disfigures the pertinent constitutional clause. As noted in the *Pocket Veto*, *Wright*, and other cases, the exercise of the pocket veto rests not solely with the definition of adjournment, but with whether the adjournment in question prevents bill return. In *Wright*, the court said, the "Constitution does not define what shall constitute a return of a bill or deny the use of appropriate agencies in effecting the return." The failure of these presidents to cite any source other than the *Pocket Veto* case underscores the fact that they are placing their entire emphasis on a dubious and self-serving definition of adjournment while ignoring the equally important matter of whether bill return is possible.

3. The eighteenth- and nineteenth-century concerns about delay and uncertainty were real concerns when Congress met for only a few months out of the year, and when travel and communications were slow, unreliable, or even impossible. Given a contemporary society

that incorporates routinely fast and reliable travel and communication, the uncertainty problem no longer exists, as the court noted in *Wright*. As for the matter of delay, the use of congressional agents to receive veto and other presidential messages obviates the problem, precisely because the executive is able to complete its constitutional responsibility to review and return veto-objectionable bills more efficiently.[34] For its part, Congress is under no obligation to act, much less act quickly, on vetoed bills. If it fails to act, then the president prevails. Furthermore, there is no constitutional objection to override attempts that are played out even many months after a veto.

4. Protective return vetoes present myriad potential problems that simply need not exist. The bogus executive claim in veto messages that the dual veto procedure is being employed to "leave no doubt" that the bill in question has been vetoed is doublespeak because protective return creates, not resolves, doubt. Furthermore, consider these scenarios:
   a. A president exercises the protective return: Congress does not attempt or does not succeed in an override attempt; either way, the bill is dead, but the legal ambiguity of how it was killed remains.
   b. A president exercises a protective return, but Congress succeeds in its override votes. Potential litigants who are harmed either by the bill's enactment (successful override) or by its defeat (through pocket veto) file suit. Furthermore, what if the president orders that the bill not be published as a law? Aside from making more work for lawyers and judges, these complications all introduce a degree of uncertainty to the lawmaking process that is not only unnecessary, but also harmful to the functioning of the lawmaking process.

The arguments in favor of sine die–only pocket vetoes are not only constitutional (as several courts have noted), but also sensible. Yet one need not embrace them to view with great skepticism, and even alarm, the means by which President George H. W. Bush and President Bill Clinton have sought to legitimize an expansive definition of the pocket veto though protective return. Despite presidential rhetoric, presidents have not used protective return to exercise a veto that could not otherwise be exercised as these presidents' own actions demonstrate. The term itself is a misnomer because it erroneously suggests preserving something that already exists.

So why, to address the question looming over this discussion, have presidents done this? Only one answer presents itself: to legitimize for the presidency an expansive pocket veto that is, for all intents and purposes, a practical absolute veto. Admittedly, the actual operation of these protective returns to date would seem to belie such a threat because Congress has treated them as return vetoes and responded with override attempts. Yet the continued assumption of the expansive definition of the pocket veto that has accompanied these dual vetoes accumulates precedent and legitimacy. If these protective returns continue unchallenged, the prospect of presidential exercise of the expansive pocket veto without bothering with simultaneous return grows. To use a simple analogy, the return veto may serve as the booster rocket by which the pocket veto capsule may be launched into the realm of constitutional legitimacy after which time the return veto booster may be jettisoned.

Even though the modern Congress works throughout the calendar year, the congressional calendar is littered with adjournments lasting longer than three days, meaning that the longer-than-three-day definition of adjournment would afford presidents with pocket veto opportunities throughout the calendar year. The net result would be a nearly unlimited absolute veto for the president. Even setting aside the Founders' strenuous objections to an absolute veto, the effects of such a power for presidential-congressional relations would be significant. Given the now-accepted realization that the veto power shapes much more of the legislative process than was once thought,[35] the prospect of a more available and versatile pocket veto would materially enhance presidential influence over the legislative process.

An analysis of bills subject to conference committees (selected because such bills tend to be important, controversial, and high profile) during the 97th (1981–1982) and 98th (1983–1984) Congresses found that 74 percent of the eighty-two bills in the 97th and 54 percent of the eighty-three bills in the 98th would have been subject to a pocket veto under the three-day rule. Admittedly, Congress could avoid at least some potential pocket vetoes through careful timing of its presentment of enrolled bills. But the legislative process does not lend itself well to such incremental manipulations, and as Kennedy[36] noted, "since Congress is virtually always in adjournment at midnight, the *reductio ad absurdum* is that virtually every piece of congressional legislation could be vulnerable to a pocket veto."

Finally, I conclude with a prediction: the George W. Bush administration will, if the opportunity arises, continue and, if possible, expand the "protective veto" practice. If the practice remains unchallenged, yet another precedent-based presidential power will eventually have been created.

NOTES

1. Robert J. Spitzer, *Presidential Studies Quarterly* 31 (2001): 720–32. Reprinted by permission of Sage Publications.

2. David Gray Adler, "The Constitution and Presidential Warmaking," *Political Science Quarterly* 103 (Spring 1988); Robert Spitzer, *President and Congress: Executive Hegemony at the Crossroads of American Government* (New York: McGraw-Hill, 1993), chap. 5; Louis Fisher, *Presidential War Power* (Lawrence: University Press of Kansas, 1995); Louis Fisher, *Congressional Abdication on War and Spending* (College Station: Texas A&M University Press, 2000).

3. Raoul Berger, *Executive Privilege: A Constitutional Myth* (Cambridge: Harvard University Press, 1974); Rozell, Mark. *Executive Privilege: Presidential Power, Secrecy, and Accountability* (Lawrence: University Press of Kansas, 2002).

4. Fisher, *Presidential War Power*; Fisher, *Congressional Abdication*.

5. Kenneth R. Mayer, *With the Stroke of a Pen: Executive Orders and Presidential Power* (Princeton, N.J.: Princeton University Press, 2001); Cooper, Phillip J. "The Law: Presidential Memoranda and Executive Orders: Of Patchwork Quilts, Trump Cards, and Shell Games," *Presidential Studies Quarterly* 31 (March 2001).

6. Marc N. Garber and Kurt A. Wimmer. "Presidential Signing Statements as Interpretations of Legislative Intent: An Executive Aggrandizement of Power," *Harvard Journal on Legislation* 24 (Summer 1987): 363–95; Christopher S. Kelley, "Faithfully Executing and Taking Care—the Unitary Executive and the Presidential Signing Statement" (Paper presented at the Annual Meeting of the American Political Science Association, Boston, Mass., August 29–September 1, 2002).

7. David Gray Adler and Michael Genevose. *The Presidency and the Law: The Clinton Legacy* (Lawrence: University Press of Kansas, 2002).

8. Cooper, "The Law," p. 138. See also Phillip J. Cooper, *By Order of the President: The Use and Abuse of Executive Direct Action* (Lawrence: University Press of Kansas, 2002).

9. The author conducted a Lexis-Nexis search for the phrase *protective return* as applied to presidential vetoes and could find no such reference in either law journal articles or those of the popular media.

10. Robert J. Spitzer, *The Presidential Veto: Touchstone of the American Presidency* (Albany, N.Y.: SUNY Press, 1988).

11. Wilbourne Benton, *1787: Drafting the Constitution*, vol. 1 (College Station: Texas A&M Press, 1986), pp. 792–818.

12. The term *pocket veto* apparently was first applied during Andrew Jackson's administration by critics including Daniel Webster (Clement E. Vose, "The Memorandum Pocket Veto," *Journal of Politics* 26 [1964]: 397), although the use of the term *to pocket* as a synonym for blocking or suppressing traces back to Great Britain. The *Oxford English Dictionary* notes that in Shakespeare's play *The Tempest*, Antonio says in Act II, scene 1, "If but one of his pockets could speak, would it not say he lies?" to which Sebastian replies, "Ay, or very falsely pocket up his report."

13. Joseph Story, *Commentaries on the Constitution of the United States* (1833; repr. Durham, N.C.: Carolina Academic Press, 1987).

14. Story, p. 324.

15. Max Farrand, *The Records of the Federal Convention of 1787*, vol. II (Stamford, Conn.: Yale University Press, 1966), p. 162.

16. Edward M. Kennedy, "Congress, the President, and the Pocket Veto," *Virginia Law Review* 63 (April 1977): 360.

17. Farrand, pp. 167, 181.

18. Farrand, pp. 199–200.

19. Spitzer, *Presidential Veto*, pp. 19–20.

20. Kennedy, pp. 362, 379; see also Lindsay Rogers, "The Power of the President to Sign Bills after Congress Has Adjourned," *Yale Law Journal* 30 (November 1920): 1–22.

21. Kennedy, p. 357. In his pocket veto message, President Johnson noted the Senate's presentment delay, having come "two days after adjournment." Johnson continued, "It is not believed that the approval of any bill after the adjournment, is authorized by the Constitution of the United States . . . [and] would be contrary to the established practice of the Government from its inauguration to the present time. This bill will therefore be filed in the office of the Secretary of State without my approval." (Richardson 1913, V, 3734, compilation of messages and papers of the president, 1789–1897, U.S. Doc.)

22. A sine die adjournment is one that means, literally, "without a day," meaning a final adjournment. Contemporary congresses adjourn sine die only at the end of a two-year congress. A non–sine die adjournment is to a fixed date, which cannot be used to end a concluding congress.

23. Benson K. Whitney, "*Barnes v Kline:* Picking the President's Pocket," *Minnesota Law Review* 70 (May 1986): 1167.

24. Charles J. Zinn, *The Veto Power of the President* (Washington, D.C.: U.S. Government Printing Offie, 1951), p. 19.

25. Even in 1929, prevailing state practices, buttressed by several state court rulings, upheld the use of gubernatorial pocket vetoes only for final, sine die adjournments of state legislatures. Bill return to agents or representatives of state legislatures during other recesses and adjournments was also widely accepted in the states, and validated in state court rulings.

26. The argument for embracing the constitutionality of congressional use of agents to receive veto messages and other documents from the president is buttressed by the fact that a similar and parallel courtesy has long been extended to the president. In a 1964 case, *Eber Bros. Wine and Liquor Corp. v. U.S.* (337 F.2d 624 (Ct. Cl.), cert. denied, 380 U.S. 950 (1965)), a bill was presented to the president on August 31, 1959, after President Dwight D. Eisenhower had left for Europe. He returned on September 7, and vetoed the bill on September 14. Even though more than ten days had passed, the court upheld the veto, and further ruled that the president could ask to have bills presented to him personally abroad, that presentment could be delayed until the president's return, or that Congress could present bills at the White House as though the president were there. The logic of parallel flexibility applied to congressional receipt of vetoed legislation supports the argument for sine die–only pocket vetoes.

27. U.S. Congress, House of Representatives, Judiciary Committee, Subcommittee on the Legislative Process, *Hearing on H.R. 849*, 101st Congress, 1st sess., May 9, 1989, p. 61. Shortly after the *Burke* case in 1987, Sen. Kennedy was informed by

the Reagan Department of Justice that it would henceforth argue that any adjournment longer than three days would justify a pocket veto. This in turn prodded the House to draft legislation to make clear that a pocket veto would only be justifiable at the end of a congress. Butler C. Derrick Jr., "Stitching the Hole in the President's Pocket: A Legislative Solution to the Pocket-Veto Controversy," *Harvard Journal on Legislation* 31 (Spring 1993): 371–94.

28. John O. McGinnis, "Pocket Veto Clause," Office of Legal Counsel, Department of Justice, May 17, 1990, pp. 103–6.

29. Robert J. Spitzer, "Presidential Prerogative Power," *PS: Political Science and Politics* 24 (March 1991): 38–42; Robert J. Spitzer, "The Constitutionality of the Presidential Line-Item Veto," *Political Science Quarterly* 112 (Summer 1997): 261–84.

30. In a June 4, 2001, interview with a lawyer at the Office of Legal Counsel (OLC) of the Department of Justice employed there since 1989, the phrase *protective return* is the term that has been used within the executive branch to describe these double vetoes. The term probably dates back to the first Bush administration. They are dubbed "protective" because, according to the lawyer, the double veto erases any doubt that a veto has in fact occurred, so that a litigant affected by the legislation in question could not claim that the bill had somehow successfully become law, thus avoiding litigation. It was also considered "protective" because the action was viewed as a way of protecting the president's pocket veto power, based on the idea that any more expansive use of the power provides useful precedent in defense of the three-day rule. Yet the OLC lawyer conceded that the protective return might provoke litigation as well. Most important, the "protective return" reflects an executive branch view that Congress's use of agents to receive veto or other messages may not be legitimate. When the OLC lawyer was probed to explain these reasons, he referred the author to testimony Department of Justice spokesperson John O. McGinnis gave before the House Judiciary Committee (U.S. Congress, 23–33) in 1990 (John O. McGinnis, *Pocket Veto: Hearing before the Subcommittee on Economic and Commercial Law of the Committee on the Judiciary*, May 9, 1990 [Washington, D.C.: U.S. Government Printing Office]).

31. Fisher, *Congressional Abdication*, p. 6.

32. "Message to the House of Representatives Returning without Approval the 'Marriage Tax Relief Reconciliation Act of 2000,'" *Weekly Compilation of Presidential Documents* 36 (August 11, 2000): 1793–94; "Message to the House of Representatives Returning without Approval the Death Tax Elimination Act of 2000," *Weekly Compilation of Presidential Documents* 36 (August 31, 2000): 1985–86; "Message on Returning without Approval to the House of Representatives the 'Intelligence Authorization Act for Fiscal Year 2001,'" *Weekly Compilation of Presidential Documents* 36 (November 10, 2000): 2784–85.

33. The Wright Court noted with approval that Congress often sent bills to the president by messenger and that presidents routinely received and returned bills through agents even when the president was away, even though the Constitution said that "'he,' the President, shall return it. . . ." The court then said:

> It is against all reason and every recognized rule of construction, when the avoidance of unnecessary delay is so clearly manifest . . . that a construction should be superimposed which would make for delay regardless of every desire and of every effort of the President and of the Congress in the situation indicated.

34. Congressional Record 2000, H 11853.

35. Spitzer, *The Presidential Veto*; Richard A. Watson, *Presidential Vetoes and Public Policy* (Lawrence: University Press of Kansas, 1993); Charles M. Cameron, *Veto Bargaining: Presidents and the Politics of Negative Power* (New York: Cambridge University Press, 2000).

34. Kennedy, p. 280.

SEVEN

Executing the Rhetorical Presidency: William Jefferson Clinton, George W. Bush, and the Contemporary Face of Presidential Power

Kevan M. Yenerall

The rhetorical presidency has been an increasingly crucial and frequently controversial element of presidential governance for nearly a century. This chapter examines this vital aspect of presidential leadership by placing it within the larger context of paradigms of presidential power and their theoretical underpinnings. In doing so, key contributions from presidential scholars are addressed. Second, the institutional-constitutional foundations, strengths, shortcomings, and evolving execution of rhetorical power in the modern age of the presidency are considered. Lastly, recent use of the rhetorical presidency is considered by reviewing two aspects of the rhetorical leadership of Bill Clinton and George W. Bush, two contemporary presidents from different political parties and ideologies who have governed during a wide variety of political and institutional dynamics and constraints, including war and peace, surplus and deficit, divided and unified government, and impeachment and contested elections.

As evidenced by their rhetorical responses to the issues of civil rights and racial harmony (Clinton) and the terrorist attacks of September 11, 2001 (Bush), presidents Clinton and Bush have used vital constitutional and national occasions to outline certain aspects of their domestic and foreign agendas, unite American society behind their policies, and even redefine the very idea of the United States itself. Their embrace of the rhetorical presidency to meet some of their core constitutional duties illustrates that the execution of the rhetorical presidency transcends political, ideological, and institutional dynamics and constraints and can be a strategic and invaluable tool in the execution of essential, constitutionally prescribed presidential duties.

PRESIDENTIAL POWER: PARADIGMS, LEADERSHIP, AND THE LITERATURE

Popular literature exploring presidential power, until roughly mid-twentieth century, focused primarily on the traditional terrain of institutional matters—constitutional duties, executive relations with the legislative and judicial branches, and, occasionally, executive leadership in foreign policy. In short, such research reflected the original—or constitutional—intent of the office. Likewise, the focus of this scholarship was generally narrow, legalistic, and descriptive, centering on the office and its formal structures, legal precedents, and clearly defined constitutional authority. Thus, for this original paradigm of presidency literature, the powers Article II of the Constitution grants to the president—as well as the philosophical underpinnings of the office and the outlining of its structure and purpose in *The Federalist*, the Pacificus-Helvidius debates, and other sources—are quite instructive.[1]

In addition, William Taft's restrained view of the office—which espoused the view that there was "no undefined residuum of power" that a president could exercise merely "because it seems to him to be in the public interest"—stands as an essential constitutionally grounded treatise examining the nature and powers of the American presidency.[2] Indeed, for former President and Chief Justice Taft, the authority and specific responsibilities of the nation's chief magistrate were unambiguously rooted in the Constitution:

> The true view of the Executive functions is, as I conceive it, that the President can exercise no power which cannot be fairly and reasonably traced to some specific grant of power or justly implied and included within such express grant as proper and necessary to its exercise. Such a specific grant must be either in the Federal Constitution or in an act of Congress passed in pursuance thereof.[3]

Taken as a whole, this approach to the study of the presidency tended to downplay or minimize politics, bargaining, and tactical maneuvering, eschewing extensive consideration of intervening variables such as the social, political, and cultural climate of the day, or the psychological disposition, personality quirks, and persuasive powers of the individual occupying 1600 Pennsylvania Avenue.[4]

However, beginning—at least in part—with Clinton Rossiter's *The American Presidency* (1960), and, especially, with Richard Neustadt's landmark *Presidential Power* (1960), presidency scholarship shifted its coverage and understanding of the office, moving beyond the original paradigm of presidency scholarship. Keeping with the basic approach of the original paradigm, Rossiter's landmark work considered the formal roles of the presidency—including chief of state, chief executive, diplomat, and legislator. Also highlighting five prominent "informal roles" increasingly portrayed by modern presidents: chief of party, voice of the people, protector of the people, manager of prosperity, and world leader, thereby moving beyond the parameters of previous presidency scholarship. With one foot in the original paradigm and one foot examining newer and more explicitly political and behavioral roles, Rossiter's book signaled a shift toward a different theoretical framework for understanding and studying the nation's highest office.

Then, with Richard Neustadt's seminal work on presidential persuasion and behavior, *Presidential Power* (1960),[5] presidential research segued into several relevant areas of interest, prompted by both Neustadt's central thesis that true presidential power is the "power to persuade," as well as the growth—in power, size, and expectations—of the presidency and the institutionalized "presidential branch" that began in earnest after the Brownlow Commission's 1937 report and continued at an accelerated pace from Franklin Roosevelt to the present.[6] The Neustadt paradigm clearly and dramatically places the president at the center of the political system. Unlike the constitutional approach which grew in part out of a historical tradition of weak executives (Jefferson, Jackson, and Lincoln aside) and earlier political thought that reflected antagonism toward strong executives—no doubt influenced by the colonial experience—this new approach to examining the presidency advocates an aggressive leader who, from the center of the government, is the undisputed architect and executor of foreign policy and, especially, a wide-ranging set of domestic policies. And although Taft and Corwin both supported assertive presidential actions, they clearly favored more restraint than Neustadt. To operate successfully from this strategic position, a president must use "personal"—not formal constitutional—power: the power of persuasion buoyed by interpersonal skill and organization and prestige earned by a solid professional reputation.

As a result of this phenomenon and the heightened expectations the legacy of Franklin Roosevelt and New Deal activism brought on, presidents have since been defined and evaluated not only by their success in fulfilling basic constitutional duties, but also by the scope of their agendas and the style of their persuasion in implementing major policies. Presidents were increasingly expected to speak directly to the American people, and—aided and abetted by radio and, later, television—many chief executives engaged in near-constant conversations on a variety of national matters. In recent years political scholars such as Samuel Kernell[7] and George Edwards,[8] among others, have examined the propensity for modern presidents to "go public"—

staging events, photo opportunities, and campaign-style stops and speeches complete with pageantry and patriotism—to push agendas and maintain high levels of popular support.

Literature chronicling the evolution and dynamics of an increasingly behavioral, modern, "personal" and "plebiscitary,"[9] "postmodern,"[10] "rhetorical,"[11] and even extraconstitutional presidency has expanded exponentially in recent years. As this rhetorical, often larger-than-life presidency has raised public expectations for omnipresent executive leadership in a wide variety of areas, some scholars contend that a once (and deliberately structured) congressional-centered political system has been transformed—not necessarily for the better—into a nondeliberative, unbalanced, and executive branch–centered "presidential republic."[12] Others have expressed concern that lofty or unrealistic presidential rhetoric, even when executed with the best of intentions, may serve to further public cynicism toward the chief executive and the institutions of government in general when such words do not translate into coherent policy action and results. Consequently, this gap between words and expectations and political reality can cause Americans to view their presidents with less reverence and more contempt.[13]

In the aftermath of Franklin Roosevelt, the New Deal, and the exponential growth in the size and scope of the presidency and the federal government, the scholarship of unabashed proponents of broad presidential power—such as Neustadt—has had to be reconciled with constitutional and contextual constraints on such grandiose visions. According to this line of reasoning, a presidency-centered government is inherently irrational if for no other reason than the fundamental fact that the U.S. political system was established as a separated, not presidency-centered, system.[14] The president is but one player in a complex system of governance. Similarly, such scholarship also cautions against the propensity of modern presidents to assume that electoral "mandates," which are largely nonexistent, will provide enough political and institutional capital to overcome the fragmentation of a separated system and implement their proposals. Other scholars warned of the abuses inherent in a presidency-dominated system in the area of foreign policy and war powers, highlighting constitutional conflicts between the legislative and executive branches and documenting the chief executive's usurping of congressional power in the post–World War II era.[15] In many cases, further contributions to the study of the presidency shifted, at least in part, to the original paradigm, using the constitutional framework to explain and evaluate the dynamics and evolution of the office[16] and the "ambivalence" of modern executive power.[17]

In recent years, the very premise that a powerful "modern presidency" was established in the twentieth century has been challenged. David Nichols asserts that however infrequent, "modern presidents" and broad exercise of executive power in domestic and foreign affairs were indeed a reality prior to the twentieth century and the oft-cited administrations of Theodore and Franklin Roosevelt and Woodrow Wilson.[18] In fact, Nichols suggests that the basis for prerogative powers and a powerful chief executive resides not in uniquely twentieth century expectations of presidential power and leadership and the precedents Theodore and Franklin Roosevelt and Woodrow Wilson set, but in Article II of the Constitution. Thus the notion "modern" presidency is a myth; presidents have always had the legal authority to wield substantial power, and ample evidence exists—from Jefferson to Jackson to Lincoln and others—that the Constitution has always provided for broad presidential power.

In addition to the criticism of the Neustadt paradigm and the very idea of a twentieth-century "modern presidency," challenges to the tenets and success of the modern, personal presidency appeared in the form of the short-lived and less-than-spectacular presidencies of the 1970s. In the aftermath of Watergate and in the midst of stagflation and the beleaguered Ford and Carter regimes, some presidency scholars hinted that the Neustadt paradigm of presidential power had run its course. Indeed, in the 1970s, due to the bouts of executive abuse and deceit Nixon and Johnson[19] engineered—coupled with the "swelling" of the Executive Office of the President and the executive bureaucracy—many believed that the era of the powerful president had ended and that the pendulum of power and influence had swung, perhaps permanently, away from the White House. Scholarly reaction to the tumult of the 1960s, 1970s, and the comparatively weak presidencies of Ford and Carter, reflected this growing sentiment.

But midway through the Reagan presidency, Erwin Hargrove and Michael Nelson[20] argued that such myopic characterizations of the office do a tremendous disservice to presidency studies. Rather than react to the most recent presidents, scandals, or election losses, political scientists examining the highest office in the land would be wise to evaluate the institution of the presidency in terms of the specific historical cycles of preparation, achievement, and consolidation. Ultimately, individual presidencies and their levels of success or mediocrity are dependent on political, constitutional, and cultural constraints and to ignore any of these dynamics is to offer an anemic analysis of a complex situation. And, as the policy successes, governing strategies, and myriad institutional and political resources of the early Reagan years clearly suggest, a powerful, effective presidency was still very much possible.[21]

THE RHETORICAL PRESIDENCY: EXECUTIVE LEADERSHIP THE MODERN AGE

Of these diverse forays into theories of presidential leadership and governance, one of most relevant concepts in terms of understanding the contemporary execution of presidential power and the setting of agendas is the phenomenon known as the *rhetorical presidency*. In an extenuation of an argument originally presented in 1981 with coauthors James Ceaser, Glen Thurow, and Joseph Bessette, Jeffrey Tulis[22] assert that, since the presidencies of Theodore Roosevelt and, particularly, Woodrow Wilson, popular or mass rhetoric has become "one of the principal tools of presidential leadership."[23] For Tulis, the history of the rhetorical presidency is best understood from the point of view of the existence of two distinct constitutional presidencies. Although the first constitutional presidency (1789–1913) was a restrained office rooted in deliberation and rare public speeches, direct appeals to the public have dominated the second constitutional presidency (1913–present). Illustrative of this new strategy of leadership is the aggressive rhetorical presidency of Woodrow Wilson (1913–1921), which ushered in the second constitutional presidency. Wilson's ambitious whirlwind speaking tour to promote the League of Nations, a monumental and stressful campaign that may have, in part, ultimately led to his stroke, personifies this new form of presidential leadership. Consequently, in the era of the second constitutional presidency, leadership by popular and mass rhetoric became the norm, whereas until Wilson, and to a lesser and different extent, Theodore Roosevelt, both the Constitution and tradition had discouraged such a public presidency.[24]

Although the rhetorical presidency carries with it tremendous promise for dynamic leadership (perhaps best exemplified by Theodore Roosevelt's successful public crusade for the Hepburn Act), Tulis is apt to point out the immediate and long-term dangers and dilemmas presented by overreliance on public oratory as a means of leadership. Presidential routinization of crisis rhetoric in the twentieth century, for example—often to gain short-term advantages—has had grave consequences for effective policy, governance, and the presidency as an institution. To demonstrate the negative effects of the rhetorical presidency, particularly when used hastily to design and implement legislation without careful deliberation, Tulis presents a brief but illustrative case study of the formulation of Lyndon Johnson's ambitious Great Society programs.

Nonetheless, since the institutionalization of the rhetorical presidency in the twentieth century, presidents have routinely used the bully pulpit (the president's strategic use of rhetoric as a "vantage point for inspiring people") to legitimize their leadership and advance their agendas by going directly to the public for popular support.[25] As Samuel Kernell points out, one prominent tactic various twentieth century presidents have used is the act of "going public," the process of bypassing the deliberative process with Congress and taking one's message directly to the public.[26] In addition to and often in concert with the process of going public is the propensity for modern presidents to create carefully orchestrated political speeches, or "spectacles," designed to gain popular support for themselves and their specific policies.[27] The political spectacle,[28] cloaked in pageantry, civil religion, and patriotism[29]—and choreographed with the most effective images, lighting, backdrops, props, symbols, and rhetoric—has become commonplace in the contemporary presidency, serving as "a kind of symbolic event, one in which particular details stand for broader and deeper meanings."[30]

As Carol Gelderman[31] asserts in *All the President's Words*, the words and speeches of our presidents have shaped the modern presidency. Yet, importantly—and perhaps, on occasion, unfortunately—the real and perceived demands and organizational requirements of the modern rhetorical presidency have also led to a situation in which most presidents in last forty years have increasingly relied on wordsmiths and image makers, who are neither close advisors nor policy experts, to draft speeches and policy presentations. Consequently, in this era, the importance of exposition and eloquence has arguably largely vanished, and the result has been not only mediocre and unfocused speeches, easy-to-swallow sound-bites, and focus group–driven initiatives, but also messages and policies that, when divorced from careful planning and attention from a president and his closest of advisors, are often incoherent and severely flawed. Yet at the same time, even with a decrease in the quality and focus of presidential oratory, the rhetorical presidency is still a valid topic for critical study. We have, after all, examples of modern presidents having at least moderate success in using rhetoric to define their administration and its focus, and scholars have offered various examples of rhetorical "eloquence in an electronic age."[32] Indeed, Carol Gelderman argues that Bill Clinton resurrected his presidency via effective, eloquent rhetoric. Moreover, as Wayne Fields[33] reminds us, presidents have throughout the history of the Republic used State of the Union addresses, inaugurations, acceptance and farewell speeches, and a variety of other vital national occasions and ceremonies to unite American society, using major addresses to redefine and recreate not only themselves and their regimes, but also the very idea of the United States itself.

With the evolution and growing expectations of the rhetorical presidency throughout the twentieth century, as well the ongoing revolution in communication technology in the twenty-first century, presidents have a potential arsenal of rhetorical tactics to advance their policy agendas and meet their constitutional duties—or, at the very least, maintain exceptional levels of public support.[34] Yet, to be a truly constitutionally sound or inspired form of presidential power, even the most gregarious, photo- and television-friendly chief executive must connect his rhetorical actions to enumerated or inherent powers. To grasp the nature, possibilities, and legitimacy of rhetorical actions more fully, let us consider how the rhetorical leadership that shapes the contemporary presidency also derives from institutional power outlined in Article II of the Constitution.

Institutional Power and Rhetorical Actions

Institutional powers are specifically enumerated in, directly related to, or reasonably inferred from Article II of the Constitution. Such powers include executing the laws, recommending to Congress "such measures" the president "shall deem necessary and expedient" (that is, proposing, promoting, and signing legislation), periodically giving Congress information concerning the state of the union (what has since evolved into the annual ritualistic State of the Union Address, beginning in earnest with President Wilson), and appointment powers (federal judiciary, ambassadors, cabinet, and so on). Other institutional powers derive from constitutional amendments and acts of Congress. Thus, due to the ratification of the Twentieth Amendment in 1933, the inaugural address that occurs a few moments after the 12:00 P.M. oath of office on January 20 every four years (the formal ceremonial and substantive beginning of a president's tenure) is a constitutionally authorized affair. Likewise, State of the Union addresses, constitutionally sanctioned events that the Washington establishment has come to view as the primary method by which president's define their agenda, are both rhetorical and inherently institutional events.[35] Signing legislation, issuing executive orders, and presenting proclamations are other prominent examples of institutional acts that can be accented and executed, at least in part, with rhetorical action.

Purely rhetorical actions, whether stump speeches; acceptance speeches; weekly radio addresses; political spectacles; going public; interviews; phone conversations; public campaigning for candidates; or the strategic use of individuals, props, and images for symbolic purposes are by themselves examples of presidential activities Article II of the Constitution does not explicitly mandate. This does not mean, however, that rhetorical actions cannot be legitimate and constitutionally sound exercises of presidential power. If such actions are instrumental in carrying out enumerated duties, then they become indispensable to presidential leadership and constitutional fidelity. Thus, rhetorical acts—including Franklin Roosevelt's famous Fireside Chats, Lyndon Johnson's proclaiming "We Shall Overcome" to a joint session of Congress, or Ronald Reagan's direct plea to the American public to support his 1981 budget package of tax cuts, military spending increases, and social spending cuts—also stand as vivid examples of rhetoric directly informed by institutional responsibilities. Roosevelt's Fireside Chats aided in promoting his legislative agenda to combat the Great Depression, as well as ease the minds of a nation facing dire poverty and, later, world war. Lyndon Johnson's words put presidential and moral force behind the execution of laws, including the right to equal protection. And Ronald Reagan's direct appeals to the public were instrumental in passing a budget package that reflected his values and enacted his major policy initiatives even in the midst of divided government.

How have recent presidents used the rhetorical presidency to fulfill part of their institutional duties? A brief examination of the rhetorical responses to domestic and foreign challenges facing two contemporary presidents—Bill Clinton and George W. Bush, who governed during divergent and occasionally mercurial political and economic climates—illustrates the ongoing capacity for the rhetorical presidency to be a vital and necessary institutional resource.

EXECUTING THE RHETORICAL PRESIDENCY: WILLIAM JEFFERSON CLINTON

> And finally, we have to find a way to live together better. . . . People still . . . define themselves in very primitive ways—they're scared of people who are different from them—different race, different religion, different ethnic group. Some are gay, some are straight. . . . The number one challenge this country faces is building one America across all the lines that divide us. And in some ways, I'm prouder of the work we've done in that than all the economic prosperity we've had.
>
> —Bill Clinton, Coral Gables, Florida, December 11, 1999[36]

> My fellow Americans, we must never, ever believe that our diversity is a weakness—it is our greatest strength. . . . We still see evidence of abiding bigotry and intolerance, in ugly words and awful violence, in burned churches and bombed buildings. We must fight against this, in our country and in our hearts.
>
> Just a few days before my second Inauguration, one of country's best known pastors, Reverend Robert Schuller, suggested that I read Isaiah

> 58:12. Here's what it says: "Thou shalt raise up the foundations of many generations, and thou shalt be called the repairer of the breach, the restorer of paths to dwell in." I placed my hand on that verse when I took the oath of office, on behalf of all Americans. For no matter what our differences—in our faiths, our backgrounds, our politics—we must all be repairers of the breach.
>
> —Bill Clinton, State of the Union Address, February 4, 1997[37]

Church Burnings and Hate Crimes

The mysterious outbreak of fires at black churches throughout 1995–1996 caused Bill Clinton to use a variety of presidential resources to help rebuild houses of worship, promote racial reconciliation, assist in the apprehension of the arsonists, and determine whether the fires were the result of conspiracy. The weekly radio addresses proved to be a particularly popular and comfortable forum for Clinton to address the church burnings, and he devoted his June 8, 1996, and January 18, 1997, addresses to the issue.[38] Using the institutional powers at his disposal, Clinton signed into law the Church Arson Prevention Act on July 10, 1996, which made hate crimes against churches a federal crime, doubled the maximum sentence for such crimes, and increased the statute of limitations from five to seven years.[39]

Clinton also created the National Church Arson Task Force on June 19, 1996, a special mobilization of the Department of Justice, and the Department of the Treasury, and the Federal Emergency Management Agency (FEMA) to assist in the investigation, provide precautionary measures, and help rebuild the churches. The task force worked in concert with state and local law enforcement agencies and provided some $6 million for law enforcement and community efforts related to the fires.[40] In addition, the Department of Justice provided $3 million in grants to aid local communities in intensifying enforcement and surveillance efforts, and Congress authorized the Department of Housing and Urban Development (HUD) to administer a $10–million loan effort to aid in the rebuilding of burned churches. John Conyers (D-MI) and Henry Hyde (R-IL) avidly supported the legislation, and the president endorsed and promoted it. Lastly, Clinton himself traveled to several of the newly rebuilt churches that had been devastated by the fires—including the Salem Missionary Baptist Church in Fruitland, Tennessee, among others—and, accompanied by cabinet secretaries and government dignitaries, officially rededicated many of the new houses of worship, speaking to the congregations, and presenting ministers with presidential plaques.[41] CNN and C-SPAN covered several of the dedications of African-American churches live, dubbing the ceremonies the Clinton Church Tour.

By the time Clinton delivered his January 18, 1997, weekly radio address detailing progress made in investigating the church burnings, some 143 suspects in connection with 107 fires had been arrested.[42]

White House Conferences and Presidential Initiatives

Citing recent hate crimes committed against African Americans and gays in Atlanta, and Washington, D.C., Clinton used his June 7, 1997, weekly radio address as a vehicle to denounce the acts. The president concluded the address by announcing that he would convene a White House Conference on Hate Crimes on November 10, 1997, to "confront the dark forces of division that still exist."[43] The first White House conference of its kind, Clinton asserted that it would bring together community and religious leaders and law enforcement officials, providing a forum in which to review shared experiences and outline relevant laws and individual- and community-based solutions to the problem of hate crimes.[44] The daylong conference, which Clinton convened at the Dorothy Betts Marvin Theater at George Washington University, was attended by 350 civil rights, law enforcement, and elected officials, as well as HUD Secretary Andrew Cuomo. At the conference, Clinton cited federal statistics indicating a 10 percent increase in hate crimes between 1995 and 1996, reaching a total of 8,759 reported crimes to the federal government.[45] Race was a factor in 63 percent of reported hate crimes, whereas religion accounted for 14 percent; ethnic origin, 11 percent; and sexual orientation, 11 percent.[46]

Along with the presentation of the blueprint for the hate crimes conference, the summer of 1997 witnessed a flurry of other quasi-institutional presidential initiatives in the arena of civil rights. On June 13, 1997, Clinton announced the creation of the highly-anticipated President's Advisory Board on Race, a seven-member panel of presidential-appointees that would conduct a yearlong investigation and discussion of racial attitudes and problems. The advisory board, chaired by John Hope Franklin, would conduct town meetings, research, and outreach initiatives designed to examine the state of race relations in the United States in the 1990s. After establishing the advisory board through an executive order, Clinton made the project official with an announcement ceremony in the Oval Office. Moreover, Clinton further outlined the mission of the advisory board during a commencement address on racial diversity at the University of California at San Diego on June 14 in which he cited the immediate negative impact that California's controversial anti–affirmative action ballot initiative, Proposition 209—which California voters passed in 1996—was having on minority college and law school admissions.[47] The speech also served as a reaffirmation of Clinton's oft-questioned commitment to affirmative action with the president citing an integrated military as a clear example of the merits of affirmative action programs.[48] Sharing the stage with Ward Connerly, the man who successfully spearheaded the ballot initiative to cease affirmative action in California, Clinton used the highly publicized occasion to make the case for proactive government programs in the areas of economic opportunity and education, among others.

Affirmative Action and Presidential Apologies

Affirmative Action: "Mend it, Don't End it." In addition to his commencement address in San Diego, Bill Clinton has frequently used other public forums and the institutional powers of the presidency to address an array of the peripheral issues surrounding the legacy of racial discrimination in the United States. On July 19, 1995, for example, he used a speech at the National Archives to outline his administration's "mend it, don't end it" approach and commitment to affirmative action programs, and he issued an executive memorandum to the heads of all executive departments and agencies designed to review all existing affirmative action programs and eliminate any initiatives that created quotas, preferences for unqualified individuals, or reverse discrimination. Simply put, while supporting affirmative action, Clinton's memorandum used the strict scrutiny guidelines established by the 1995 Supreme Court decision *Adarand v. Pena*, which involved set-asides for minority contractors.[49] At a dual sermon/campaign speech delivered from the pulpit of St. Paul's African Methodist Episcopal Church in Tampa, Florida, on November 3, 1996, Clinton donned his role of repairer of the breach and devoted his address to closing the divisions in U.S. society, urging the congregation and America to "rise above the 'politics of division and gridlock' and to say 'no to racial and religious hatred.'"[50]

Presidential Apologies. With his infamous "I feel your pain" comment to an HIV-positive individual during the 1992 campaign, Bill Clinton's ability to empathize with individuals and certain segments in society—or shamelessly pander, if one takes a more cynical view of Clinton's leadership style—has become one of the more readily recognizable of Bill Clinton's traits as candidate and president. Even many of Clinton's most severe critics grudgingly admit that, whether sincere or not, the empathy can be quite effective in shepherding popular support and, occasionally, transmitting that mass appeal into support for his policy agenda.

Clinton has embraced a similar empathetic approach—on a broader scale—when offering formal national apologies for severe violations of civil rights in America's past. In addition to his oft-cited apologia condemning U.S. participation in the slave trade while on a major state tour of Africa in 1998, Bill Clinton has harnessed the imagery and symbolic dimensions of the presidency to make pleas for national forgiveness in other areas involving racial and social justice. In May 1997, for instance, Clinton used two events—an official White House press conference on May 16 and a May 18 commencement address at the predominantly African-American Morgan State University in Baltimore—to offer a formal national apology for the Tuskegee syphilis study.[51]

The Legacy of Dr. Martin Luther King Jr.

Throughout his tenure in the White House and his initial campaign for the presidency, perhaps no one leader has been referenced as often as Martin Luther King Jr. From symbolic proclamations and sermons across the country, to State of the Union addresses and political spectacles, to annual celebrations and service projects in Dr. King's honor, Bill Clinton has consistently used the prestige of the office to cement further King's message and legacy in the national psyche. Several instances reflect this dynamic. On November 13, 1993, Clinton chose to deliver a sermon on race, youth violence, and the breakdown of the family in Memphis, Tennessee, at the Church of God in Christ, the same hallowed pulpit where Martin Luther King delivered his final sermon—the "Mountaintop" address—on April 3, 1968.[52] In addition to public speeches, a variety of small yet symbolic institutional gestures further cement Clinton's homage to the late civil rights leader and the issue of racial reconciliation, including: a weekly radio address praising King and establishing January 14, 1995, as a National Day of Service; the signing of HR 4236, the Omnibus Parks and Public Lands Management Act of 1996, establishing a King Memorial in Washington, D.C., and the Selma-Montgomery National Historic Trail; and a proclamation naming January 20, 1997, a National Day of Hope and Renewal in honor of King.

In this vein, Clinton has also used well-staged and timed public addresses to revisit the legacy of race in the United States. On the morning of the Million Man March on October 16, 1995, Clinton gave a major address on race relations at the University of Texas at Austin. Alluding to the of role of Louis Farrakhan in organizing the Million Man March without mentioning the controversial Nation of Islam leader by name, Clinton declared: "one million are right to be standing up for personal responsibility, but [one] million men do not make right one man's message of malice and division."[53] And, not by coincidence, as mentioned, Clinton staged a speech concerning race and affirmative action at the University of California at San Diego, a school system directly affected by California's Proposition 209, which ended affirmative action in state policies. Clinton's second inaugural address, which fell on the national King holiday, featured a tribute to the slain civil rights leader.

In the spirit of promoting King's legacy, Clinton made a point to make major presidential addresses—and visits—to commemorate seminal events in the civil rights movement. In 1997 he was on hand to honor the struggles of the Little Rock Nine, who desegregated Little Rock Central High School in 1957. Speaking from the steps of the high school forty years later, Clinton memorialized the students and warned of resegregation in education.[54] That same year he was also on hand at Shea Stadium to celebrate the fiftieth anniversary of Jackie Robsinson's historic breaking of the color barrier in Major League Baseball. On March 5, 2000, Clinton traveled to Selma, Alabama—with various cabinet members and dignitaries, such as AmeriCorps director Harris Wofford and Ethel Kennedy—to commemorate the thirty-fifth anniversary of the march across the Edmund Pettis Bridge and the passage of the landmark Voting Rights Act of 1965. Joined on the dais by civil rights pioneers John Lewis (D-GA), Coretta Scott King, Hosea Williams, Jesse Jackson, among others, Clinton cited several contemporary "bridges to cross" in the area of civil rights, economic opportunity, education, and healthcare. Before beginning the symbolic march across the bridge, Clinton closed his speech with this message:

> My fellow Americans, this day has a special meaning for me, for I, too, am a son of the South—the old, segregated South. And those of you who marched thirty-five years ago set me free, too, on Bloody Sunday. Free to know you; to work with you; to love you; to raise my child to celebrate our differences and hallow our common humanity. I thank you all for what you did here. Thank you, Andy and Jesse and Joe, for the lives you have lived since. Thank you, Coretta, for giving up your beloved husband and the blessings of a normal life. Thank you, Ethel Kennedy, for giving up your beloved husband and the blessings of a normal life. And thank you, John Lewis, for the beatings you took and the heart you kept wide open. Thank you for walking with the wind, hand in hand with your brothers and sisters, to hold America's trembling house down. Thank you for your vision of the beloved community, an America at peace with itself. I tell you all, as long as Americans are willing to hold hands, we can walk with any wind; we can cross any bridge. Deep in my heart I do believe we shall overcome.[55]

The lingering South Carolina Confederate flag controversy also warranted select presidential statements from President Clinton. By early 2000, passions on both sides of the issue were running high: the National Association for the Advancement of Colored People (NAACP), led by President Kweisi Mfume, called for an economic boycott of South Carolina, and more than 50,000 citizens protested the flag during a rally at the state capitol on Martin Luther King Jr. Day. In early April 2000, Charleston Mayor Joseph Riley led advocates of removing the flag on a 100-mile march from Charleston to Columbia. When they arrived in Columbia, they were met by several pro-flag supporters. During the presidential primaries, the Confederate flag was center stage. On the Republican side, George W. Bush declared that the matter was best handled by the state, and John McCain also echoed the Texas governor's position. On the campaign trail, McCain also declared that although the flag's meaning was certainly open to interpretation and disagreement, he personally viewed it as a symbol of heritage.[56] At a dinner honoring Rep. Jim Clyburn (D-SC), chairman of the Congressional Caucus on March 29, Clinton suggested that South Carolina remove the flag from atop the Capitol dome, where it had flown since 1962. Clinton, who had also addressed Confederate flag issue during his address in Selma on the thirty-fifth anniversary of the voting rights march, reiterated his position on the flag, telling the partisan audience: ". . . as long as the waving symbol of one American's pride is the shameful symbol of another American's pain, we still have bridges to cross in our country. And we better go on and get across them."[57] Clinton also placed the symbolic, emotional debate over the flag in the context of lingering global hatreds from Ireland to Pakistan to Rwanda:

> This flag controversy here, you shouldn't be surprised by how tough this has been. Why are the Catholics and Protestants still fussing in Northern Ireland? Why did the Orthodox Christians run the Albanian Muslims out of Kosovo—a million of them? Why did 800,000 people in Rwanda get killed in a tribal war in 100 days? . . . Why can't we make peace in the Middle East. . . . I think the South has something to show the rest of the country, and to help our country teach the rest of the world. We've got to let this go. . . .[58]

Yet, as several previous examples illustrate, not all of Clinton's efforts in the area of racial justice and civil rights were merely symbolic and rhetorical and void of concrete results achieved via substantial institutional efforts. Two examples reveal attempts by the Clinton administration to recover substantial funds for civil rights enforcement, as well as and remedy past injustices in the area of housing practices. On January 18, 1999, Martin Luther

King Jr. Day, Clinton announced that HUD had reached a monumental $6.5-billion discrimination settlement with Columbia National, Inc., a Washington, D.C.–based mortgage-lending company.[59] HUD investigated the mortgage-lending institution for violating the 1968 Fair Housing Act by discriminating against minorities seeking home mortgages.

According to HUD and Clinton—who made the mortgage bias pact announcement at a news conference at a Washington, D.C., retirement home during a series of Martin Luther King Jr. Day events—the multibillion dollar settlement included $6 billion in home mortgage loans over five years and roughly $530 million for home rehabilitation loans, advertisements in minority-oriented media, and closing-cost assistance. About $1 million was earmarked for training Columbia National staff to deal with fair lending issues.[60] Although Columbia National claimed that they had been cleared of any discriminatory practices based on the Fair Housing Act and were "flabbergasted" by HUD's report, Clinton and HUD maintained that the pact between HUD and Columbia National was indeed an "enforcement agreement."[61] In 1998 HUD had also negotiated a significant $2.1-billion settlement with the Dallas-based AccuBanc Mortgage for discriminating against black and Hispanic loan applicants. The federal investigation commenced after the Dallas and Fort Worth Human Relations Commissions filed complaints with HUD.

Meanwhile, as the 2000 campaign loomed overhead, Vice President Gore officially announced the Clinton administration's request for additional funds for enforcing the country's civil rights laws. Flanked by President Clinton; Washington, D.C., Mayor Anthony Williams; and Delegate Eleanor Holmes Norton at a senior citizen apartment complex, Gore unveiled the administration's proposed $84-million increase for spending on six federal civil rights agencies. If allocated by the Republican-controlled Congress, the budget for the six agencies would grow to $683 million. Gore also revealed the Clinton budget request at the Ebenezer Baptist Church in Atlanta the previous day, asserting that the administration's budget request for civil rights enforcement—a 15 percent hike—represented "the largest single increase in the enforcement of our civil rights in nearly two decades."[62] In actuality, the additional $84-million request was roughly equal to the previous year's 15 percent increase request ($86 million)—of which Congress appropriated $64 million.[63] Nonetheless, the budget requests represented concrete executive efforts to aid the civil rights enforcement arms of the federal government—specifically, agencies in the departments of Justice, Labor, Education, HUD, and Agriculture (which recently announced a landmark settlement of a lawsuit filed by African-American farmers). Especially in need of financial assistance was the Equal Employment Opportunity Commission (EEOC), which faced a backlog of 52,000 discrimination cases.[64] Clinton and Gore estimated that the new budget hikes would cut the backlog of cases in half.

EXECUTING THE RHETORICAL PRESIDENCY: GEORGE W. BUSH

As several scholars have indicated, the inaugural address has become the seminal national event for presidents to simultaneously pledge fidelity to the past, outline their administration's domestic and foreign agenda, and redefine America's purpose in a new political age. This was true of Bill Clinton's message of seasonal renewal and fidelity to a "New Covenant" in 1993, and was evident in George W. Bush's 2001 inaugural address. Citing America's longstanding ability to confront and solve crises, Bush outlined the immediate and future challenges at home and abroad, signaling specific policies, values, and action in a number of key areas: from education, Medicare, and Social Security at home to the proliferation of weapons of mass destruction abroad. In addition, he articulated how his agenda was in concert with America's enduring values:

> Our national courage has been clear in times of depression and war, when defending common dangers defined our common good. Now we must choose if the example of our fathers and mothers will inspire us or condemn us. We must show courage in a time of blessing by confronting problems instead of passing them on to future generations.
>
> Together, we will reclaim America's schools, before ignorance and apathy claim more young lives.
>
> We will reform Social Security and Medicare, sparing our children from struggles we have the power to prevent. And we will reduce taxes, to recover the momentum of our economy and reward the effort and enterprise of working Americans.
>
> We will build our defenses beyond challenge, lest weakness invite challenge.
>
> We will confront weapons of mass destruction, so that a new century is spared new horrors.
>
> The enemies of liberty and our country should make no mistake: America remains engaged in the world by history and by choice, shaping a balance of power that favors freedom. We will defend our allies and our

> interests. We will show purpose without arrogance. We will meet aggression and bad faith with resolve and strength. And to all nations, we will speak for the values that gave our nation birth.[65]

In addition, Bush, like many of his predecessors, imbued his inaugural address with a mixture of sacred and secular text and inspiration. Like Ronald Reagan invoking the sacred promise of a country that was a shining "City on the Hill," Bush revisited the notion of America's divinity and promise, drawing from the civil religious terrain of the Declaration of Independence and its Framers, as well as the more specific religious grounds of Christian scripture, to make his point:

> After the Declaration of Independence was signed, Virginia statesman John Page wrote to Thomas Jefferson: "We know the race is not to the swift nor the battle to the strong. Do you not think an angel rides in the whirlwind and directs this storm?"
>
> Much time has passed since Jefferson arrived for his inauguration. The years and changes accumulate. But the themes of this day he would know: our nation's grand story of courage and its simple dream of dignity.
>
> We are not this story's author, who fills time and eternity with his purpose. Yet his purpose is achieved in our duty, and our duty is fulfilled in service to one another.
>
> Never tiring, never yielding, never finishing, we renew that purpose today, to make our country more just and generous, to affirm the dignity of our lives and every life.
>
> This work continues. This story goes on. And an angel still rides in the whirlwind and directs this storm.[66]

September 11 and the War on Terror: The Rhetoric of Commander in Chief and Head of State

In times of great tumult and crisis, presidents are expected to provide direction, take decisive executive action, and, increasingly, soothe a tense or grieving nation. After the cataclysmic events of September 11, 2001, in which roughly 3,000 people were killed in terrorist attacks in New York City; the Pentagon; and Somerset, Pennsylvania, George W. Bush focused his attention on fulfilling the president's specific constitutional duty of commander in chief as well as the ceremonial role of head of state. A chief tool in executing these vital institutional roles is rhetoric, as evidenced in Bush's

"Address to a Joint Session of Congress and the American People" on September 20, 2001. Bush's comments at the outset of his speech address both of the aforementioned presidential roles:

> In the normal course of events, Presidents come to this chamber to report on the state of the Union. Tonight, no such report is needed. It has already been delivered by the American people. . . . Tonight we are a country awakened to danger and called to defend freedom. Our grief has turned to anger, and anger to resolution. Whether we bring our enemies to justice, or bring justice to our enemies, justice will be done.[67]

After explicating the reason for the speech and the initial responses of the United States and the world to the terrorist attacks, Bush executed his role as commander in chief by outlining the central questions surrounding the attacks and as well as America's specific plan of action:

> Americans are asking: How will we fight and win this war? We will direct every resource at our command—every means of diplomacy, every tool of intelligence, every instrument of law enforcement, every financial influence, and every necessary weapon of war—to the disruption and to the defeat of the global terror network.

In putting forth his administration's plans to combat terrorism, Bush differentiated between the nature and tactics of the current course of U.S. action from recent military operations:

> This war will not be like the war against Iraq a decade ago, with a decisive liberation of territory and a swift conclusion. It will not look like the air war above Kosovo two years ago, where no ground troops were used and not a single American was lost in combat.
>
> Our response involves far more than instant retaliation and isolated strikes. Americans should not expect one battle, but a lengthy campaign, unlike any other we have ever seen. It may include dramatic strikes, visible on TV, and covert operations, secret even in success. We will starve terrorists of funding, turn them one against another, drive them from place to place, until there is no refuge or no rest. And we will pursue nations that provide aid or safe haven to terrorism. Every nation, in every region, now has a decision to make. Either you are with us, or you are with the terrorists. From this day forward, any nation that continues to harbor or support terrorism will be regarded by the United States as a hostile regime.[68]

In addition, Bush announced domestic efforts to coordinate antiterrorism and homeland security efforts: the creation of a new cabinet-level position, the Office of Homeland Security. According to Bush, this new office would oversee and coordinate a "comprehensive national strategy to safeguard our country against terrorism, and respond to any attacks that may come":

> Our nation has been put on notice: We are not immune from attack. We will take defensive measures against terrorism to protect Americans. Today, dozens of federal departments and agencies, as well as state and local governments, have responsibilities affecting homeland security. These efforts must be coordinated at the highest level. So tonight I announce the creation of a Cabinet-level position reporting directly to me—the Office of Homeland Security.[69]

Tom Ridge, then governor of Pennsylvania, whom Bush called "a military veteran, an effective governor, a true patriot, a trusted friend," was announced as Bush's choice to lead the new office.[70]

Rhetoric, Civil Religion, and Religiosity:
Beyond the September 20 Address

Like Bill Clinton, George W. Bush used a host of rhetorical actions to promote, explain, and execute institutional action. And, similar to Clinton, Bush often permeated these speeches, proclamations, and executive orders with ample civil religious and religious references. This dynamic is especially evident in Bush's September 20, 2001, address to the nation, in which he painted an unambiguous picture of right and wrong, freedom and fear, and the fight against terrorism:

> The course of this conflict is not known, yet its outcome is certain. Freedom and fear, justice and cruelty, have always been at war, and we know that God is not neutral between them.
>
> Fellow citizens, we'll meet violence with patient justice—assured of the rightness of our cause, and confident of the victories to come. In all that lies before us, may God grant us wisdom, and may He watch over the United States of America.[71]

Bush then used a variety of presidential resources to advance the spirit of that stirring statement. One such action was issuing a presidential proclamation. On September 13, 2001, Bush issued a presidential proclamation declaring Friday, September 14, 2001, a National Day of Prayer and Remembrance for the Victims of the Terrorist Attacks on September 11, 2001. In the proclamation, the president asked "that the people of the United States and places of worship mark this National Day of Prayer and Remembrance with noontime memorial services, the ringing of bells at that hour, and evening candlelight remembrance vigils." In addition, the proclamation encouraged "employers to permit their workers time off during the lunch hour to attend the noontime services to pray for our land," and invited "the people of the world who share our grief to join us in these solemn observances."[72] This action suggests that, as his immediate predecessor had done consistently throughout his years in the White House, Bush cloaked his executive action with religiosity while reprising the presidential role of mourner in chief:

> We mourn with those who have suffered great and disastrous loss. All our hearts have been seared by the sudden and senseless taking of innocent lives. We pray for healing and for the strength to serve and encourage one another in hope and faith.
>
> Scripture says: "Blessed are those who mourn for they shall be comforted." I call on every American family and the family of America to observe a National Day of Prayer and Remembrance, honoring the memory of the thousands of victims of these brutal attacks and comforting those who lost loved ones. We will persevere through this national tragedy and personal loss. In time, we will find healing and recovery; and, in the face of all this evil, we remain strong and united, "one Nation under God."[73]

CONCLUSION: A CONSTITUTIONAL CASE FOR THE RHETORICAL PRESIDENCY

As the aforementioned aspects of the rhetorical presidencies of Bill Clinton and George W. Bush illustrate, a virtual "rhetorical branch" exists within the executive branch: an arsenal of speeches, symbolism, and myriad institutional and communication resources at the presidents' disposal to advance domestic and foreign policy. Presidents' exhortations, substantive and symbolic, whether concerning war, peace, or civil rights, when rooted in a solid foundation (that is, the constitutional responsibilities embodied in Article II and precedent reasonably related to essential duties) are legitimate and constitutionally valid forms of executive action. Clinton's use of the rhetorical presidency to promote and execute his civil rights agenda and Bush's rhetorical efforts after September 11 are prime examples of rhetoric informed and in large part directed by presidential duties.

Obviously, this does not mean that contemporary presidents, including Clinton and Bush, have not used the smorgasbord of rhetorical resources at their disposal to veer into purely political, personal, and symbolic terrain that is not reasonably related to essential constitutional duties and presidential roles. Clearly they have—and on many occasions—and we have no reason to believe that future presidents will avoid using rhetorical action to engage in behavior that is dramatically removed the constitutional course. Moreover, serious dangers are inherent in wanton or cynical use of the rhetorical presidency. Shortsighted and politically expedient use of the rhetorical presidency may very likely exacerbate an already hypercynical and apathetic citizenry (and, in many cases, media) predisposed to view politics, policy, and the presidency as a series of irrelevant games and tactics. In addition, such use of stagecraft, buzzwords, and theater devoid of meaning or institutional duty may alienate key players in the legislative branch and further frustrate and infuriate the media. A steady diet of images and fluff is no healthy way to feed a Republic hungry for substance and action.

However, although the rhetorical presidency is often denigrated as pure politically driven gobbledygook far removed from the Framers' intent and the specific powers enumerated in Article II of the Constitution, it can, in many forms, be a constitutionally sound and legitimate exercise of presidential power. Rhetorical leadership can have dramatic policy and agenda-setting impact, shaping the debate on important issues of national concern. And such outcomes are certainly within the realm of presidential responsibility. Witness Clinton's eloquence after the 1995 Oklahoma City bombing and his creative use of executive action to promote civil rights and religious freedom throughout his tenure in office. Similarly, George W. Bush's response to September 11 stands as proof that the rhetorical powers of the office can be harnessed to perform essential executive functions.

Indeed, whereas presidents will most likely continue to use the rhetorical presidency for political and personal purposes, their use of speeches, symbolism, policy declarations, and proclamations also indicates in areas of domestic policy and national security evidence that rhetorical leadership need not be the province of pollsters and popularity. It may very well be a tool in setting national priorities, promoting and passing legislation aimed at enhancing security, promoting civil rights, and healing—and mourning with—a grieving nation. These goals are reasonably traced to presidential duties outlined in and informed by our constitutional foundation, and as such, make a constitutional case for the rhetorical presidency.

NOTES

1. For the first two sections of this chapter—namely, presidential leadership, paradigms, and the rhetorical presidency—see Kevan M. Yenerall, *The Cultural Pulpit: Rhetoric, Executive Power, and the Clinton Presidency* (Ph.D. diss., Miami University, 2000), and "The Presidency as a Cultural Pulpit" in *Presidential Frontiers: Underexplored Issues in White House Politics*, Ryan J. Barilleaux, ed. (Greenwood, Conn.: Praeger, 1998), pp. 151–78.

2. William Howard Taft, *Our Chief Magistrate and His Powers* (New York: Columbia University Press, 1916), pp. 138–45; cited in James P. Pfiffner and Roger H. Davidson, *Understanding the Presidency* (New York: Longman, 1997), p. 27.

3. Taft, p. 28.

4. See Taft; Edward Samuel Corwin, *The President, Office and Powers* (New York: New York University Press, 1940).

5. Richard Neustadt, *Presidential Power and the Modern Presidents* (New York: Free Press, 1990).

6. See John Hart, *The Presidential Branch: From Washington to Clinton*, 2nd ed. (Chatham, N.J.: Chatham House, 1995).

7. Samuel Kernell, *Going Public*, 3rd ed. (Washington, D.C.: Congressional Quarterly Press, 1997).

8. George C. Edwards III, *The Public Presidency* (New York: St. Martin's Press, 1983).

9. Theodore Lowi, *The Personal President* (Ithaca, N.Y.: Cornell University Press, 1995); Robert Schmuhl, *Statecraft and Stagecraft* (Notre Dame, Ind.: University of Notre Dame, 1990; Craig Rimmerman, *Presidency by Plebiscite* (Boulder, Colo.: Westview, 1995).

10. Ryan J. Barilleaux, *The Postmodern Presidency* (New York: Praeger, 1988); Richard Rose, *The Postmodern President: The White House Meets the World* (Chatham, N.J.: Chatham House, 1988).

11. Jeffrey Tulis, *The Rhetorical Presidency* (Princeton, N.J.: Princeton University Press, 1987); Martin Medhurst, ed., *Beyond the Rhetorical Presidency* (College Station: Texas A&M University Press, 1996); Richard Ellis, ed., *Speaking to the People* (Amherst: University of Massachusetts Press, 1998).

12. Gary L. Gregg, *The Presidential Republic* (Lanham, Md.: Rowman and Littlefield, 1997).

13. Thomas Langston, *With Reverence and Contempt* (Baltimore: Johns Hopkins University Press, 1995).

14. Charles O. Jones, *The Presidency in a Separated System* (Washington, D.C.: Brookings Institution Press, 1994).

15. Louis Fisher, *Constitutional Conflicts between Congress and the President* (Lawrence: University Press of Kansas, 1991), and *Presidential War Power* (Lawrence: University Press of Kansas, 1994).

16. Sidney M. Milkis and Michael Nelson, *The American Presidency*, 3rd ed. (Washington, D.C.: Congressional Quarterly Press, 1998); Daniel P. Franklin, *Extraordinary Measures* (Pittsburgh: University of Pittsburgh Press, 1991); Terry Eastland, *Energy in the Executive* (New York: Free Press, 1992).

17. Harvey C. Mansfield, *Taming the Prince* (New York: Free Press, 1989).

18. David K. Nichols, *The Myth of the Modern Presidency* (University Park: Pennsylvania State University Press, 1994).

19. See Arthur Schlesinger Jr., *The Imperial Presidency* (Boston, Mass.: Houghton-Mifflin, 1973).

20. Edwin Hargrove and Michael Nelson, *Presidents, Politics, and Policy* (New York: Knopf, 1994).

21. Barilleaux, *Postmodern Presidency*.

22. James Ceaser et al., "The Rise of the Rhetorical Presidency," *Presidential Studies Quarterly* 11 (Spring 1981): 158–71.

23. Ryan J. Barilleaux et al., "Forward to the Past: Paradigm Shifts in Presidential Studies" (paper presented at the American Political Science Association Annual Meeting, San Francisco, Calif., September 1996), p. 9.

24. According to Tulis, the lone exception to the norm of the deliberative presidency in the first constitutional presidency (1789–1913) was Andrew Johnson, who stumped relentlessly throughout the 1866 midterm elections, attacking his enemies in the House and Senate in public broadsides. Two of the articles of impeachment later brought against Johnson—Articles 10 and 11—cited, as a basis for his removal from office, the president's inflammatory speeches during the 1866 congressional elections, speeches that, according to the articles, sought to bring Congress into "disgrace, ridicule, hatred, contempt, and reproach." See "Articles of Impeachment against Andrew Johnson," in *The Evolving Presidency*, Michael Nelson, ed. (Washington, D.C.: Congressional Quarterly Press, 1999), pp. 82–92.

25. Gil Troy, *See How They Ran* (New York: Free Press, 1991), p. 3

26. Kernell.

27. Bruce Miroff, "The Presidency and the Public: Leadership as Spectacle," in *The Presidency and the Political System*, Michael Nelson, ed. (Washington, D.C.: Congressional Quarterly Press, 1994).

28. Murray Edelman, *Constructing the Public Spectacle* (Chicago: University of Chicago Press, 1988).

29. Robert Bellah, "Civil Religion in America," *Daedalus* 96 (Winter 1967): 1–21; Richard V. Pierard and Robert D. Linder, *Civil Religion and the Presidency* (Grand Rapids, Mich.: Academic Books, 1988); and Langston.

30. Bruce Miroff, "The Presidency and the Public: Leadership as Spectacle," in *The Presidency and the Political System*, Michael Nelson, ed. (Washington, D.C.: Congressional Quarterly Press, 1994), p. 274.

31. Carol Gelderman, *All the Presidents' Words* (New York: Walker, 1997).

32. Kathleen Hall Jamieson, *Eloquence in an Electronic Age* (New York: Oxford University Press, 1988).

33. Wayne Fields, *Union of Words* (New York: Free Press, 1995).

34. Charles Jones recently wrote, "in the era of the permanent campaign the 'lame duck' flies"; in other words, even a president—such as Bill Clinton—who cannot overcome divided government and other institutional constraints, and whose legislative agenda is seemingly diminished in the final years of a lame-duck second term, can appear (and perhaps actually be) relevant and remain quite popular with the masses, due, at least in part, to the use of the rhetorical presidency and the very public "permanent campaign" style of presidential governance. See Charles Jones, "Nonstop! The Campaigning Presidency and the 2000 Presidential Campaign," *Brookings*

Review 18 (Winter 2000): 12–16. Also, see Jones's attention to the phenomenon of "presidential voice" and Bill Clinton's effective campaign-style leadership strategies in *Passages to the Presidency* (Washington, D.C.: Brookings Institute Press, 1999).

35. See Paul Light, *The President's Agenda* (Baltimore: Johns Hopkins University Press, 1991), pp. 1–12.

36. WHPR, "Remarks by the President at Unity Reception," December 11, 1999.

37. WHPR, "Remarks by the President in State of the Union Address," February 4, 1997.

38. WHPR, "Radio Address by the President to the Nation," June 8, 1996; WHPR, "Radio Address of the President to the Nation," January 18, 1997.

39. WHPR, "Remarks by the President on the Church Arson Prevention Act," July 10, 1996.

40. WHPR, July 10, 1996.

41. Bill Clinton, "Remarks at the Salem Missionary Baptist Church in Fruitland, Tennessee," *Weekly Compilation of Presidential Documents* 32 (August 26, 1996): 1468–71.

42. WHPR, "Radio Address of the President to the Nation," January 18, 1997.

43. WHPR, "Radio Address of the President to the Nation," June 7, 1997.

44. WHPR, June 7, 1997.

45. Michael A. Fletcher, "Conference Explores Rise in Reports of Hate Crimes," *Washington Post*, November 11, 1998, p. A8; WHPR, "Remarks by the President at the White House Conference on Hate Crimes," November 10, 1997.

46. Fletcher, *Washington Post*, November 11, 1997, p. AO8

47. WHPR, "Executive Order: President's Advisory Board on Race," June 13, 1997; WHPR, "Remarks by the President in Meeting with the Advisory Board to the President on Race," June 13 1997.

48. Alison Mitchell, "Clinton Presses a Campaign to Bridge Racial Divide," *New York Times*, June 15, 1997, p. A1.

49. WHPR, "Memorandum for Heads of Executive Departments and Agencies—Subject: Evaluation of Affirmative Action Programs," July 19, 1995; WHPR, "Remarks by the President on Affirmative Action," July 19, 1995.

50. Alison Mitchell, "Avoid 'Politics of Division,' Says Clinton," *New York Times*, November 4, 1996, p. A1.

51. WHPR, "Remarks by the President in Apology for Study Done at Tuskegee," May 16, 1997.

52. WHPR, "Remarks by William Jefferson Clinton, 86th Annual Holy Convocation, The Church of God in Christ, November 13, 1993, Memphis Tennessee," November 13, 1993.

53. See WHPR, October 16, 1995; see also Carol Gelderman, *All the Presidents' Words* (New York: Walker, 1997), pp. 172–73. Gelderman points out that this dramatic and oft-cited line was penned by speechwriter Donald Baehr. Clinton, who worked closely with his speechwriters on the Austin address, was significantly aided by speechwriters David Shipley and Terry Edmonds, who, along with Clinton took over entire responsibility for the speech after Baehr's initial contribution. Said Shipley of the Austin speech on race relations and the close collaboration with the Clinton, "There's not a word in that speech untouched by the president. . . . Our text was

a little bit of yeast for him." Edmonds—the first black presidential speechwriter—added that the speech was "a good team effort, an ideal collaborative process" and a "defining speech" (p. 173).

54. Kevin Sack, "On 40th Anniversary of Little Rock Struggle, Clinton Warns against Resegregation," *New York Times*, September 26, 1997, p. A1.

55. WHPR, "Remarks by the President to the People of Selma, Alabama Commemorating the 35th Anniversary of the 1965 Voting Rights March," March 5, 2000.

56. In April 2000 McCain, who lost his bid for the Republican presidential nomination to George W. Bush and suspended his campaign in March, returned to South Carolina to declare that he did not support the Confederate flag flying atop the state capitol. McCain informed a South Carolina audience that he did not take such a position in the Republican primaries because he feared that he could not win South Carolina if he took an anti-Confederate flag stance.

57. Charles Babington, "Clinton Challenges S.C. on Flag Conflict," *Washington Post*, March 30, 2000, p. A9.

58. Babington, p. A9.

59. Kirstin Downey Grimsley, "Clinton, HUD Unveil Mortgage Bias Pact," *Washington Post*, January 19, 1999, p. E1.

60. Grimsley, p. E1.

61. Grimsley, p. E1.

62. Howard Kurtz, "Gore to Announce Plan to Hike Budget for Civil Rights by 15%," *Washington Post*, January 18, 2000, p. A7.

63. Kurtz, p. A7.

64. Kurtz, p. A7.

65. George W. Bush, "President George W. Bush's Inaugural Address," January 20, 2001, http://www.whitehouse.gov/news/inaugural-address.html (accessed October 25, 2002).

66. Bush, "Inaugural Address."

67. George W. Bush, "Address to a Joint Session of Congress and the American People," Office of the Press Secretary, September 20, 2001, http://www.whitehouse.gov/news/releases/2001/09/20010920–8.html (accessed October 28, 2002).

68. Bush, "Address to a Joint Session of Congress."

69. Bush, "Address to a Joint Session of Congress."

70. Bush, "Address to a Joint Session of Congress."

71. Bush, "Address to a Joint Session of Congress."

72. Bush, "Address to a Joint Session of Congress."

73. George W. Bush, "National Day of Prayer and Remembrance for the Victims Of the Terrorist Attacks on September 11, 2001," Office of the Press Secretary, September 13, 2001, http://www.whitehouse.gov/news/releases/2001/09/20010913–7.html (accessed October 25, 2002).

EIGHT

Unsettling the New Deal: Reagan's Constitutional Reconstruction and the Rehnquist Court's Federalism

George Thomas

Ronald Reagan consciously drew parallels between himself and Franklin Delano Roosevelt. So much so, in fact, that after his acceptance speech at the 1980 Republican Convention, the *New York Times* lead editorial ran under the title, "Franklin Delano Reagan."[1] But as William Leuchtenburg writes, "Reagan presented himself as Rooseveltian . . . not in order to perpetuate FDR's political tradition but for exactly the opposite purpose: to dismantle the Roosevelt coalition."[2] Indeed, we might push this even further: Reagan did not simply seek to break the New Deal coalition to create one of his own because the New Deal party system was already under stress. Far more ambitiously, Reagan sought to unsettle the "Constitutional Revolution of 1937"[3] and reconstruct our constitutionalism. Or, as Reagan himself put it, much like Franklin Roosevelt before him had, he sought a return to constitutional first principles, which the New Deal had fallen away from and the Supreme Court had sorely distorted beyond recognition. Here the parallel between Reagan and FDR is striking. Reagan was the first president since FDR to insist that he had the authority to interpret the Constitution in his own right and was not bound by Supreme Court opinions. Much like FDR, in articulating his own constitutional vision Reagan was prepared to wrestle with the Supreme Court for constitutional authority because he flatly rejected the notion that he was bound by the Supreme Court's reading of the Constitution as handed down in its opinions.

This chapter analyzes Reagan's attempted constitutional reconstruction. Although Reagan has been treated as a "reconstructive" president,[4] a president who attempted to "engage the nation in a struggle for its constitutional soul,"[5] the so-called Reagan Revolution is generally seen as a stalled constitutional revolution because it did not bring about the kind of constitutional reconstruction or transformation that Roosevelt's New Deal wrought. Even if true, this overlooks an important point. The recognition that presidents play a profound role in constructing constitutional meaning is an important one that supplements our focus on the Supreme Court. Too often this is seen as great presidents transforming the Constitution in extraordinary moments of constitutional politics;[6] yet Reagan unsettled the existing order without bringing on a full-scale constitutional transformation. Constitutional change and discontinuities may come in more subtle forms, suggesting that constitutional politics may be an ordinary, rather than extraordinary, feature of U.S. constitutionalism.

On federalism and the enumerated powers of the national government, Reagan articulated a constitutional vision that was at odds with the "Constitutional Revolution of 1937," and one that, after a lag, the Rehnquist Court began to articulate. This chapter seeks to connect judicial appointments to questions of constitutional interpretation and development, what Bruce Ackerman has called "transformative judicial appointments."[7] Judicial appointments may not only serve as a way for the president to put forth his constitutional vision, but also may, if successfully pursued, become the mechanism whereby he alters or overturns past Supreme Court opinions. The literature on judicial appointments is rarely integrated into larger questions of constitutional theory and development[8] but the evidence is at least suggestive that Reagan's determination to overturn long-standing Supreme Court interpretations of the Constitution—and thereby articulate a "constitutional reconstruction"—has been partly accomplished by his Rehnquist Court appointees.

How judicial appointments are connected to questions of constitutional interpretation is a neglected area of study in the debate about judicial supremacy. If we look only at Supreme Court opinions, we are likely to see the judiciary settling constitutional issues (if the other branches remain silent). But this misses the larger background. The Court's opinions may be based on the president's constitutional vision. So even if we have the appearance of judicial supremacy, the political branches may be behind it. Ironically, the Reagan justices have been the most vocal articulators of judicial supremacy in recent years, despite the fact that the president who appointed them rejected this very notion. Even so, Reagan's constitutional vision has found acceptance by the justices who have revived a judicial defense of constitutional federalism. This suggests that the executive may play a central role in determining constitutional meaning even in the absence of a great "constitutional moment."

Although the Rehnquist Court has begun articulating Reagan's view of federalism, thereby reopening constitutional questions that have been settled since the New Deal, whether Congress has accepted the Court's limitations on its power under the guise of federalism, or, for that matter, the Court's claims to judicial supremacy, is not clear. Reagan unsettled these meanings. They remain, however, in state of constitutional flux that will most likely be settled in the political arena, revealing how constitutional politics play out on a smaller scale.

PRESIDENTIAL RECONSTRUCTION AND CONSTITUTIONAL POLITICS

Presidential scholars have long recognized the president's connection with constitutional maintenance, even if it has not been fully integrated into much of public law scholarship.[9] In *The Federalist Papers*, Alexander Hamilton insists on the necessity of executive independence as a way to preserve the Constitution against the transient whims of the public as well as legislative aggrandizement.[10] This comes from the man who insisted in *Federalist 78* that "the complete independence of the courts of justice is peculiarly essential in a limited Constitution."[11] Public law scholars—and especially legal scholars—remain fixated on *Federalist 78*, insisting that the judiciary is the final arbiter of constitutional meaning. Indeed, when Reagan's Attorney General Edwin Meese announced that the president could interpret the Constitution in his own right and was not, therefore, bound by judicial opinions in the broad sense of adhering to them as a matter of constitutional principle,[12] many in the legal academy acted as if Meese was out to subvert—rather than maintain—constitutional government.[13] Yet Meese's claim on Reagan's behalf was consistent with the claims of past presidents and part of a robust lineage in constitutional interpretation. Indeed, we should note that all of the agreed-on "great presidents" were departmentalists when it came to constitutional interpretation. Jefferson, Jackson, Lincoln, and Franklin Roosevelt all claimed the power to interpret the Constitution independently of Supreme Court opinions. Jackson, Lincoln, and Roosevelt confronted the Supreme Court directly, arguing that they were not bound by specific Supreme Court opinions. It is not just that they ventured—as a matter of constitutional theory—that they were capable of independent constitutional interpretation; rather, they struggled with the Court for constitutional authority. And, not coincidentally, such struggles "reconstructed" our constitutionalism.[14] Stephen Skowronek's reconstructive presidents "reset the very terms and conditions of constitutional government"; Mark Landy and Sidney Milkis's great presidents "taught the citizenry about the need for great change but also about how to reconcile such change with American constitutional traditions and purposes."[15] Bruce Ackerman has connected such presidential struggles with dramatic constitutional change leading to the creation of new constitutional regimes.[16] In a similar vein, Keith Whittington has suggested that "reconstructive" presidents have a unique capacity to challenge judicial supremacy and "play the role of constitutional prophet."[17] Whereas Skowronek and Landy and Milkis only touch on the Supreme Court incidentally, Ackerman and Whittington see the inherited Court, committed to the old regime, as the principal challenger to a president's ability to remake our fundamental constitutional commitments. Such moments of presidential reconstruction are extraordinary moments after which the Supreme Court once again takes the primary responsibility for maintaining the Constitution. The cyclical unfolding of founding, decay, and regeneration places great presidents in the role of "perpetuator" of our "republican institutions." The common theme of the narrative is presidential interpretation as an extraordinary moment of constitutional politics after which we return to a more ordinary politics. We find a good deal of truth in this, especially the recognition of punctuated moments of constitutional change, but it misses the way significant constitutional change can come incrementally, absent extraordinary transformation or clear-cut political realignment.

Reagan is frequently placed with Jefferson, Jackson, Lincoln, and Franklin Roosevelt as a departmentalist president who sought to refound our constitutionalism, but most view his attempt as falling short of past presidential reorderings: "For all that the New Beginning changed the terms and conditions of national politics, it proved far less successful than the New Deal in reconstructing American government."[18] As Milkis and Landy put it, "Reagan's emphasis on presidential politics and executive administration relegated his administration to the task of managing—even reinforcing—the state apparatus it was committed to dismantling."[19] Ackerman speaks specifically of Reagan's "failed" constitutional transformation.[20] Concurrent with pronouncements of Reagan's failed constitutional reconstruction, legal scholars began speaking of the "Rehnquist Court's federalism revolution" as auguring a post–New Deal jurisprudence. Some directly accused the Court of "unconstitutionally" rejecting the New Deal's constitutional settlement, of reopening settled constitutional questions.[21] Others praised the Court for returning to the constitutional scheme of federalism.[22] In the 1995 case

United States v. Lopez, the Court rejected a congressional act as beyond the scope of the commerce clause for the first time since the New Deal revolution of 1937.[23] Are we living in a constitutional moment?[24] Just how far the Court's revival of federalism will reach remains to be seen, but since *Lopez* the Court has continued down this path. Nearly all agree that we are in a transitory period, even while disagreeing on whether it is a major constitutional shift or a mild departure, a mere corrective that leaves the New Deal essentially intact.[25] More important, a consensus seems to exist that the emerging constitutional debate must be measured against the backdrop of the New Deal, the last great constitutional moment in our history. Debates about the legitimacy of the Court's new federalism serve as a proxy, in some ways, for debates about the legitimacy of the New Deal state. If rather obviously, a connection exists between Reagan's attempted constitutional reconstruction and the revival of federalism on the Rehnquist Court: Reagan appointed four of the five justices behind the revival, and George H. W. Bush, "faithful son" of the Reagan Revolution, appointed the fifth.[26]

REAGAN'S RECONSTRUCTION

Reagan was the first president living in the shadow of Franklin Roosevelt who squarely rejected the New Deal state. Flipping Roosevelt on his head, in his first inaugural address Reagan insisted, "In the present crisis, government is not the solution to our problem; government is the problem." The election of 1980 brought federalism and the notion of a limited government of enumerated powers back to the political agenda in a way that challenged the continuing validity of the New Deal administrative state; it looked like the long-awaited political realignment. The first full year of the Reagan administration seemed to fulfill this promise as Reagan pushed through sizeable tax cuts and a reduction in government expenditures, aiming specifically at rolling back the New Deal state. Comparisons to Roosevelt and the 100 Days Congress were inevitable. Yet the Reagan Revolution seemed to stall in the election of 1984. Reagan won a landslide victory, but the Republicans failed to gain control of the House of Representatives. Reagan's personal victory was not translated into a constitutional transformation that dramatically rejected New Deal constitutionalism. In 1986 Democrats won back control of the Senate and the Reagan Revolution fizzled out in the Iran-Contra scandal.[27]

Reagan was able to challenge the New Deal Constitution in part because it was already showing signs of strain. Indeed, the New Deal Constitutional order was perplexed by deep incongruities at its heart, made evident in the constitutional debates over *Griswold* and *Roe*, which I will address later. The New Deal order appeared to be degenerating because the administrative state seemed unwieldy and the political coalition that sustained Roosevelt began to disintegrate, which made reconstructive efforts timely. Some scholars of political realignment pronounced the New Deal coalition dead in 1968 if not earlier. Nevertheless, even Nixon, who insisted on a "strict construction" of the Constitution and spoke more actively of federalism than any president until Reagan, never questioned the fundamentals of the New Deal constitutional order in terms of governmental power. Some have even suggested that Nixon was the last New Deal president.[28] Thus the New Deal order remained coherent in terms of governmental power, but was beset with tension from the outset in the realm of "civil liberties." In this merging the Warren Court with the New Deal order is difficult; rather, the Warren Court brought out the tensions in New Deal constitutionalism and revealed how Lyndon Johnson's Great Society followed the path of the New Deal in one area (national regulation) and inherited its discontinuities in another (the role of the Court in relation to civil liberties). Thus, the so-called New Deal Constitution was already revealing unsettled constitutional issues in some areas with consensus in others.[29] Against this backdrop of discontent with the New Deal order Reagan offered a limited constitutional vision, which required less from government; indeed, as I have already noted, he wanted to "get the government off the people's backs." In this, he was more like Jefferson and Jackson than Roosevelt. Accomplishing this constitutional change required an alteration in public expectations: the people must demand less of the national government; they must be weaned away from national administrative programs. In some ways, such a project seemed well suited to Reagan's rhetorical leadership, itself an outgrowth of the modern presidency, rather than the earlier style of Calvin Coolidge whom Reagan often trumpeted as an ideal president. And to a degree Reagan succeeded. In the wake of Reagan, "Democrats now talk like Republicans."[30] Democratic President Bill Clinton, after all, pronounced the "the era of big government is over" and he ended welfare as we know it, whereas his greatest failure as president was the New Deal–style attempt at government-mandated universal health care. If Reagan did not bring about a Republican realignment, he seems to have changed the ideological dimension of both parties in a more conservative direction.[31] At the same time, using the tools of the New Deal—a reliance on administration and the courts to bring about constitutional change—Reagan seemed trapped by the old order and unable to reconstitute the government's fundamental commitments.[32] Here Reagan failed to bring about his whole constitutional vision in an immediate way. Still, the Reagan Revolution succeeded in reopening a debate about the terms of our constitutionalism and placed the legitimacy of the New Deal Constitution squarely at the center of this debate—a debate that is very much alive.

In this, Reagan did instigate a constitutional revolution of sorts. Or, perhaps more aptly, he succeeded in unsettling fundamental constitutional questions that the politics of the New Deal had settled. Whether he is a "reconstructive" president may remain to be seen, but he surely disrupted the old order, leaving the contours of our constitutionalism the subject of intense debate (which is true of Roosevelt as well on many constitutional issues). Reagan did this, moreover, in an area that cut to the heart of the New Deal: federalism. And, what is more, he did it in a peculiarly New Deal style: by way of transformative judicial appointments. Ackerman himself argues that one of the fundamental changes the New Deal wrought was the "self-conscious use of *transformative judicial appointments* as a central tool for constitutional change."[33] Yet Ackerman paints Reagan's attempted constitutional transformation as a failure. Unlike Roosevelt, Reagan did not win a solid Republican majority in the Congress in the 1984 election, and in 1986 the Republicans lost the Senate, which most likely resulted in the defeat of Reagan's nomination of Judge Robert Bork to the Supreme Court. Bork's confirmation, for Ackerman, combined with Reagan's earlier elevation of William Rehnquist to Chief Justice and the appointment of Antonin Scalia to the Court, may well have culminated in a series of transformative constitutional opinions—namely the overruling of *Roe v. Wade*,[34] the Supreme Court's controversial 1973 opinion recognizing a woman's constitutional right to have an abortion. Instead, failing to win widespread support for his constitutional vision, Reagan was forced to appoint the more moderate Anthony Kennedy to the Court, who brought constitutional politics to a crashing halt when he joined Justice O'Connor, another Reagan appointee, and Justice Souter, a Bush appointee, in a plurality opinion upholding *Roe* in *Planned Parenthood v. Casey*—or so Ackerman suggests.[35]

What is odd about Ackerman's argument is that he sees the failure to overturn *Roe* as a rejection of Reagan's constitutional vision. The New Deal Constitution stands because the Reagan Revolution failed. But *Roe* itself is hard to reconcile with the New Deal constitutional regime. If anything, *Roe* highlights the discontinuities in New Deal constitutionalism, which makes speaking meaningfully of a New Deal constitutional regime difficult. Nothing in the New Deal constitutional revolution justified the Court's opinion in *Roe*, which embraced the very substantive due process arguments that the Court had rejected in 1937, clearing the way for the New Deal.[36] Indeed, at the center of the New Deal was a need to tether judicial power against the kind of reasoning (so to speak) we see in *Roe*. Dissenting in *Roe*, Justice Rehnquist drew attention to the fact that, "while the Court's opinion quotes from the dissent of Mr. Justice Holmes in *Lochner*, the result it reaches is more closely attuned to the majority opinion of Mr. Justice Peckham in that case."[37] Rehnquist's dissent echoed an earlier dissent by Justice Hugo Black, Roosevelt's first appointment to the Court, in a case recognizing a married couple's right to contraception:

> The Due Process Clause with an "arbitrary and capricious" or "shocking the conscience" formula was liberally used by this Court to strike down economic legislation in the early decades of this century, threatening, many people thought, the tranquility and stability of the Nation. See, e.g., *Lochner*. That formula, based on subjective considerations of "natural justice," is no less dangerous when used to enforce this Court's views about personal rights than those about economic rights. I had thought that we had laid that formula, as a means for striking down state legislation, to rest once and for all in cases like *West Coast Hotel Co.*[38]

The return of substantive due process in *Roe* highlighted the fractured state of New Deal jurisprudence and provoked many legal scholars who had been weaned on the New Dealer's critique of the old court—on the ghost of *Lochner*—to cry foul.[39] For New Dealers, *Lochner*—with its embrace of substantive due process—was synonymous with judicial lawmaking and a political Court. For all the tensions within New Deal jurisprudence, for all that it left unsettled, the retreat from substantive due process was a unifying theme.[40] Reagan's call for a return to a jurisprudence of "original intent" highlighted the tension between rejecting *Lochner* and embracing *Roe*, drawing heavily on the condemnation of *Lochner* as handed down by the New Dealers themselves. As expounded on by Bork and Scalia, originalism rejected the very notion of substantive due process whether of the *Lochner* or *Roe* variety and in this way digested a central tenet of New Deal constitutionalism. For originalists, these decisions were of a piece, which placed these jurists squarely with the Constitutional Revolution of 1937 on this issue; that is, on the need to tether judicial will.[41] The preoccupation with reconciling judicial review with democratic government and the suggestion that any attempt to define substantive rights beyond constitutional text was all politics, were inheritances from the New Deal critique of the Old Court.[42] Having criticized the Court's use of judicial review as illegitimate, New Dealers became preoccupied with grounding judicial review in a way that clearly limited judicial power. As Professor Herbert Wechsler's posed this dilemma, "The problem for all of us became: How can we defend a judicial veto in areas where we thought it helpful in American life . . .

and at the same time condemn it in the areas where we considered it unhelpful?"[43] Originalism's preoccupation with the legitimacy of judicial review—viewing it in countermajoritarian terms—and its attempt to ground judicial will in "original intent" draws squarely on this New Deal inheritance. Whether this is accurate constitutional history insofar as original intent itself is concerned, it was a forceful critique of *Roe* that illuminated its tensions with the New Deal regime—illuminated, in fact, the tension at the heart of the Constitutional Revolution of 1937.[44] The New Deal constitutional order was coming apart because the Court had already instituted constitutional change that fell away from its foundations (in part because those foundations were essentially contested from the beginning). Reagan's originalism was in part an attempt to recover constitutional foundations—albeit an attempt of a different sort.

Reagan's originalism traveled easily with the New Deal's critique of *Lochner*, but it posed a challenge to the New Deal Constitution with regard to federalism. Although the New Deal court abandoned substantive due process, it also embraced a far-reaching view of Congress's power to regulate interstate commerce, rejecting arguments that federalism or the Tenth Amendment were limitations on national power.[45] On these issues, Reagan's constitutional vision squarely challenged the New Deal Constitution and its institutional arrangements. As Bork described it, "The [New Deal] Court's refusal to enforce limits of any kind simply abandoned this aspect of the Constitution. That worked a revolution in the relationship of the federal government to the state governments and to the people, and the revolution did not have to await a constitutional amendment."[46]

By focusing on *Roe* and *Casey* while neglecting the Reagan Court's federalism decisions, Ackerman is able to claim that the Reagan Revolution failed to legitimate constitutional change and, from there, claim that we are still living under the New Deal Constitution. This is troublesome because the link between *Roe* and the New Deal is specious. But more important, the resurgence of federalism represents a challenge to the New Deal order and shows signs that Reagan's challenge to that order was at least partly successful. In fact, Ackerman's scholarship in and of itself seems to reflect the potency of Reagan's challenge: by rooting our current Constitution in the New Deal, Ackerman proffers a sort of "New Deal Originalism" as a preemptive strike against Reagan's call for original intent, which rejected New Deal foundations with regard to federalism and limited government.[47] Reagan's failure to overturn *Roe* amounts, then, to a failure to ratify his constitutional vision, which then makes the Rehnquist Court's departure from New Deal foundations "unconstitutional." Ackerman is surely right that Reagan failed on this count. But he makes too much of the failure. Reagan spoke often about overturning *Roe* and frequently criticized what he called judicial lawmaking. He insisted, again and again, that he would put men and women on the bench who would interpret the law rather than legislate—a clear criticism of *Roe*. Even so, such moves were largely rhetorical. Castigating the Court's judicial lawmaking was a sure and easy way to affirm Reagan's commitment to pro-lifers and religious groups. And whereas numerous scholars focus on this aspect of Reagan's constitutional vision, a danger of overplaying it exists.[48] As Landy and Milkis argue:

> Reagan the divorcé', the TV huckster, the casual churchgoer, the signer of the California abortion bill coexisted uneasily with Reagan the Savonarola. As long as the Democrats kept control of at least one house of Congress, he did not need to resolve his ambivalence. He could continue to rhetorically support a whole host of conservative initiatives without having to actually put them into practice.[49]

Reagan's commitment to limited government and federalism, on the other hand, were at the very core of his political vision. Reagan and Meese's vision of originalism brings this out. What was most egregious about decisions such as *Roe* was not that they allowed abortion; it was the fact that they removed the decisions from where they properly belonged: in the hands of the states. The states themselves might choose to allow abortion, but constitutional principles of federalism commanded that the issue be decided there and not by the Supreme Court.[50]

In the wake of *Casey*, Ackerman says, "we have returned to normal politics."[51] But this is not true. Or, to vary the formula, ordinary politics itself contains constitutional politics, which we see in the realm of civil liberties under the New Deal regime, so whether we ever left such politics behind is not clear. Reagan and the Rehnquist Court are more likely just a particularly vivid and potent form of constitutional politics in an area that had been settled. The very same year that *Casey* was handed down, the Court reopened a debate on the meaning of the Tenth Amendment that had been settled since the New Deal.[52] Three years later the Court, in *Lopez*, clearly struck down a law as beyond the scope of Congress's commerce clause power for the first time since the New Deal. Since that time the Court has shown that it is willing to police the boundaries between the states and the national government: limiting Congress's power under the commerce clause,[53] breathing life into the Tenth Amendment,[54] and recognizing the sovereign immunity of the states.[55] Just how far the Reagan justices of the Rehnquist Court will go is an open question, as is whether this line of federalism decisions will be solidified over time.

Reagan's Transformative Appointments

Sheldon Goldman argues that, much like Roosevelt before him, Reagan "self-consciously attempted to use the power of judicial appointments to place on the bench judges who shared [his] general philosophy."[56] In fact, Reagan saw a transformation of the judiciary as key to his political agenda and, in Goldman's terms, policy considerations drove his judicial appointments. Unlike Roosevelt, the Court did not play spoiler to Reagan directly. To return to a more limited vision of government, the administration could cut government spending and taxes and let the states and local governments take up their more traditional roles. As long as the government acted in such a fashion, it could bring about significant change without confronting the Court. So although Reagan articulated a departmentalist vision, he was not forced to act on it directly. Yet absent a significant change in our constitutional vision or a fundamental change on the Court, Reagan's return to limited government would be transitory rather than foundational. To solidify a return to "dual sovereignty," he turned to judicial appointments. His quarrel with the Court was largely rhetorical, insisting that it let states and local governments return to their traditional functions. The Supreme Court opinions he was most critical of—those forcing school busing, forbidding prayer in public schools, and nationalizing abortion and criminal rights—prevented the states from making choices he thought they were constitutionally vested with the power to make. This required a change in judicial philosophy: getting justices to police the boundaries of federalism in a way that had not been done since the pre–New Deal years. The rhetoric, much like Roosevelt's before, was an insistence on judicial restraint: let state legislatures make these decisions, not federal courts. Judicial restraint, however, was only part of the picture. At the national level a constitutionally mandated return to federalism might require a much more active judiciary. If the national government had a broader vision of its constitutional power than the Reagan administration did, it would very likely come into conflict with a Court dedicated to federalism. Perhaps more than any administration since Franklin Roosevelt's, Reagan was committed to this jurisprudential shift; indeed, the administration started vetting candidates for the Supreme Court before there were even any vacancies.[57]

Reagan's reliance on judicial appointments to bring about constitutional change was in part due to the fact that he was not in direct conflict with the Court. But it also reveals the degree to which Reagan was working within an inherited institutional order even while attempting to change that very order. To alter the existing constitutional order, Reagan worked primarily through the instruments of the modern executive: through administration and presidential rhetoric, not large-scale legislative change. These instruments are part of the most profound constitutional change of the twentieth century and Reagan's use of them to foment constitutional change reflected just how rooted Franklin Roosevelt's administrative executive was.[58] Through judicial appointments, the Department of Justice, Office of Legal Policy, and by way of executive orders and presidential signing statements, Reagan attempted to shift constitutional thinking in legal terms.[59] And although Reagan criticized a "political" Court, most of the action was contained in the legal arena—the stuff of lawyers and courts, not high-level constitutional politics.[60] Reagan's rhetorical efforts seemed to promise more.

Here again, Reagan embraced the modern presidency: he was *the* rhetorical president.[61] But there was a twist. Reagan's rhetoric, unlike many modern presidents, raised "important constitutional concerns."[62] Of course, Reagan also used rhetoric to mobilize and flatter his political supporters. (One wonders, even, if much of his constitutional rhetoric on abortion and the like was of this nature.) Reagan's rhetoric provoked a constitutional debate that freed his administration from the Court monopoly of constitutional norms. Much of Reagan's rhetoric in this regard seemed to be precisely so that the administration could offer its own constitutional views independently of what the Court had said or done. Most famously, Reagan insisted that he was not bound by Court opinions on constitutional questions and could—in fact, *must*—interpret the Constitution independently of Supreme Court opinions. As with Lincoln before him, Reagan did not reject Court opinions as binding on the parties to the case, but he rejected the broader rule that the Court had articulated most forcefully in *Cooper v. Aaron*, that once the Court has spoken on a constitutional issue, it definitively settled that issue for all the branches of government.[63] Attorney General Meese explicitly rejected this line of reasoning. Meese set off a maelstrom by innocuously arguing that the duty to interpret the Constitution is a duty of all the branches of government and not just a duty of the Court. Meese went on to say that, given this, *Cooper v. Aaron* "was, and is, at war with the Constitution, at war with the basic principles of democratic government, and at war with the very meaning of the rule of law."[64] The very rhetoric of originalism suggested that the Court had fallen away from the Constitution and that the president was thereby better positioned to speak for the Constitution than the Court, to return to constitutional first principles. Reagan brought this to light in speeches on federalism, insisting that the states had created the national government, not the other way around. Reagan even invoked Alexis de Tocqueville in a 1981 television address, suggesting that federalism was key to American democracy.[65] Meese, once again, echoed this thinking by directly taking on the Supreme Court's opinion in *Garcia v. San Antonio Metropolitan Transit Authority*, where the Court, reversing the only significant federalism opinion of a generation, held that Congress could reach state employees by way of its power to regulate interstate commerce. Moreover, the Tenth Amendment was rejected as a limitation on national power and the Court, per Justice Blackmun, went so far as to say that the judiciary was ill equipped to police the boundaries of state and national power. It was an affirmation of the New Deal Constitution. Meese insisted that in *Garcia* "the Court displayed—in the view of the administration—an inaccurate reading of the text of the Constitution and a disregard for the Framers' intention that state and local governments be a buffer against the centralizing tendencies of the national leviathan." Pushing this further, Meese noted that "the administration's view is that federalism is one of the most basic principles of our Constitution," and added "we hope for a day when the Court returns to the basic principles of the Constitution as expressed in *Usery*." In *National League of Cities v. Usery*, a case out of line with the New Deal view of federalism, Rehnquist argued that the Tenth Amendment limited congressional power. The very year that *Garcia* overturned *Usery*, Reagan elevated Rehnquist to Chief Justice. And dissenting in *Garcia*, Rehnquist turgidly noted, "I do not think it incumbent on those of us in dissent to spell out further the fine points of a principle that will, I am confident, in time again command the support of a majority of this Court."[66] Rehnquist has led just such a resurgence that has its roots in Reagan's constitutional vision. And although Reagan's rhetorical efforts are important, they seem to supplement his more concerted effort through administrative and legal channels. In this manner Reagan brought about his most fruitful constitutional change.

WHITHER THE CURRENT REGIME?

We might see the Rehnquist Court as part of Reagan's national governing coalition, part of the current political regime. Federalism emerged as a political and constitutional issue on the national agenda, addressed by both the political parties, long before the Rehnquist Court's revival of it. Whether "the Court has led a 'federalism revolution,'" as much as "followed national political trends" is not clear.[67] Submerged in the Reagan years, however, was the possibility of an active Court. A return of the Court's policing state-federal boundaries would almost surely require judicial activism if the national government did not restrain itself and recognize a wide arena for state autonomy.[68] In the last decade the Court has taken on this role, striking down an unprecedented number of congressional acts in the arena of federalism. Critics have been quick to point to the Court's judicial activism of which Reagan was so critical.[69] So is the Court thwarting congressional will? This question should draw our eye to a central point: the foundations of judicial power are political. While the Court has taken up the role of enforcer of federalism in the constitutional order—with rather dramatic claims to judicial supremacy—this was brought about, after a lag, by Reagan and has strong political support in the current regime. Much like the New Dealers before them, those who criticized judicial power in the 1980s have grown comfortable with it in the 1990s, whereas past supporters have suddenly started invoking notions of judicial restraint and accusing the Court of second guessing the political branches. It is ironic, no doubt, that the president who brought forth the current Court was an advocate of departmentalism, whereas the Court itself has rejected anything short of judicial supremacy. Still, how solid the current foundation is, including the Court's claims to judicial supremacy, remains to be seen. The fact that so many of these decisions are 5–4 symbolizes the tensions within our constitutionalism and the difficulty, once more, of speaking of constitutional regimes.

Constitutional change does not necessarily emerge all at once as in Ackerman's great constitutional moments; nor does it unfold in a neat evolutionary manner with subtle changes in judicial doctrine. The recognition that presidents—especially great presidents—may remake the constitutional order, and often against the Court, is an important one. Even so, this recognition mirrors some of the problems with conventional notions of judicial supremacy. Indeed, to some degree presidential reconstructions supplement judicial supremacy. In remaking the constitutional order, great presidents engage in departmentalist constitutional rhetoric, displace the current constitutional understandings as the Supreme Court articulates, and restructure our constitutional views and institutions. The Court, by and large, then returns to its role as the articulator of the new constitutional order.[70] So judicial supremacy is the norm with moments of constitutional politics as extraordinary events. Although surely a more accurate rendering of our constitutional history than simple judicial supremacy, this narrative also misses moments of constitutional dialogue, conflict, discontinuity, unsettlement, and innovation that bring about significant constitutional change. Indeed, the ebb and flow of constitutional meaning may capture the ordinary functioning of our system far more aptly than grand presidential reconstructions or simple judicial enforcement.[71] Constitutional disjunctions may break with the past order without bringing about full-scale constitutional change. Although Reagan did not overturn Roe, whether *Roe* was part of the existing constitutional order in the first place, or that the question of a constitutional right to abortion has truly been settled is difficult to say.[72] We see this with Reagan's revival of federalism: the Rehnquist Court has broken with the New Deal, but in doing so has continued, rather than settled, a constitutional debate.

Undoing the New Deal

The 5–4 federalism decisions in recent years have often amounted to a debate about the New Deal between the majority and dissenting justices. In *Lopez*, when the Court struck down the Gun-Free School Zones Act of 1990, Justice Souter, writing in dissent, raised the specter that the Court may be returning to a pre-1937 reading of the commerce clause. He even accused the majority of "ignoring the painful lesson learned in 1937."[73] And Justice Breyer's dissenting opinion, which was joined by Stevens, Ginsburg, and Souter, insisted that Rehnquist's opinion for the majority "runs contrary to modern Supreme Court cases" with particular emphasis on *Wickard v. Filburn*, which solidified the New Deal understanding of the commerce power. It is appropriate that Justice Robert Jackson, who as Roosevelt's Solicitor General had articulated the New Deal constitutional vision to a usually hostile Court. Now on the bench, Jackson solidified this constitutional vision, symbolized all the more by the fact of not a single dissenting opinion. In *Wickard*, the Court upheld a congressional regulation that limited the amount of wheat a farmer could grow for home consumption even though it did not move in interstate commerce. In doing so, the Court held that it must look at the totality of effects, so even purely local matters might, taken cumulatively, have an effect on interstate commerce. Therefore, such local activities were within the reach of the commerce power. Rehnquist's opinion slyly evades the logic of *Wickard*, noting that at least it purported to regulate commercial activity, whereas *Lopez* was not regulating commercial activity at all. But as Justice Breyer pointed out, "the Wickard Court expressly held that Wickard's consumption of home grown wheat, '*though it may not be regarded as commerce*,' could nevertheless be regulated—'whatever its nature'—so long as 'it exerts a substantial effect on interstate commerce.'"[74] *Lopez* does not sit easily with *Wickard* and looks like a departure. That is surely why Rehnquist, although speaking of *Wickard*, rested *Lopez* on the logic of an earlier New Deal case: *Jones and Laughlin Steel*. This watershed case upheld the National Labor Relations Act (the Wagner Act) against a commerce clause challenge, thus allowing a key piece of New Deal legislation to go forward, even while reminding the Congress:

> the scope of this power [the interstate commerce power] must be considered in the light of our dual system of government and may not be extended so as to embrace effects upon interstate commerce so indirect and remote that to embrace them, in view of our complex society, would effectually obliterate the distinction between what is national and what is local and create a completely centralized government.[75]

This is just what *Wickard* did four years later. In returning to the logic of *Jones and Laughlin Steel*, the Rehnquist Court may not have been returning fully to pre-1937 understandings of the commerce clause, but it was just as surely rejecting the full fruit of the New Deal as put forward in *Wickard*.[76]

The Court had opened up another such departure in *New York v. The United States*, where it held that the Congress may not "commandeer" the states by forcing them to take action to implement a federal program. For our purposes, *New York* is significant in that its reading of the Tenth Amendment revived the notion of "dual sovereignty" all but buried in the Constitutional Revolution of 1937. O'Connor explained:

> The Tenth Amendment . . . restrains the power of Congress, but this limit is not derived from the text of the Tenth Amendment itself, which, as we have discussed, is essentially a tautology. Instead, the Tenth Amendment confirms that the power of the Federal Government is subject to limits that may, in any given instance, reserve power to the States. The Tenth Amendment thus directs us to determine, as in this case, whether an incident of state sovereignty is protected by a limitation on an Article I power.[77]

Similar to what the Chief Justice would later do in *Lopez*, O'Connor held that this was consistent with New Deal precedent, quoting Stone's opinion in *United States v. Darby*, "The Tenth Amendment 'states but a truism that all is retained which has not been surrendered.'"[78] O'Connor uses this truism, however, to breathe life into the Tenth Amendment as a substantive limit on congressional power by restoring the notion of dual sovereignty. This is exactly what Stone was rejecting: *Darby* was meant to bury the notion that dual sovereignty placed any substantive limits on congressional power and place such a reading of the Tenth Amendment in the dustbin of history. Again, while not necessarily returning to a pre–New Deal jurisprudence, the five Reagan/Bush appointees were signaling a significant departure from the New Deal Constitution—and on the very issues it had in fact settled.[79]

The Court's break became evident in *United States v. Morrison* when it struck down the Violence against Women Act (VAWA) even though Congress had offered substantial findings "that gender-motivated violence affects interstate commerce." This was something Congress had not done in *Lopez*. The Court made apparent the meaning of *Lopez* when Rehnquist insisted, "whether particular operations affect interstate commerce sufficiently to come under the constitutional power of Congress to regulate them is ultimately a judicial rather than a legislative question."[80] In its commerce clause opinions since *Wickard*, the Court had always insisted that—theoretically—a limit on what Congress could regulate existed under the guise of its commerce power, but the reasoning of the Court's opinions had suggested that Congress's power was plenary. By itself *Lopez* might have been a simple recognition of this outer limit. But *Morrison* made clear that the Court would police the "distinction between what is truly national and what is truly local." This gave federalism a bite that although possible in the Court's earlier opinions, was simply not there in practice, a point Rehnquist made explicit:

> Although Justice Breyer argues that acceptance of the government's rationales would not authorize a general federal police power, he is unable to identify any activity that the States may regulate but Congress may not. Justice Breyer posits that there might be some limitations on Congress' commerce power . . . [but] these suggested limitations, when viewed in light of the dissent's expansive analysis, are devoid of substance.[81]

The so-called federalist five made clear that they would give substance to these limitations on congressional power and, even if *sub silentio*, broke from the New Deal.[82]

Morrison solidified the Court's federalism on another front as well. In addition to the commerce clause analysis, Rehnquist's opinion rejected the idea that Congress may federalize traditional state matters, such as violence against women, under Section 5 of the Fourteenth Amendment. Federalism was held to limit Congress's power to enforce the terms of the Fourteenth Amendment. Here federalism bled into the Court's stunning insistence on judicial supremacy in *City of Boerne v. Flores*, on which *Morrison* rested squarely. In *Boerne*, Justice Kennedy, appointed by a president who insisted that he could interpret the Constitution independently of what the Court had said, insisted that constitutional interpretation was a job for the Court alone. "Congress," Justice Kennedy lectured, "has been given the power 'to enforce,' not the power to determine what constitutes a constitutional violation. Were it not so, what Congress would be enforcing would no longer be, in any meaningful sense, the 'provisions' of [the Fourteenth Amendment.]"[83] The Constitution, for Justice Kennedy, is what the Court says it is. Congress, then, can enforce the Court's reading of the Constitution, but not its own. This is surely at odds with Meese, who had a heavy hand in appointing Kennedy, insisting:

> once we understand the distinction between constitutional law and the Constitution, once we see that constitutional decisions need not be seen as the last words in constitutional construction . . . we can grasp a correlative point: constitutional interpretation is not the business of the Court alone, but also properly the business of all branches of government.[84]

The majority, however, has been quite insistent on the Court as the definitive interpreter of constitutional meaning. Does this suggest a return to judicial supremacy, solidifying a departmentalist president's constitutional vision?

Congress and Court

Many scholars suggest we seem to have entered a new constitutional regime, but one whose foundation is remarkably tenuous.[85] We might better understand these developments as consistent with ordinary political change—the political Constitution at work—which itself is part or our constitutional development. The persistence of the 5–4 decisions on federalism issues highlights this fact. The four dissenting justices make as coherent a bloc as the Reagan/Bush appointees and are convinced that the Court is wrong. As Justice Breyer put it squarely in dissent at the end of the Court's 2002 term, in yet another 5–4 federalism decision: "[the majority opinion] reaffirms the need for continued dissent."[86] Both sides have solid political support within the political system. The path of federalism may well depend on the next few appointments to the Court. And yet, remarkably, although the Supreme Court played a limited role in the last presidential election, federalism was not the key issue.[87] Rather, the Court factored in, yet again, as a way for both sides to flatter supporters and gain their votes by highlighting *Roe v. Wade*. The rhetorical presidency persists. But this may also say something about the Court's conflict with Congress over the last decade.

The Congress appears reluctant simply to accept the Court's recent decisions, but it appears just as reluctant to challenge the Court boldly. After the Court struck down the Gun-Free School Zones Act in *Lopez* and the Religious Freedom Restoration Act (RFRA) in *Boerne*, Congress refused to simply let the Court settle the issue. In passing the VAWA in 1999, the Congress touched on both of these cases. The act rested on both Congress's commerce power and its power under Section 5 of the Fourteenth Amendment.

In *Lopez*, the Court had rejected the federal regulation of guns in school zones as far too tenuously linked to the regulation of interstate commerce. So in passing the VAWA, Congress compiled a "mountain of data" to show "the effects of violence against women on interstate commerce." Here, Congress was engaging the Court and attempting to work within the contours of its opinion. The Court, as we have seen, rejected Congress's attempt to do this and signaled how serious it was about the limits of Congress's commerce power. Whether Congress will accept this remains to be seen. In the same act, however, Congress did challenge the Court's recent opinion in *Boerne*. By also resting the VAWA on its Section 5 power, Congress was attempting to define substantive rights under the amendment, which the Court, in *Boerne*, insisted Congress could not do. But even here Congress attempted to engage the Court: it tried to show that these rights were not being preserved in the states, which therefore justified congressional action (something it did not clearly show in the RFRA).

Congress itself has been ambivalent about the Court's power and has even tacitly indulged it. In passing legislation that is constitutionally controversial, Congress often defers to the Court's ultimate judgment by enacting fast-track provisions that allow for direct appeal to the Supreme Court so that it may settle the constitutional question. Its reluctance to work out controversial constitutional questions by deferring to the Court for political cover neglects its role as an independent interpreter of the Constitution. Perhaps most important, much of the legislation the Rehnquist Court has struck down is "symbolic" or "message politics."[88] This is particularly evident in the Gun-Free School Zones Act. Here Congress was responding to a perceived national problem to get credit for "doing something." In passing such legislation—which in many cases simply mirrors state legislation—Congress gets political credit. When the Court strikes down such legislation, Congress is not held accountable for the failure; indeed, members of Congress have already received the biggest benefit: recognition from interest groups and their constituents for addressing the issue. Nor, however, are members of Congress necessarily troubled by the Court's decisions because such decisions do not truly keep congressional members from responding to constituent demands. In fact, many members of Congress may well support the Court's general turn to federalism even while supporting legislation they think the Court very likely to strike down to reap the benefits for responding to interest groups and constituents. This is perhaps why the Court has drawn far more fire from interest groups and Court watchers than from members of Congress. And this says something important about the actions of the Rehnquist Court.

The Rehnquist Court, in contrast to the New Deal Court, has not yet prevented political actors from achieving significant political goals. The Court is not consistently thwarting a powerful national agenda Congress supports (or even that the public and the president support). Particular political groups may be miffed at the Court, and thus Congress may be reluctant to simply accept the Court's path, but neither has it mounted a serious challenge to the Court's authority. (And many members are quite content with the Court.) Congress, much like the President with signing statements, engages in a sort of independent constitutional interpretation on the cheap. It asserts this power on occasion, and refuses to simply follow Court opinions (often flatly ignoring them), but it does not flatly reject the Court's claims to judicial supremacy. But this also indicates a sort of judicial supremacy on the cheap. Whereas the Court has insisted on its unique role in settling constitutional questions, the foundations of such a role are not necessarily solid. We may indulge the Court as long as it is generally in line with a political consensus or not directly thwarting the President and Congress's political will. How long this will hold may depend on how far the Court pushes, but it will almost certainly depend on external political developments. As the four dissenting justices have continually warned, the "consequences of the court's approach [may] prove anodyne."[89] But, depending on events, the Court's approach may also prove destructive. Justice Souter, the lone outlier of the Reagan/Bush appointees on federalism issues, reiterated this warning in his dissenting opinion in *Morrison*:

> All of this convinces me that today's ebb of the commerce power rests on error, and at the same time leads me to doubt that the majority's view will prove to be enduring law. There is yet one more reason for doubt. Although we sense the presence of [pre–New Deal decisions] once again, the majority embraces them only at arm's-length. . . . Cases standing for the sufficiency of substantial effects are not overruled; cases overruled since 1937 are not quite revived. The Court's thinking betokens less clearly a return to . . . conceptual straightjackets . . . than to something . . . unsteady, a period in which the failure to provide a workable definition left this Court to review each case ad hoc. As our predecessors learned then, the practice of such ad hoc review cannot preserve the distinction between the judicial and the legislative, and this Court, in any event, lacks the institutional capacity to maintain such a regime for very long.[90]

The dissenting justices persist in insisting the Court's federalism jurisprudence is not tenable and that it may, once again, have to relearn the lessons of 1937. Yet, depending on the trajectory of current politics (or a possibly emerging regime), the Rehnquist Court's federalism may prove a constitutional moment that leaves the lessons of 1937 as a remnant of the New Deal Constitution. The outcome will depend on the constitutional politics of the next few years. We are, in the meantime, in a state of constitutional drift, but such a state is far more familiar in U.S. constitutional history then we often suppose; it is not a stretch to suggest this is politics as usual.

CONCLUSION

Reagan's counterrevolution against the New Deal—playing Franklin Roosevelt in reverse—did not bring on the kind of sweeping constitutional and political change that Roosevelt himself did. Partly this is a result of circumstance. The gradual disintegration of the New Deal coalition in the 1970s was very different from the sharp political crisis of the early 1930s. In fact, Reagan's movement from enthusiastic New Dealer to outspoken critic of the New Deal state over the course of four decades mirrored many Americans' growing frustrations with national centralization. Reagan sought to dismantle New Deal institutions by turning away from Washington, D.C., and returning political responsibility back to local and state governments. Most important, he saw this as not just smart politics, but as constitutionally mandated. The Reagan Revolution has succeeded in this far more modest task: it has brought federalism back to the table as a constitutionally robust principle. But this is a work in progress—with the distinct possibility of failure.

In this way, Reagan's constitutional reconstruction reflects the ebb and flow of constitutional change, rather than the dramatic politics of constitutional transformation. Here we see Reagan's break with the New Deal as well as his indirect affirmation of its legacy. The Rehnquist Court's federalism opinions have broken with the New Deal Constitution on the enumerated powers of the national government and the meaning of the Tenth Amendment. Yet, the fact that the most significant aspects of Reagan's constitutional reconstruction worked through the legalistic and administrative realm attests to the continuing presence of New Deal institutions—and reveals, in fact, the institutional and constitutional overlap of different "orders."[91] The Reagan Court, as we might properly call the Rehnquist Court when it comes to federalism, has assumed the task of policing the federal system and, in doing so, has unsettled the New Deal Constitution. Leuchtenburg concluded the Constitutional Revolution of 1937 by noting, "'When the extreme negativist position of 1935–36 was forsaken, as it had to be, the Court could find no stopping place short of abdication.' In 1937 the Supreme Court began a revolution in jurisprudence that ended, it appeared forever, the reign of laissez-faire and legitimated the arrival of the Leviathan State."[92] In U.S. constitutional development things rarely last forever.[93] A return to a laissez-faire state seems unlikely, but the Rehnquist Court is once again attempting to draw a line between national and state authority and, thereby, rejecting the Leviathan state. The fragility of this constitutional shift is highlighted by the fact that it seems to turn on the vote of a single Supreme Court justice. Although the Court is in the forefront of this constitutional development, this should not blind us to the politics that underlie the Court. For far more than a single Supreme Court justice, the fate of the current federalism revival will depend on the course of U.S. politics more generally. We are no longer living under the New Deal Constitution, but neither has a coherent constitutional vision replaced it.

NOTES

1. Quoted in Sidney Milkis, *The President and the Parties: The Transformation of the American Party System Since the New Deal* (New York: Oxford University Press, 1993), p. 263.

2. William Leuchtenburg, *In the Shadow of FDR: From Harry Truman to Bill Clinton* (Ithaca, N.Y.: Cornell University Press, 1993), p. 225.

3. William Leuchtenburg, *The Supreme Court Reborn: The Constitutional Revolution in the Age of Roosevelt* (New York: Oxford University Press, 1995), p. 213.

4. Stephen Skowronek, *The Politics Presidents Make: Leadership from John Adams to George Bush* (Cambridge, Mass.: Harvard University Press, 1993), p. 416.

5. Marc Landy and Sidney Milkis, *Presidential Greatness* (Lawrence: University Press of Kansas, 2000), p. 198.

6. See especially Bruce Ackerman, *We the People: Transformations* (Cambridge, Mass.: Harvard University Press, 1998).

7. Ackerman, *We the People*, 26.

8. In pursuit of what Sheldon Goldman calls a president's "policy agenda." Goldman, *Picking Federal Judges: Lower Court Selection from Roosevelt to Reagan* (New Haven, Conn.: Yale University Press, 1997), p. 3. See also Terri Perreti, *In Defense of a Political Court* (Princeton, N.J.: Princeton University Press, 1999), who makes this connection explicit.

9. Keith Whittington, "The Political Foundations of Judicial Supremacy," in *Constitutional Politics: Essays on Constitutional Making Maintenance, and Change*, Sotirios Barber and Robert P. George, eds. (Princeton, N.J.: Princeton University Press, 2001), is one such attempt. Earlier studies, such as Robert Scigliano's *The President and the Supreme Court* (New York: Free Press, 1971), drew on the special connection, but largely deferred to judicial supremacy.

10. Alexander Hamilton, James Madison, and John Jay, *The Federalist Papers* (New York: Mentor, 1999) Nos. 71, 73, 400, and 410. See also Jeffrey Tulis, *The Rhetorical Presidency* (Princeton, N.J.: Princeton University Press, 1986), pp. 39–40.

11. *Federalist 78*, p. 434.

12. Edwin Meese III, "Perspective on the Authoritativeness of Supreme Court Decision: The Law of the Constitution," *Tulane Law Review* 61 (1987): 979–89.

13. Michael Kinsley called it "Meese's stink bomb" *Washington Post*, October 29, 1986, p. A19; Ronald Dworkin, *Freedom's Law* (Cambridge, Mass.: Harvard University Press, 1996); essays that originally appeared in the *New York Review of Books*; Laurence Tribe, *Constitutional Choices* (Cambridge, Mass.: Harvard University Press, 1985).

14. Skowronek, *The Politics Presidents Make*, p. 39.

15. Landy and Milkis, *Presidential Greatness*, p. 4.

16. Ackerman, however, focuses only on Lincoln and Franklin Roosevelt, neglecting Jefferson and Jackson, and explicitly arguing that Reagan's attempted transformation failed. *We the People*, pp. 390–403.

17. Whittington, "The Political Foundations of Judicial Supremacy," p. 274.

18. Skowronek, *The Politics Presidents Make*, p. 428.

19. Landy and Milkis, *Presidential Greatness*, p. 225.

20. Ackerman, *We the People*, p. 391.

21. Stephen Gottlieb, *Morality Imposed* (New York: New York University Press, 2000). Arguably, this is the message of Ackerman's *We the People* as well.

22. Steven Calabresi, "Federalism and the Rehnquist Court: A Normative Defense" *The Annals of the American Academy of Political and Social Science* 574 (2001): 24–36.

23. As an isolated case, which I address later, Rehnquist's opinion for the Court in *National League of Cities v. Usery* (1976) held out limitations on Congress's power under the commerce clause, but did so indirectly by way of state sovereignty. Moreover, *Garcia* overturned it nine years later. Although, as I argue later, this was surely an initial probing that laid out Rehnquist's view of federalism, which the Court would start to articulate fully and consistently after *Lopez*.

24. Mark Tushnet, "Living in a Constitutional Moment? *Lopez* and Constitutional Theory," *Case Western Reserve Law Review* 46 (1996): 845–75; and *The New Constitutional Order* (Princeton, N.J.: Princeton University Press, 2003).

25. To name but a few, Dean Alfange Jr., "The Supreme Court and Federalism: Yesterday and Today," in *Politics and Constitutionalism: The Louis Fisher Connection*, Robert Spitzer, ed. (Albany: SUNY Press, 2000), pp. 107–62; Tinsley E. Yarbrough, *The Rehnquist Court and the Constitution* (New York: Oxford University Press, 2000); John Dinan, "The Rehnquist Court's Federalism Decisions in Perspective," *Journal of Law and Politics* 15 (Spring 1999): 127–93; Timothy Conlan and Francois Vergniolle de Chantal, "The Rehnquist Court and Contemporary American Federalism," *Political Science Quarterly* 116 (2001): 253–75; Richard Fallon, "The 'Conservative' Paths of the Rehnquist Court's Federalism Decisions," *University of Chicago Law Review* 69 (2002): 429–93; Christopher Schroeder, "Causes of the Recent Turn in Constitutional Interpretation," *Duke Law Journal* 51 (2001): 307–60; Neal Devins, "Congress as Culprit: How Law Makers Spurred on the Court's Anti-Congress Crusade," *Duke Law Journal* 51 (2001): 435–63; Keith Whittington, "Taking What They Give Us: Explaining the Court's Federalism Offensive," *Duke Law Journal* 51 (2001): 477–519, all see the see the shift as significant, even while disagreeing profoundly over particulars. For an interesting demurer, see Robert Nagel, *The Implosion of American Feder-*

alism (New York: Oxford University Press, 2001), who argues that nationalism reigns supreme and that the recent move to federalism is minor at best.

26. Skowronek, *The Politics Presidents Make*, p. 429.

27. Reagan's election may look more like 1896 than 1932 if it ushers in a period of constitutional uncertainty much like 1895–1925, rather than the sharp change of 1935–1941.

28. Milkis, *The President and the Parties*, p. 228.

29. Tushnet attempts to merge the Great Society and New Deal as a single constitutional order, which neglects the way in which ordinary political change—even simple judicial appointments—helped bring in constitutional change that revealed the tensions at the heart of the New Deal. See his *The New Constitutional Order*. On judicial appointments and the Great Society, see Goldman, *Picking Federal Judges*, pp. 154–97.

30. Tulis, *The Rhetorical Presidency*, p. 181.

31. At least at the presidential level, although this is not true at the congressional level and whether it will hold as Al Gore ran to the left of Clinton in 2000, remains to be seen.

32. Skowronek, *The Politics Presidents Make*, pp. 416–29 and Landy and Milkis, *Presidential Greatness*, pp. 219–26.

33. Ackerman, *We the People: Transformations*, p. 26 (emphasis in original).

34. *Roe v. Wade*, 410 U.S. 113 (1973)

35. *Planned Parenthood v. Casey*, 505 U.S. 833 (1992).

36. *West Coast Hotel Company v. Parrish*, 300 U.S. 379 (1937).

37. *Roe* at 174.

38. *Griswold v. Connecticut*, 381 U.S. 479, 522 (1965), Justice Black dissenting.

39. Most notably John Hart Ely, who spun out Harlan Fiske Stone's famous *Carolene Products* footnote four into a full fledged theory of judicial review in *Democracy and Distrust: A Theory of Judicial Review* (Cambridge, Mass.: Harvard University Press, 1980), objected to *Roe*. Ely argued that *Roe* was not just bad constitutional law, but not constitutional law at all. "The Wages of Crying Wolf: A Comment *on Roe v. Wade*," *Yale Law Journal* 82 (1973): 920–48. See also, Laura Kalman, *The Strange Career of Legal Liberalism* (New Haven, Conn.: Yale University Press, 1996), pp. 1–10.

40. This argument repeatedly flared up between Felix Frankfurter and Hugo Black. See Mark Silverstein, *Constitutional Faiths: Felix Frankfurter, Hugo Black, and the Process of Judicial Decision-Making* (Ithaca, N.Y.: Cornell University Press, 1984), and C. Herman Pritchet, *The Roosevelt Court: A Study in Judicial Politics and Values, 1937–1947* (New York: Macmillan Company, 1948).

41. Robert Bork, *The Tempting of America* (New York: Free Press, 1990), p. 57.

> In my history-book, the Court was covered with dishonor and deprived of legitimacy by *Dred Scott v. Sandford* (1857), an erroneous (and widely opposed) opinion that it did not abandon, rather than by *West Coast Hotel* (1937), which produced the famous "switch in time" from the Court's erroneous (and widely opposed) constitutional opposition to the social measures of the New Deal.

Scalia's originalism is different from Bork's because he has shown a willingness to draw on unenumerated rights that are clearly part of our history and tradition. See, for example, Scalia's opinion in *Michael H. v. Gerald D.*, 491 U.S. 110 (1989).

42. See Holmes's dissenting opinion in *Adkins v. Children's Hospital*, 261 U.S. 525 (1923).

43. Quoted in Leuchtenburg, *The Supreme Court Reborn*, p. 234.

44. For an interesting take on constitutional originalism and the rise of the New Deal see Howard Gillman, "The Collapse of Constitutional Originalism and the Rise of the Notion of the 'Living Constitution' in the Course of American State-Building," *Studies in American Political Development* 11 (October 1997): 149–89.

45. See especially, *United States v. Darby*, 312 U.S. 100 (1941).

46. Bork, *The Tempting of America*, p. 57. See also, Raoul Berger, *Federalism: The Founder's Design* (Norman: University of Oklahoma Press, 1987).

47. George Thomas, "New Deal 'Originalism,'" *Polity* 33 (Fall 2000): 151–61. See also G. Edward White, *The Constitution and the New Deal* (Cambridge, Mass.: Harvard University Press, 2000), p. 27. Indeed, Reagan's turn to original intent could be seen as widely successful in that it has reshaped the debate about constitutional interpretation. When the Reagan administration brought "original intent" back to the table, the debate was often described as a debate between "interpretivists" and "non-interpretivists." But in the wake of Reagan, we are all interpretivists now. Once powerful critics of originalism such as Ronald Dworkin now speak its very language. In a way the argument is over who has the better form of "originalism." See Dworkin's *Freedom's Law* (Cambridge, Mass.: Harvard University Press, 1996). See also Akhil Reed Amar, *The Bill of Rights: Creation and Reconstruction* (New Haven, Conn.: Yale University Press, 1998). Ackerman's scholarship itself should be placed in the context of U.S. constitutional development because his argument can only be understood against its trajectory.

48. Donald Grier Stephenson, *Campaigns and the Court* (New York: Columbia University Press, 1999), focuses almost exclusively on the Court and abortion. James Simon's *The Center Holds* (New York: Simon and Schuster, 1996) speaks about the failure of the conservative revolution, but does not even have a chapter on federalism!

49. Landy and Milkis, *Presidential Greatness*, p. 224. Which is not to say that Reagan was not committed to these socially conservative issues, but he seemed unwilling to spend political capital to achieve them.

50. David E. Kyvig, *Explicit and Authentic Acts: Amending the U.S. Constitution, 1776–1995* (Lawrence: University Press of Kansas, 1996), argues that Reagan supported many conservative amendments for the same kind of rhetorical purposes, pp. 447–55.

51. This is not even true for abortion. In the 2000 partial birth abortion case, *Carhart v. Stenberg*, Justices Kennedy and O'Connor argued with one another over the very meaning of *Casey*. And the Congress passed the Born Alive Infants Act in July 2002, which may well have dramatic ramifications for abortion.

52. *New York v. United States*, 505 U.S. 144 (1992). O'Connor's majority opinion on the Tenth Amendment does not easily square with *Darby*. Again, *Usery* foreshadows these opinions, but placed in context it seems an isolated case.

53. *Lopez* and *United States v. Morrison*, 529 U.S. 598 (2000).

54. *New York v. United States* and *Printz v. United States*, 521 U.S. 898 (1997).

55. *Seminole Tribe of Florida v. Florida*, 517 U. S. 44 (1996); *Florida Prepaid Post-secondary Education Expense Board v. College Savings Bank*, 527 U.S. 627 (1999); *Col-*

lege Savings Bank v. Florida Prepaid Postsecondary Education Expense Board, 527 U.S. 666 (1999); *Alden v. Maine*, 527 U.S. 706 (1999); *Kimel v. Florida Board of Regents*, 528 U.S. 62 (2000); *Trustees of the University of Alabama v. Garrett*, 531 U.S. 356 (2001).

56. Sheldon Goldman, *Picking Federal Judges*, p. 285.

57. David Yalof, *Pursuit of Justices: Presidential Politics and the Selection of Supreme Court Nominees* (Chicago: University of Chicago Press, 1999), p. 143. David O'Brien suggest that the Reagan judges may well be his most enduring legacy, "The Reagan Judges: His Most Enduring Legacy?" in *The Reagan Legacy: Promise and Performance*, Charles O. Jones, ed. (Chatham, N.J.: Chatham House, 1988). See also Goldman, *Picking Federal Judges*, pp. 285–345

58. Milkis, *President and the Parties*.

59. See Kenneth Mayer, *With the Stroke of a Pen: Executive Orders and Presidential Power* (Princeton, N.J.: Princeton University Press, 2001).

60. What Cornell Clayton calls the "judicialization of politics." *The Politics of Justice: The Attorney General and the Making of Legal Policy* (New York: Sharpe, 1992), pp. 146–55.

61. Tulis, *The Rhetorical President*, pp. 189–202

62. Tulis, *The Rhetorical President*, p. 192.

63. *Cooper v. Aaron*, 358 U.S. 1, 18 (1958).

64. Edwin Meese, "The Law of the Constitution," p. 987.

65. *Congressional Quarterly*, (October 3, 1981): 1922.

66. *Garcia v. San Antonio Metropolitan Transit Authority*, 469 U.S. 528, 580 (1986; Justice Rehnquist dissenting).

67. J. Mitchell Pickerill and Cornell Clayton, "Politics and the Safeguards of Federalism during the Rehnquist Court" paper presented at the 2002 annual meeting of the Law and Society Association (Vancouver, B.C., 2002). Pickerill and Clayton examine the party platforms of both parties noting federalism issues. This is especially true of the Republican Party platforms, which speak "a decentralization of the federal government and efforts to return decision making power to state and local elected officials."

68. On this aspect of conservative jurisprudence, see Tom Keck, "The Rehnquist Court's Revival of Federalism and the Contradictions of Contemporary Conservatism." See also Thomas Keck, "Activism and Restraint on the Rehnquist Court: Timing, Sequence, and Conjuncture in Constitutional Development," *Polity* 35 (2002): 121–52.

69. Writing in *New Republic* ("Our Discriminating Court: Federal Offensive," April 9, 2001), p. 24, Jeffrey Rosen insisted that the Court's federalism opinions put the "New Deal legacy of a powerful federal government" at stake. Rosen has gone on to suggest, "the resurrection of a tradition of liberal judicial restraint . . . seems more relevant today than at any time since the New Deal," "Breyer Restraint: A Modest Proposal," *New Republic*, January 14, 2002, p. 21. Linda Greenhouse, "The High Court's Target: Congress," *New York Times*, February 25, 2001, p. 3.

70. Ackerman, Whittington, Skowronek, and Landy and Milkis all go with this narrative to varying degrees.

71. Louis Fisher, *Constitutional Dialogues: Interpretation as Political Process* (Princeton, N.J.: Princeton University Press, 1988). See also *Politics and Constitutionalism: The Louis Fisher Connection* (collected essay in tribute to Fisher).

72. Not only does continued and vehement constitutional debate exist on the issues, with large sections of the political community refusing to view *Roe* as legitimate, but also the Court itself continues to dispute the meaning of *Roe*. This is evident in *Casey* itself and, most recently, with Justices Kennedy and O'Connor disputing the meaning of *Casey* in relation to *Roe* in *Stenberg v. Carhart*, 530 U.S. 914 (2000).

73. *Lopez* at 609 (Justice Souter dissenting).

74. *Lopez* at 628 (Justice Breyer dissenting; emphasis in original).

75. *Jones and Laughlin* at 37.

76. Justice Thomas's concurring opinion helps draw this out as he urges a complete repudiation of the New Deal cases and a return to pre-1937 understanding of the commerce power. *Lopez* at 585 (Justice Thomas concurring).

77. *New York* at 156–57.

78. *Darby* at 124.

79. In *New York v. United States*, Justice Souter supplied the fifth vote and Clarence Thomas was not yet on the Court. In subsequent opinions, Souter would change his vote and become a leading critic of the Court's federalism decisions, whereas Thomas supplied the fifth vote. The sovereign immunity cases are perhaps the Court's most novel departure, but I do not address them because they are less central to the New Deal Constitution and Reagan's attempted reconstruction. For a critique of the Court's sovereign immunity jurisprudence, which does not reject the Court's return to a more limited view of Congress's commerce power, see George Thomas, review of John Noonan, *Narrowing the Nations Power: The Supreme Court Sides with the States* (Berkeley: University of California Press, 2002), and *Law and Politics Book Review* 12 (December 2002), http://www.bsos.umd.edu/gvpt/1pbr.

80. *Morrison* at 614. Ronald Rotunda, "The Commerce Clause, the Political Questions Doctrine, and Morrison," *Constitutional Commentary* 18 (2001), argues that, in fact, the dissenting opinions in these cases represent the significant departure from past cases insofar as they argue for a complete judicial abdication in this area.

81. *Lopez* at 564–65.

82. Dean Alfange Jr., "The Supreme Court and Federalism," and Tinsley E. Yarbrough, *The Rehnquist Court and the Constitution*, see the New Deal as restoring John Marshall's view of the Constitution, much like Edward Corwin, *Constitutional Revolution, Ltd.* (Claremont, Calif.: Claremont Colleges, 1941), and Alpheus Thomas Mason, *Harlan Fiske Stone: Pillar of the Law* (New York: Viking, 1956). Originalists such as Bork and Raoul Berger, however, see the New Deal as a departure from Marshall's Constitution on federalism issues.

83. *City of Boerne v. Flores*, 521 U.S. 507, 535–36 (1997).

84. Edward Meese, *The Law of the Constitution*, p. 978.

85. Tushnet suggests this new constitutional regime is not a radical departure, but one where constitutional aspiration (of, no doubt, a progressive variety) remains chastened. *The New Constitutional Order*.

86. *Federal Maritime Commission v. South Carolina State Ports Authority* (2002), http://supct.law.cornell.edu/supct/html/01–46.ZDI.html (Justice Breyer dissenting). Breyer again invoked the New Deal:

> An overly restrictive judicial interpretation of the Constitution's structural constraints (unlike its protections of certain basic liberties) will undermine the

Constitution's own efforts to achieve its far more basic structural aim, the creation of a representative form of government capable of translating the people's will into effective public action. This understanding, underlying constitutional interpretation since the New Deal, reflects the Constitution's demands for structural flexibility sufficient to adapt substantive laws and institutions to rapidly changing social, economic, and technological conditions.

87. Other than deciding it in *Bush v. Gore* (2000)! (I mean during the election and not in the aftermath.) Although critics have insisted that *Bush v. Gore* is not consistent with the Court's commitment to federalism, this need not be so. Even these justices argue that national questions rooted in the Constitution will trump state actions. But most important, however one comes down on *Bush v. Gore*, the federalism revolution of the Court has continued.

88. Devins, "Congress as Culprit," and Whittington, "Taking What They Give Us."

89. *Federal Maritime Commission v. South Carolina State Ports Authority.*

90. *Morrison* at 654–55 (Justice Souter dissenting).

91. Karren Orren and Stephen Skowronek, "Beyond the Iconography of Order: Notes for a 'New Institutionalism,'" in *The Dynamics of American Politics: Approaches and Interpretations*, Lawrence C. Dodd and Calvin Jillson, eds. (Boulder, Colo.: Westview, 1994).

92. Leuchtenburg, *The Supreme Court Reborn*, p. 236.

93. And Leuchtenburg himself is too sanguine about the Court's view of its role in the wake of this constitutional transformation, suggesting the Warren Court comes easily out of the New Deal revolution in "The Birth of America's Second Bill of Rights," in *The Supreme Court Reborn*, pp. 237–58.

NINE

Democratic Politics and Constitutional Creation: The Paradoxes of Presidential Policy toward the Judiciary

Kevin J. McMahon

> History teaches us, I think, that even a "strong" president determined to leave his mark on the Court, like Lincoln, or Franklin Roosevelt, is apt to be only partly successful. Neither the President nor his appointees can foresee what issues will come before the Court during the tenure of their appointees, and it may be that none had thought very much about these issues. Even though they agree as to the proper resolution of current issues, they may well disagree as to future cases involving other questions. . . . [T]he Supreme Court is an institution far more dominated by centrifugal forces, pushing towards individuality and independence, than it is by centripetal forces pulling for hierarchical ordering and institutional unity.
>
> —Associate Justice William Rehnquist, October 19, 1984[1]

> [T]he Supreme Court is not a subdivision of the executive branch, and a President must be steadfast in avoiding the temptation to treat the Court as an institution that is expected to hew to a particular ideological position.
>
> —Judge Irving R. Kaufman, U.S. Court of Appeals, December 9, 1984[2]

Despite lawyerly admonishments against the effectiveness or appropriateness of such action, presidents often attempt to alter judicial interpretation. From George Washington to George W. Bush, presidents have historically used the appointment process, the threat of court-curbing legislation, and the powers of the Department of Justice to influence future decisions of federal courts, especially the Supreme Court. In particular, some say, "realigning" presidents—those who have succeeded in, or appear to be on the verge of, bringing about a new dominant electoral coalition—have aspired to transform the federal judiciary, believing that if left "unreformed," its composition and doctrine will continue to advance the interests of the vanquished alliance. With this in mind, most have suggested that presidents, believing that success in constitutional construction will better secure their legacies, use their administration's policy toward the judiciary to alter the nature of judicial interpretation in ideological terms.[3] As Nixon White House advisor John Ehrlichman explained, second in importance to foreign affairs was Nixon's

> ability to change the domestic situation through the creation of a long-lived strict-constructionist Supreme Court, composed of young Justices who would sit and rule in Nixon's own image. He guessed he'd always be thwarted by Democrats in the Congress; the likelihood of winning broad domestic legislative changes—a Nixon New Deal—was slim or nonexistent. But if he could get his Supreme Court nominees confirmed by the Senate, fundamental domestic changes could be effected by the third branch of the Federal Government.[4]

This chapter analyzes Richard Nixon's and Ronald Reagan's policy toward the judiciary. Building on earlier research that focused on Franklin Roosevelt's "judicial policy,"[5] I suggest that presidential attempts to alter judicial interpretation are by definition designed to enhance the constitutional power of the presidency by extending its influence into the judicial arena. However, I argue that presidential judicial policy is not only driven by ideology, but also that presidents are motivated by a complexity of factors.[6] The most important of these motivations include: (1) consolidating or expanding an electoral coalition; (2) achieving a president's immediate legislative policy preferences; and (3) implementing a president's "constitutional vision," defined as his image of institutional order designed to best advance his values. Yet, an analysis of these motivations reveals only part of the story. To understand the likelihood of presidential success in altering judicial doctrine, gauging the amount of political authority a particular president possesses during his time in the White House is also necessary. Borrowing from Stephen Skowronek's work, "reconstructive" presidents, in theory, would have the most authority to alter the terms of judicial doctrine. Presidents in other moments of "political time" would either have less desire to challenge the Court's work or confront greater opposition in their efforts to do so. The comparison between Nixon and Reagan is therefore a useful one because Nixon fits well under Skowronek's definition of a "preemptive" president and Reagan nearly reaches the status of a "reconstructive" president.[7] Under these terms, Nixon would be expected to face more resistance to an ideological-driven effort to remake the Court, whereas Reagan would most likely have an easier time. And indeed, these expectations ring true. Nevertheless, in constructing their policy toward the judiciary, the desire to alter the nature of judicial interpretation in ideological terms still had to compete with electoral and legislative concerns in both administrations. In the pages that follow, I outline how these battles of emphasis lessened the ideological nature of both Nixon's and Reagan's judicial policy while still considering the importance of political time.

My conclusions suggest that given the divided nature of presidential judicial policy, scholars should avoid judging presidential success simply in ideological terms.[8] The end of the chapter argues that the partial success of Nixon's and Reagan's efforts to alter the ideological outlook of the Court has had positive (even if unintended) consequences for today's Republican Party.

RICHARD NIXON AND THE SILENT MAJORITY

Following the death of Chief Justice Warren Burger in 1995 and the retirement of his Minnesota Twin Harry Blackmun in 1994, commentators were quick to reevaluate the work of the Burger (that is, Nixon) Court.[9] With an eye toward the staunch conservatism of the Reagan administration's approach toward the Court, most argued that Nixon's first two appointees had failed to fulfill the president's promise to send only "strict constructionists" to the high bench. After all, Blackmun, with Burger in the majority, authored *Roe v. Wade* (1973), that generation's most controversial constitutional ruling and a striking example of judge-made law for jurists supposedly committed to conservative restraintism. In other areas as well, such as affirmative action, sex discrimination, and separation of church and state, both of these justices, but especially Blackmun, aided in the continuation of the Warren Court's liberal activism, albeit at a more moderate pace. Certainly, in some spheres, namely school desegregation and criminal procedure, these justices (along with Nixon's other two appointees, Lewis Powell and William Rehnquist) led the Burger Court's drive to limit the alleged radicalism of its predecessor, writing opinions that changed the path of judicial doctrine. The Nixon justices' role in blocking some post-Warren initiatives—such as attempts to "constitutionalize" the right to welfare and the right to education—should also not go unmentioned.[10] Nevertheless, the crux of the analysts' reassessments was that the Burger years had failed to furnish the expected conservative counterrevolution in judicial interpretation.[11] Alas, they proclaimed, this was yet another example of how a president cannot control the Court.[12]

In my analysis of the Nixon administration's policy toward the judiciary, I argue that the president's judicial policy was driven not only by ideology, but also was heavily influenced by one of the overriding themes of his presidency, the construction of a new electoral majority. This is not to say that Nixon simply used this policy as a tool to "play politics." He was clearly committed to remaking the Court into a more conservative institution, a commitment driven by his constitutional vision. However, his desire to construct a Republican majority often tempered the conservative nature of his policy toward the judiciary. The result was a judicial policy that combined selective attempts at interpretation alteration with anti–Warren Court rhetoric—Nixon and his political strategists believed that to do otherwise was too dangerous to the quest for a Republican realignment. In other words, it was thought that pressing the Court to reverse itself on all—or even most—aspects of the Warren-led legal revolution was sure to upset the balances of Nixon's emerging "new majority." Such a move would surely attract disaffected Democrats, but it might also convince traditional Republicans to simultaneously bolt from the Republican Party. Thus, in the end, Nixon's attempt to use this policy to both build an electoral and legislative majority and "conservatize" the Court limited his ability to do the latter.

To be sure, the mixed nature of his judicial policy was not simply the result of Nixon's personal brinkmanship. It was also the product of Nixon's level of political authority as president. As a "preemptive president," Nixon faced a preexisting government order that retained significant legitimacy when he entered office. According to Skowronek, "aggressive leaders" in such positions "tend to get themselves impeached, de facto if not de jure."[13] Although Nixon would later meet this fate, in his first term, his judicial policy reflected his uncertainty on how best to precede, an uncertainty the absence of a fully developed conservative critique of the courts, the presence of divided government, and the reality of a Republican party torn asunder exacerbated. Put another way, the nature of the political time significantly hindered Nixon's ability to implement fully a conservative policy toward the judiciary. Two examples display how the combination of Nixon's decision-making and the political temper of the times shaped his administration's positioning on judicial matters.

The first involves the fate of Nixon's two failed Supreme Court nominees, Clement Haynsworth and Harold Carswell. Because the Warren Court's approach toward civil rights still commanded a degree of respect among Republicans during the late 1960s, Nixon could not successfully issue overt attacks on its racially liberal decisions without some political consequences. After all, the leading figure of the Warren Court, the Chief Justice himself, was a Republican of the liberal sort. Another, Justice Brennan, was a Democrat Eisenhower appointed. In addition, no Republican president would have attempted to alter the Court in the manner Nixon desired in 1968. Success by a liberal Republican such as Nelson Rockefeller or George Romney in that year would have resulted in a much different presidential policy toward the federal judiciary. Thus, Nixon's bold attempt to remake the Court with southern strict constructionists was destined to confront dissent from members of his own party. Indeed, in the end, many liberal Republican senators did not approve Nixon's second two Supreme Court nominees. With some Republican conservatives—citing either the ethics or the qualifications of the nominees—joining in, a bipartisan coalition voted to reject both Haynsworth and Carswell. Strikingly, when the tally was in, 40 percent of the Senate's Republicans did not support Haynsworth, and 32 percent of those voting did not favor Carswell.[14] Given such a split in the Republican Party, Nixon could not simultaneously attract disgruntled southern Democrats and northern Catholics while retaining traditional Republicans. Racial and social issues simply spilt the parties too evenly. As Nixon angrily concluded, any southerner of his stripe would confront hostile territory in the Senate. He instead settled on the confirmable Blackmun, a choice that eventually lessened the conservatism of the Burger Court.

The second example involves the Office of the Solicitor General during Nixon's first term. During this time, the Office of the Solicitor General, under the leadership of Erwin Griswold, often presented arguments that seemed to diverge from the stated intentions of the president and the apparent legal philosophies of his nominees to the Court. These contradictions are highlighted by John Ehrlichman's astonishing claim that in selecting a southern strict constructionist to fill Abe Fortas's seat in 1970, "Nixon exulted . . . with this one we'd stick it to the liberal, Ivy League clique who thought the Court was their own private playground (people like *Erwin Griswold*, Robert Morgenthau and the Kennedys.")[15] Of course, Nixon knew that Griswold was his own advocate before the Supreme Court, but he apparently felt too constrained by the politics of the time to replace him. Still, given this attitude and the apparent importance the president placed on changing judicial interpretation, that Solicitor General Griswold lasted into the president's second term and was allowed to take positions in court that were often inconsistent with the policy preferences of the Nixon White House is remarkable.[16] While the oddity of this personal decision deserves further study, it nevertheless suggests a concern on Nixon's part about aggressively pursuing broad-based legal change.

In this sense, two competing electoral strategies concerning the future shape of the Republican Party influenced the Nixon administration's judicial policy in the president's first term. On the one hand, the much-maligned "southern strategy"—emphasizing a move away from the Republican Party's traditional liberal constituency (located largely in New England and New York) toward more conservative white southerners and northern Catholics—tended to serve as the administration public voice on judicial matters and as a guide to some of the president's choices for the High Court. On the other hand, the less radical "battleground state strategy"—encouraging the creation of a grand center coalition that would both retain the party's traditional liberal voters and attract new converts—tended to shape the administration's policies and positions in court.[17] (The presence of George Wallace in the political scene significantly influenced these two strategies. The first was designed to attract the Alabama governor's supporters and dissuade him from running as an Independent again in 1972. If Wallace did run, however, Nixon would need to secure his Republican base, making the second strategy crucial.)[18] After all, Republican strategist Kevin Phillips had acknowledged that if the party adopted his ideas of a rightward shift "several million liberal Republican voters from Maine and Oregon to Fifth Avenue" would be lost.[19] At times, Nixon seemed willing to accept this loss. At other times, he thought Phillips had "flipped." As Nixon White House aide Lee Huebner summed it up in 1974:

> Despite the fact that Phillips dedicated his book to Richard Nixon and John Mitchell, "the architects of the emerging Republican majority," and despite conservative efforts to label the Phillips book as the "Bible of the Nixon administration," its views were never fully adopted by the new administration's most powerful strategists. The strategy of writing off any sizable group of Republicans was risky and unnecessary, they said. The new Republican majority must be built by inclusion and not exclusion. The party would therefore attempt to join the South and the cities, the suburbs and small towns, in a grand new coalition of the center.[20]

Although Huebner's analysis is informative, in actuality Nixon and Attorney General John Mitchell vacillated between adopting Phillips's proposal and attempting to construct the grand center coalition, never deciding on which would best support their pragmatic style of conservatism. This vacillating, moreover, was in part the result of Nixon's position as a "preemptive president." When he did make an aggressive move with his two southern strategy appointments, both Democrats and leading members of his own party rebuked his efforts. A major reason why the counterrevolution in judicial interpretation never came, then, was because President Nixon never authorized a full-scale effort. Instead, he seemed caught in the cross fire of the notion of an "emerging Republican majority" and that of a grand center coalition based on the Republican Party's traditional constituency.

Thus although Nixon wanted to impose his constitutional vision on the Court, with an unstable electoral coalition, a fractured party, the lack of conservative scholars from which to draw ideas and talent, and the corresponding arrival of divided government, the implementation of this vision was impeded for most of his presidency. Shaped partly by the spirit of this political time, Nixon never appeared confident enough to pursue his vision of a more conservative institutional arrangement vigorously. Instead, his judicial policy reflected his tendency to stress pragmatic positions over conservative principles. Whereas obvious differences exist, many have reached similar conclusions about the Burger Court.

RONALD REAGAN, THE RIGHTS REVOLUTION, AND THE RELIGIOUS RIGHT

The consequences of the conservative effort to undermine the judicial doctrine of much of the Warren and Burger Courts are still unfolding. The Rehnquist Court's 2000 decision in *Bush v. Gore* appeared to confirm that the long effort to secure a conservative majority on the nation's highest tribunal had—by the narrowest of margins—finally succeeded. But the Court's liberal turn in 2003, with decisions upholding affirmative action and expanding gay rights, displayed that this group of justices could not be defined in strictly conservative terms. Nevertheless, the Rehnquist Court was clearly the product of the political alignment that created it, one that was decidedly conservative but one that was never without serious challenge. In this sense, the Nixon administration's mixed contributions to the creation of a conservative court are as much the result of the president's fragile electoral and legislative coalitions and the inchoate nature of the conservative legal reform movement as they are the product of his indecision.

In contrast, by the time Republican delegates selected Ronald Reagan as their party's presidential nominee in 1980, forces calling for a more coherent and solidly conservative judicial policy had developed more fully. As a result, once he reached the White House, Reagan was able to undertake a much more ideological attack on the legacy of the Warren Court. Nevertheless, despite reports on the intensity of the Reagan administration's campaign to alter judicial interpretation in a rightward direction, conservative principles still had to compete with Republican hopes for a full realignment and the administration's economic and military policy goals. Although this was true throughout the president's time in office, it was especially apparent during his first term. Moreover, perhaps reflecting Reagan's near status as a reconstructive president, when the Reagan Department of Justice challenged the Court's doctrine on social issues, the intention was often not simply to attain a specific ruling but rather to work toward the realization of president's constitutional vision.

Unlike Richard Nixon, Ronald Reagan benefited from the emanation of two related but distinct drives against existing judicial doctrine. The first—centered in the neoconservative movement—focused its attack on the increasing cooperation between the federal courts and Congress, which according to its leaders, had lead to the expansion of rights and the federal government's involvement into realms state action previously dominated. The second was primarily devoted to overturning the Supreme Court's constitutional declarations on social and religious-related concerns. The first of these two drives concentrated its sights on the revolution taking place in statutory rights, and sought to undo regulatory and welfare state statutes that (in the minds of the drive's leaders) sapped the economic and social freedom of all Americans, and drained the states' authority. Indeed, beginning in the 1960s and blossoming in the 1970s, a combination of "rights talk," judicial activism, and a new institutional alliance between courts, Congress, and friendly federal administrators led to the unparalleled extension of statutory rights. As R. Shep Melnick explains:

> In the 1960s and 1970s [a] surge in government activity coincided with a swing toward a more assertive role for the courts. At the very time that Congress and the president were creating new agencies, distributing more public benefits, and imposing more controls on the states and the private sector, the federal courts were becoming increasingly suspicious of claims of bureaucratic expertise. The courts began to rely more heavily on legislative history and their understanding of statutes' purposes. This new judicial activism did not reflect a desire to protect the private sector or the states from new intrusions by the federal government. To the contrary, most of these doctrinal changes were tied to efforts to increase the federal government's activity—to extend benefits to those meeting statutory criteria, to force administrators to perform nondiscretionary duties, and to secure greater federal control over the states.[22]

As divided government consistently defined the U.S. political scene, moreover, Congress increasingly encouraged the courts to employ this new activism against executive activities. As Melnick notes, "Congress passed a number of rights-based statutes, and the courts interpreted them liberally to require large-scale change in public private practices." In the tradition of the Warren Court's egalitarian opinions, federal courts at all levels began reading statutes in a manner sympathetic to proponents of a more active and expansive federal government. Coupled with observant interest groups' growing use of rights language, a revolution erupted. "Using statutory as well as constitutional interpretation, the courts . . . put new issues on the public agenda and enlarged the programs created by the other branches."[22] Although Nixon's role in this rights-expanding project was considered somewhat ambiguous in 1980—he signed some contributing pieces of legislation, rejected others, and attempted to create an administrative presidency that arguably strengthened the resolve of the Congress/courts alliance—candidate Reagan's was not. As a member of the Goldwater wing of the Republican Party, his opposition to a more expansive role for the federal government in regard to economic regulation and "social engineering" was well rooted.[23] Thus, according to the administration's second solicitor general, Charles Fried, the ensuing Reagan Revolution was designed to achieve "a more confident society and a less intrusive government." As he explains:

> The campaign was fought on two fronts. First, tax reduction was supposed to starve politicians of the resources with which they would regulate the economy, pursue their favorite projects, redistribute wealth, and reward clients who kept them in office. The other was the legal front. That battle was fought in the courts, which had for years been complicit in the aggrandizement of government. In many respects the courts themselves had become a major bureaucratic actor, enthusiastically, self-consciously enlisting in the movement to substitute the judgments and values of the nonproductive sector of society—lawyers, judges, and bureaucrats, politicians—for the self-determination of the entrepreneurs and workers who create wealth. Egged on by aggressive litigators, the legal professoriate, and the liberal press, the courts had become a principal engine for redistributing wealth and shackling the energies and enterprise of the productive sector.[24]

Although the Goldwater right, which Reagan represented, was primarily upset with the role the courts played in retarding economic initiative, in earning his party's nomination, the former California governor also benefited from a second more energetic antifederal court drive. This second drive, which had only recently asserted itself on the national scene, was based on a different strand of conservatism. Although clearly connected with the Wallace candidacy of 1968 (as well as his others),[25] the emergence of the religious right as a solidly Republican presidential ally was a significant factor in eliminating the electoral uncertainty Nixon faced with his flirtation with socially conservative voters. Unlike the drive to halt the revolution in statutory rights, this drive focused almost exclusively on the justices of the nation's highest tribunal and sought to reverse the way they had construed the language of the Constitution and (to a lesser extent) the civil rights legislation of the mid-1960s.[26] As neoconservative scholar Nathan Glazer writes, "almost every issue in the [Reagan] social agenda [was] an issue created by new and path-breaking (and to conservative legal scholars, unfounded) interpretation of the Constitution by the Supreme Court."[27] Nixon had tried to appeal to this breed of conservatism—based mainly in the ideology of the white evangelical Christian South and the Catholic North—but his rhetoric had hardly inspired the Court to listen. Instead, the Burger Court issued rulings on abortion, busing, parochial school aid, and pornography that either extended or only slightly scaled back the "liberalism" of its predecessor. Strikingly, however, if the Court had turned out the kind of decisions that many conservatives had hoped, the Reagan revolution may have never occurred. Rather, despite his promises, Nixon's Court created doctrine that mobilized religiously minded voters for negative reasons rather than the anticipated positive ones. Ronald Reagan, the standard bearer of the Goldwater right, was in perfect position to link up with the religious right to lead the Republican Party back into the White House.

And in 1980 Ronald Reagan succeeded in bringing several rather diverse groups together by emphasizing an economic, political, and patriotic message that appealed to all in his coalition and linked up the two conservative antijudiciary drives. To soothe those more interested in social issues rather than economic ones, Reagan called for the adoption of several constitutional amendments and the appointment of more strict constructionists to the courts—presumably stricter than Nixon's nominees. Still, he understood that these amendments were unlikely to be written into the Constitution. More important, if they were, his coalition risked rupturing. Ironically, his actions suggested a belief that his alliance of voters was built on a foundation that weakened with significant success in transforming judicial interpretation or with fundamental alterations of the nation's ruling document. It might endure as a minority or as a faction equal in strength to the Democrats, but its chances for majority status would last only as long as the most popular aspects of the Warren and Burger courts' activism stood.

Most important, on the issue of abortion, the Republican strategists feared that a GOP majority might be undermined if *Roe v. Wade* were reversed. As one Republican delegate noted in 1980: "If we get a court reversal, there would be a splintering. We have many people who would never vote for Ronald Reagan except for this issue."[28] In contrast, others—

particularly women Republicans—would not have backed his position either if the issue was returned to the state legislatures because *Roe* was overturned or if Congress initiated the constitutional amendment process. This possibility was especially problematic after the emergence of the gender gap in the 1980 election. With this in mind, we should not be surprised that Reagan continued to emphasize economic and foreign policy matters once he reached the Oval Office and that he chose as his first Supreme Court appointee a woman who had once voted for legislation liberalizing abortion laws (as governor of California, Reagan signed similar legislation). Reagan's attention to other concerns was not only more consistent with his own policy preferences, but he and his advisers believed that he would have difficulty completing the Republican realignment if he highlighted his social agenda. By attempting to solve the nation's social ills spotlighted by social conservatives, he would seemingly disrupt his electoral alliance. That was the conundrum Reagan faced during his presidency. This is not to say that attaining favorable rulings in court was not important for the Reagan administration. It was, however, particularly in his first term, the president seemed unwilling to employ his vast political capital to spotlight these "judicial" issues. Still, more than most presidents, Reagan was intent on formulating his judicial policy to undermine court decisions that he thought to be in the interests of the Democratic Party. And after his election days were over in 1984, Reagan put more effort behind the effort to alter judicial interpretation—most famously with the nomination of Judge Robert Bork to the Supreme Court.[29] As part of Reagan's reconstruction, moreover, the nature of this campaign was as much about installing his constitutional vision—an institutional design that potentially "got government off our backs" and returned the "judicial" issues of the past generation to the democratic process—as it was about adopting the social agenda of the religious right. As Charles Fried explained in 1991:

> Abortion seemed to be a principal preoccupation of my tenure, but for me *Roe* was just a symptom of a mistaken approach that confused and threatened the ideal of the rule of law. The struggle against quotas and racial preferences, imposed in the name of affirmative action, was another persistent theme of my work. But here too there was a deeper worry. I was concerned about government taking over too many of the prerogatives that in a healthy, liberal society properly belong to individuals and to private institutions. And I was worried as well about courts imposing a collectivist conception of equality that had no warrant in the Constitution, the civil-rights laws, or our traditions as a society.[30]

Not surprisingly, this theme resonates in the mixed message of the recent products of the Rehnquist Court. This Court has clearly noted its hostility to federal power, but with few exceptions, it has not delivered the decisions social conservatives have waited for more than a generation.

DOES SUCCESS EQUAL FAILURE?

My conclusions differ from those made by then Associate Justice Rehnquist in the quote opening this chapter. To be sure, issues appear on the Supreme Court's agenda that were never foreseen by "strong" or realigning presidents interested in transforming the essence of the law, but more often than not, these issues reach the justices' agenda toward the end of a party system. Thus, with few exceptions, the issues that have dominated the Burger and Rehnquist Courts were generally—if not specifically—those "judicial" issues in which Nixon (and Ford) and Reagan (and Bush) advanced while in office. More important, these presidents have had substantial success in altering judicial doctrine on these issues. In most areas (with notable exceptions), the Court has moved significantly closer to their "stated" positions even if it has not endorsed them entirely.

Although presidents Nixon and Reagan were not wholly successful in shaping doctrine to match their articulated policy preferences, extensive success is often politically undesirable. Put simply, because the Court has historically acted on issues that divide a dominant political alliance, overwhelming success by a president in achieving his articulated positions can have detrimental consequences for his party. The simple conclusion concerning the political consequences of a president's judicial policy is as follows: success has led to conflict within his party whereas partial success or failure has often served to maintain his party's balance. For instance, today's Republican Party remains split over the issue of abortion, and a Supreme Court ruling overturning *Roe v. Wade* would potentially disrupt the Republican coalition of voters. In this sense, while Justices O'Connor, Kennedy, and Souter have not lived up to conservative expectations, they may have aided (intentionally or not) the construction of a Republican majority. Recall that the New Deal coalition survived and thrived for decades because civil rights was a secondary issue in the party system. When the Court moved civil rights to the top of the political agenda with its decision in *Brown v. Board of Education*, the Democratic Party's lines of cohesion ruptured. First President John Kennedy and then President Lyndon Johnson had to decide which section of the Democratic Party they would align with on this issue. When Johnson acted by signing the Civil Rights Act of 1964, the party split. Success in modifying judicial doctrine, then, can produce a problematic alliance. In contrast, partial success can keep coalitions together and provide enduring issues for candidates to campaign on. For example, twenty-eight years after Nixon's election, Republican presidential candidate Bob Dole continued to employ "law and order" rhetoric similar to his mentor's in his campaign against President Bill Clinton. He pursued this course of action despite having voted to confirm every sitting justice on the Supreme Court and the vast majority of the judges on the lower courts. Four years later, George W. Bush openly discussed his affection for Justices Antonin Scalia and Clarence Thomas, seemingly suggesting that the Court remained out of sync with the core of conservatism. Thus, success in court may at times equal failure on some political level, apparently revealing a counterintuitive inverse relationship between the effectiveness of the judicial policies of presidents and the cohesiveness of their coalitions.

CONCLUSION

My brief analysis of the judicial policies of the Nixon and Reagan administrations, then, suggests that scholars who fail to take into account the complexities of this action may misrepresent its success or failure. They may do so by not examining the factors that most influence presidents in the formulation of their policy toward the judiciary, thereby leading to inaccurate assumptions about the intent of this policy. Although ideology—as structured through the president's constitutional vision—clearly carries significant weight in the construction of an administration's judicial policy, others motivations are at play as well. And when the intent of a president's judicial policy is properly understood, its effectiveness (both in terms of policy and politics) can be analyzed more accurately. For example, in the case of Nixon and Reagan, attitudinalists Jeffrey A. Segal and Harold J. Spaeth, focusing exclusively on ideology, conclude that "the more moderate Richard Nixon had a much greater impact in pulling the Court to the right" than did his more conservative successor, Ronald Reagan.[31] In reaching this conclusion, however, Segal and Spaeth place a great deal on emphasis on something presidents have little control over, the ideology of the departing justices. In turn, such judgments seemingly fail to capture the ability of a particular president to extend his constitutional authority into the courts while still advancing the other goals of his administration.

NOTES

1. William Rehnquist, "Presidential Appointments to the Supreme Court," delivered at the University of Minnesota, October 19, 1984. He later notes that it is

"normal and desirable for Presidents to attempt to pack the Court," *The Supreme Court* (New York: Alfred A. Knopf, 2001), p. 236.

2. Irving R. Kaufman, "Keeping Politics Out of the Court," *New York Times Magazine*, December 9, 1984, p. 72.

3. Along with other scholars, attitudinalists Jeffrey A. Segal and Harold J. Spaeth put significant weight on ideology with regard to presidential appointments to the Court. As they write, "a model using the ideology of the President, median senator, and Supreme Court explains 80 percent of the variance in the ideology of presidential nominees," *The Supreme Court and the Attitudinal Model Revisited* (New York: Cambridge University Press, 2002), pp. 185–86.

4. Ehrlichman, *Witness to Power* (New York: Simon and Schuster, 1982), p. 115.

5. McMahon, *Reconsidering Roosevelt on Race* (Chicago: University of Chicago Press, 2004).

6. I outline this presidency-focused approach in detail in *Reconsidering Roosevelt on Race*, 14–20.

7. Skowronek, *The Politics Presidents Make* (Cambridge, Mass.: Belknap Press, 1993).

8. Segal and Spaeth, *The Supreme Court and the Attitudinal Model Revisited*, 217–22.

9. Like Burger, Blackmun was born and reared in Minnesota. The two were friends from childhood, and after two failed attempts to put a southern on the Court, the Chief Justice proposed Blackmun to President Nixon for nomination. In their early years on the Court, their common voting record gained them the nickname the Minnesota Twins. Later on, their judicial opinions would diverge.

10. On welfare, see *Shapiro v. Thompson*, 394 U.S. 618 (1969), *Goldberg v. Kelly* 397 U.S. 284 (1970), *Dandridge v. Williams* 397 U.S. 471 (1970), and *Jefferson v. Hackney* 397 U.S. 821 (1971). On education, see *San Antonio v. Rodriguez* 411 U.S. 1 (1973).

11. The remarks of news commentators were numerous, but in evaluating the work of the Burger Court most comments amounted to an exaggerated version of what constitutional scholar David Currie had written a few years earlier. In *The Constitution in the Supreme Court* (Chicago: University of Chicago Press, 1985), Currie concluded:

> The big story of the Burger years . . . was the counterrevolution that did not come. With the announced intention of changing the Court's direction, Republican Presidents had appointed six Justices by 1981. Nevertheless, though the remaining pillars of the Warren Court dissented from decisions of the Burger period with great frequency, outside the criminal-procedure field the major accomplishments of the Warren revolution were not merely preserved but in many respects actually extended. . . . In short, only part of the explanation of the Burger Court's failure to reverse the Warren revolution lies in the fact that it was not until 1975 that the new Justices constituted a majority. Equally important is the fact that at least three of them (Blackmun, Stevens, and Powell) turned out to be not as "conservative" as those who selected them may have hoped they would be. (pp. 598, 600)

See also, Blasi, *The Burger Court* (New Haven: Yale University Press, 1983); Schwartz, *The Burger Years* (New York: Viking, 1987); Funston, *Constitutional Counterrevolution?* (Cambridge, Mass.: Schenkman Publishing Company, 1977); and Abraham, *Justices, Presidents, and Senators* (Lanham, Md.: Rowman and Littlefield Publishers, 1999), pp. 251–89.

12. The two most popular presidential quotes in this context come from Harry Truman and Dwight Eisenhower. Truman apparently said, "packing the Supreme Court simply can't be done . . . I've tried it and it won't work. . . . Whenever you put a man on the Supreme Court, he ceases to be you[r] friend. I am sure of that," O'Brien, *Storm Center* (New York: W. W. Norton, 2005), p. 84. Eisenhower's famous comment, made toward that end of his presidency, came in response to a question about his greatest mistakes during his tenure. He replied, "Two of them [meaning Warren and Brennan] are sitting on the Supreme Court," quoted in Abraham, *Justices, Presidents, and Senators*, p. 200.

13. Skowronek, *The Politics Presidents Make*, p. 44.

14. See Massaro, *Supremely Political* (Albany, N.Y.: SUNY Press, 1990), for the roll call votes for Haynsworth and Carswell, pp. 209–12.

15. Ehrlichman, *Witness to Power*, p. 118 (emphasis added).

16. Griswold was solicitor general until June 1973, staying on six months after Nixon nominated his replacement Robert Bork.

17. These strategies are most clearly explained in Kevin Phillips's *The Emerging Republican Majority* (Garden City, N.Y.: Anchor Books, 1970), and John Ehrlichman's interpretation of Scammon and Wattenberg's *The Real Majority* in his *Witness to Power* (New York: Coward-McCann and Geognegan, 1971), pp. 212–20.

18. As the second term commenced, signs that the president favored the southern strategy became more evident, but before long the Nixon Department of Justice became mired in the affairs of Watergate and notions of a more conservative campaign in the courts stalled.

19. Phillips's argued that "the changed makeup and outlook of the GOP reflects its switchover . . . from orientation towards the establishmentarian Northeast(especially the Yankee and industrial bailiwicks of New England, upstate New York, Michigan and Pennsylvania—to representation of the rising insurgency of the South, the West, the New York City Irish and middle-class suburbia." However, he also pointed out that even after the 1968 election "the silk-stocking voters and Yankees . . . remained (diminishingly) Republican; and even though the Democrats were losing strength among Northern Catholics, the blue-collar Poles, Slavs, French-Canadians, Italians and Irish of industrial cities from Saco to Sault Ste. Marie (but excluding New York City) remained the bulwark of Northeastern Democratic hegemony" (*The Emerging Republican Majority*, pp. 26, 32). Nevertheless, he asserted that "although the appeal of a successful Nixon administration and the lack of a Wallace candidacy would greatly swell the 1972 Republican vote in the South, West, Border, and the Catholic North, the 1972 Republican Party may well simultaneously lose a lesser number of 1968 supporters among groups reacting against the party's emerging Southern, Western and New York Irish majority," pp. 464–65.

20. Heubner, p. 3044; Ehrlichman, *Witness to Power*, p. 118. Phillips later agreed, "until the spring of 1972, the Nixon people did not think a watershed Republican opportunity would materialize. . . . Would anybody who saw the massive electoral opportunity coming have given G. Gordon Liddy a go-ahead on an inane political attempt at espionage?" Kevin Phillips, *Post-Conservative America: People, Politics and Ideology in a Time of Crisis* (New York: Random House, 1982), pp. 56–57.

21. R. Shep Melnick, *Between the Lines* (Washington, D.C.: Brookings Institution Press, 1994), p. 15.

22. R. Shep Melnick, *Between the Lines* (Washington, D.C.: Brookings Institution Press, 1994), pp. 15–16. See also Mary Ann Glendon, *Rights Talk* (New York: Free Press, 1991). As Glendon writes:

> The marked increase in the assertion of rights-based claims, beginning with the civil rights movement of the 1950s and 1960s, and the parallel increase in recognition of those claims in the courts, are sometimes described as a right revolution. If there is any justification for using the overworked word "revolution" in connection with these developments, it is not that they have eliminated the ills at which they were aimed. Indeed, the progress that has been made, substantial as it is, serves also to heighten our awareness of how deep, stubborn, and complex are the nation's problems of social justice. What do seem revolutionary about the rights-related developments of the past three decades are the transformations they have produced in the roles of courts and judges, and in the way we now think and speak about major public issues. (p. 4)

23. See William C. Berman, *America's Right Turn* (Baltimore: Johns Hopkins University Press, 1994), and Harvey C. Mansfield, Jr., *America's Constitutional Soul* (Baltimore: Johns Hopkins University Press, 1991).

24. Charles Fried, *Order and Law*, 17.

25. For example, in speaking about the connection between the old and new right, Kevin Phillips writes, "it is fair to say that the New Right is a partial heir of the Wallace movement. In any case, the key leaders of the New Right—Richard Viguerie, Paul Weyrich, Howard Phillips, Rev. Jerry Falwell, among others—are far more upset with the *moral* and *cultural* tone of 1970s liberalism than with its effect on free-market economics," *Post-Conservative America: People, Politics and Ideology in a Time of Crisis*, p. 47.

26. In his 1964 "A Time for Choosing" speech, Reagan had attacked the whole rights-distributing system:

> Our natural unalienable rights are now presumed to be a dispensation of government, divisible by a vote of the majority. The greatest good for the greatest number is a high-sounding phrase but contrary to the very basis of our nation, unless it is accompanied by recognition that we have certain rights which cannot be infringed upon, even if the individual stands outvoted by all of his fellow citizens. Without this recognition, majority rule is nothing more than mob rule," Erickson, *Reagan Speaks* (New York: New York University Press, 1985), p. 134.

27. Glazer, "The 'Social Agenda,'" in *Perspectives on the Reagan Years*, John Logan Palmer, ed. (Washington, D.C.: Urban Institute Press, 1986), p. 23.

28. Quoted in Michael J. Malbin, "The Conventions, Platforms, and Issue Activists," in *The American Elections of 1984*, Austin Ranney, ed. (Durham, N.C.: Duke University Press, 1985), pp. 106–7.

29. However, Reagan's second term still had limits. As Howard Fineman later explained, after the battle over Bork, political strategists for the Republican Party did not want another ardent conservative nominee. "It reminds voters, baby boomers in particular, why there are thing that they don't like about the Republican Party." After

Bork's replacement, Douglas Ginsburg, was forced to withdraw his name from nomination, Reagan chose Anthony Kennedy—an "80-percenter," a jurist who would most likely vote in Bork fashion 80 percent of the time. Quotes appear in Mark Gitenstein's *Matters of Principle* (New York: Simon and Schuster, 1992), p. 328.

30. Fried, *Order and Law*, p. 20.

31. Segal and Spaeth, *The Supreme Court and the Attitudinal Model Revisited*, p. 217.

TEN

The "Imperial Presidency" Triumphant: War Powers in the Clinton and Bush Administrations

Michael Cairo

The question of who has authority to deploy and use U.S. military troops and force abroad is controversial and one that has been present since the Republic's founding. In contemporary U.S. politics, the controversy has been decided in favor of the president. As Arthur Schlesinger Jr. argues, "presidential primacy, so indispensable to the political order, has turned into presidential supremacy," and we have seen an "appropriation by the Presidency . . . of powers reserved by the Constitution and by long historical practice to Congress."[1] According to Schlesinger, this is particularly evident in war powers, where presidents have repeatedly claimed sweeping and unilateral authority, threatening to create an "imperial presidency."

The imperial presidency threatened to emerge during the era of Vietnam and Watergate. Following President Richard Nixon's resignation, however, Congress was resurgent and the foreign policy power of the presidency appeared to be waning. Despite this appearance, President Ronald Reagan's abuse of powers leading to the Iran-Contra affair demonstrated that the imperial presidency had not vanished. Contrary to efforts to leash presidential power in foreign affairs, that power has continued to grow, especially with regard to war powers.

In the post–September 11 era, this issue is particularly important. In dealing with terrorism and the threats it presents to the United States, the George W. Bush administration pushes the boundaries on presidential use of

---

I would like to thank my wife, Carey, for her excellent comments and suggestions.

force and threatens the constitutional balance between the executive and legislative branches. This trend, however, extends back to the Clinton administration, where a similar abuse of presidential war powers occurred.

Historically, the constitutional ambiguity of war powers has produced tension between the executive and legislative branches, but the Clinton and George W. Bush administrations have advanced the abuse of presidential power in the use of force and exacerbated the already-existing tension. This surprised some because both presidents lacked foreign policy experience when they entered the White House and the cold war was no longer an emphasis for policymakers. These factors led some to suggest that Congress would be more assertive in foreign policy and recapture its war powers.[2] However, the nature of the new threats that emerged and the ambiguity of the world political environment worked against the rise of a more resolute Congress and served to enhance presidential war power. In addition, and to the chagrin of many, presidents Clinton and Bush used the United Nations (UN) in expanding their presidential power.

This chapter examines war powers with a particular emphasis on the Clinton and George W. Bush administrations. It begins with a discussion of war powers and the Constitution, demonstrating the ambiguity and the shared nature of war powers. It then proceeds to examine cases of war powers in the Clinton and George W. Bush administrations, focusing on the war on terrorism and Iraq. Finally, the chapter summarizes the issues and draws some conclusions, arguing that war powers no longer reflect the balance of shared powers the Constitution established. Instead, presidents have claimed and exercised unilateral decision-making authority with regard to war powers. Presidents Clinton and Bush have further contributed to the abuse of war powers not only by subverting Congress and its constitutional authority, but also by using the United Nations as the basis of presidential claims of unilateral war powers. In the area of war powers, the Constitution no longer reflects the idea of "separated institutions sharing powers,"[3] but rather a triumph of the "imperial presidency."

WAR POWERS AND THE CONSTITUTION

To the casual observer, the president, as commander in chief, appears entitled to unilateral military powers when deploying and using U.S. troops and forces abroad. One of the many arguments in favor of presidential war powers is the Minority Report of the Congressional Committees Investigating the Iran-Contra Affair. According to the report, no fewer than 118 occasions of force occurred without prior legislative authorization. "The relevance of these repeated examples of the extensive use of armed force," it argues, "is that they indicate how far the President's inherent powers were assumed to have reached when Congress was silent, and even in some cases, where Congress had prohibited an action."[4] Former Senator John Tower also argued that Congress should not encumber presidents in the foreign policy process.[5] Robert Bork concurs, arguing that morality should be a president's guide and Congress should abstain from decisions on the use of force.[6] Supreme Court Justice George Sutherland presented the strongest argument on behalf of presidential war powers, however, in 1936. In his written opinion in *U.S. v. Curtiss-Wright Export Corp. et al.*, Sutherland wrote that the president is the "sole organ of the federal government in the field of international relations" and has "plenary and exclusive" power as president. Congress, he suggested, was meant to play a secondary role in U.S. foreign policy.[7]

Presidential practice has also relegated Congress to a backseat in decisions on the use of force. Since World War II, Congress has never specifically declared war. In the Korean War, the Truman administration argued, "the President's power to send Armed Forces outside the country is not dependent on Congressional authority."[8] Secretary of Defense Richard Cheney echoed this sentiment prior to the Persian Gulf War. Cheney explained that he did "not believe the president requires any additional authority from Congress" to engage U.S. forces abroad.[9] During his 1992 presidential election campaign, President George H. W. Bush stated that he did not need "some old goat" in Congress to evict Saddam Hussein from Kuwait.[10]

Contrary to these arguments and presidential practice in general, the Founders did not intend to grant presidents exclusive authority in war powers. The belief that Congress should not get in the president's way when national security matters arise is clearly popular, but the Constitution contradicts this. According to the Constitution, Congress and the president are given specific foreign policy powers and each plays a role to ensure that U.S. foreign policy is effective. In fact, the Constitution grants broad power to Congress, not the president. Although the president is given the powers to nominate ambassadors, negotiate treaties, and direct the armed forces as commander in chief, the Congress is granted the powers to regulate commerce, raise and support armies, provide and maintain a navy, and declare war. Thus, the Constitution originally empowered Congress in military matters.

In drafting the Constitution, the Founders were concerned about correcting the deficiencies of the Articles of Confederation. The Articles bestowed all legislative and executive authority in the Congress. Article 6 gave Congress control over conduct of foreign affairs, and Article 9 gave Congress "the sole and exclusive right and power of determining on peace and war."[11] Unlike the Articles, the Constitution was founded on the principle of separation of powers—a division of authority between government branches. In foreign policy, that division was ambiguous. Experience under the Articles led the Founders to favor greater centralization of executive authority in the Constitution. Alexander Hamilton, writing in *Federalist 70*, explains, "energy in the Executive is a leading character in the definition of good government."[12] When constructing the Constitution, however, the Founders favored less centralization based on their experiences with the monarchy.

Nothing was more crucial than the successful conduct of foreign policy and the Founders agreed that national safety could best be ensured through trade. The Constitution gave clear priority to commercial relations and vested control over commerce in Congress. Congress was also brought into the treaty-making power. Unlike the monarch, who could approve treaties without Parliament, presidents would have to consult Congress and receive its acceptance of treaties. Congress was also given other weighty powers in foreign policy, including appropriations, and the power to declare war.[13] The Constitution makes clear that the Founders were determined to deny presidents the sole prerogative of making war and peace. The Founders designed a system that, according to James Wilson, would not "hurry us into war; it is calculated to guard against it. It will not be in the power of a single man, or a single body of men, to involve us in such distress."[14] In fact, the Founders chose not to mention the presidency in the war-making power.

This, however, did not deny presidential powers. The Constitution vested the command of the Army and Navy in the presidency. The president's power as commander in chief provided presidents with the ability to respond to national emergencies. The Founders clearly agreed with John Locke that in an emergency responsible rulers could resort to exceptional power. Legislatures were too large and unwieldy to capably cope with a crisis. According to Locke, when the executive perceived an emergency, he could initiate extralegal, or even illegal, measures but the leader would only be vindicated in these actions if the legislature and public sanctioned his actions.[15]

Prerogative is not found in the Constitution, but the Founders believed in the doctrine. Despite possessing prerogative, the executive clearly was expected to report to Congress after acting so that the Congress could judge the action. As a last resort, when the executive abused the power of prerogative, Congress was granted the power of impeachment.

The Constitution thus established a shared system. This constitutional division of foreign affairs powers only served to cause confusion. Almost immediately after the founding of the new republic, the question of war powers emerged as a prominent issue of debate. In 1793 President George Washington unilaterally proclaimed U.S. neutrality in the war between France and Great Britain despite the existence of an alliance with France. Alexander Hamilton defended the action, arguing that foreign policy was an executive function and the powers of declaring war and ratifying treaties bestowed on Congress were "exceptions out of the general 'executive power' vested in the President." These powers were to be "construed strictly, and ought to be extended no further than is essential to their execution." Although Congress had the right to declare war, the president had the duty to preserve peace until the Congress did so. "The legislature," he argued, "is still free to perform its duties, according to its own sense of them; though the executive, in the exercise of constitutional powers, may establish an antecedent state of things, which ought to weigh in the legislative decision." In short, each branch had a duty to exercise its power, possessing concurrent authority.[16]

James Madison responded to Hamilton's defense of Washington's proclamation of neutrality, denying that the powers of making wars and treaties were inherently executive. The fact that they were royal prerogative, Madison argued, did not make them presidential prerogatives. The power to declare war must include everything necessary to make that power effective, including the congressional right to judge whether the United States was obliged to declare war. According to Madison, this judgment could not be foreordained by presidential decisions.[17] Thus, whereas Hamilton saw congressional power to declare war as limited, Madison viewed it as very powerful.

The issue was never truly settled because the argument remains today. The question that continues to plague the United States is not whether Congress can declare war, but whether Congress must declare all types of war, both general and limited. According to the Founders, hostilities, whether general or limited, appear to require congressional sanction. In 1801 Chief Justice John Marshall wrote, "the whole powers of war being vested in Congress . . . the Congress may authorize general hostilities . . . or partial war."[18]

The Founders clearly divided war powers, but the ambiguity of the Constitution left the door open to conflict. Although Congress is given the sole power to initiate offensive war, the Constitution allows presidents to initiate defensive war; this has easily been enlarged. In the nineteenth and twentieth centuries, presidents strengthened their control of information and secured a monopoly on diplomacy and war.

WAR POWERS IN THE CLINTON AND BUSH ADMINISTRATIONS

With the end of the cold war and the emergence of a new world order, war powers appeared to diminish as an important issue. However, war powers reemerged with a vengeance in the Clinton and Bush administrations. Despite the belief that a new world order would mean a new era of peace, it has brought greater conflict and more opportunities for war. The uncertainty of world politics has given presidents greater latitude in the use of force. Presidents Clinton and Bush both claimed unilateral presidential powers in the use of force. Although this is similar to past presidential claims, the nature of the threat environment led many to accept their claims with greater ease.

With the collapse of the Soviet Union in 1991 and the subsequent end of the cold war, the United States became the lone superpower. The prospects for international peace seemed considerably better. Many had hopes that the end of the cold war would mean the end of conflict, yet one could argue that conflict has been more prevalent than during the cold war era. Conflict has also not focused on any one issue, but rather multiple issues, including ethnic conflict, civil war, genocide, and terrorism. The uncertainty of the post–cold war environment has increased presidential power because the use of force in U.S. foreign policy remains a key component in this uncertain world.

In dealing with terrorism and Iraq, in particular, presidents Clinton and Bush abused their power. Both of these cases offer good examples for multiple reasons. First, these issues span both presidencies and analysis can uncover patterns. Second, both issues have been central to U.S. national security since the end of the cold war. Finally, both issues demonstrate how each president used the United Nations to justify his use of power.

The Clinton Administration and Saddam Hussein

On August 2, 1990, Saddam Hussein, the leader of Iraq, invaded and annexed Kuwait, seizing Kuwait's vast oil reserves and liquidating billions of dollars of loans provided by Kuwait during the Iran-Iraq War. Within months, the George H. W. Bush administration assembled a coalition of forces, supported by the United Nations, to remove the Iraqi army from Kuwait. On January 17, 1991, Operation Desert Storm, which was authorized by UN Resolution 678 and by a congressional vote endorsing the action, ensued.

The international coalition proved victorious and instituted UN Resolution 687, giving the UN Special Commission (UNSCOM) complete access to Iraqi facilities to search for weapons of mass destruction. In addition, the

UN Security Council also passed UN Resolution 688, condemning Iraqi actions against the Kurdish population and authorizing relief organizations to provide humanitarian aid. Pursuant to these resolutions, but without specific UN Security Council authorization, a no-fly zone was established, prohibiting Iraqi flights in northern and southern Iraq.

President-elect Clinton inherited this policy toward Iraq and a hostile Hussein. Almost immediately, Clinton faced mounting tensions between the United States and Iraq. In April 1993 former President Bush visited Kuwait. Prior to his visit, the Central Intelligence Agency (CIA) and Federal Bureau of Investigation (FBI) uncovered an assassination plot against Bush and linked the Iraqi government to that plot. As a response to this plot, Clinton responded with an attack, using precision-guided missiles. Clinton justified the bombings in a statement to Congress, noting "our inherent right to self-defense as recognized in Article 51 of the United Nations Charter and pursuant to [his] constitutional authority with respect to the conduct of foreign relations and as Commander in Chief."[19] In an address to the American public about the strikes, Clinton added, "There should be no mistake about the message we intend these actions to convey to Saddam Hussein. . . . We will combat terrorism. We will deter aggression. . . . While the cold war has ended, the world is not free of danger. And I am determined to take the steps necessary to keep our Nation secure."[20]

In 1996 Clinton used force against Hussein in support of Iraq's Kurdish population. One Kurdish faction, the Patriotic Union of Kurdistan (PUK), accepted arms from Iran and Hussein responded by attacking the PUK's headquarters in northern Iraq, attempting to crush the opposition. In response, Clinton ordered a missile attack on targets in southern Iraq. In justifying this attack, Clinton relied on humanitarian arguments stressing UN Resolution 688 explaining, "Earlier today I ordered American forces to strike Iraq. Our missiles sent the following message to Saddam Hussein: When you abuse your own people . . . you must pay a price."[21] During his weekly radio address, Clinton added, "America's policy has been to contain Saddam, to reduce the threat he poses to the region, and to do it in a way that makes him pay a price when he acts recklessly."[22]

The next major crisis with Iraq occurred in 1998 when Saddam Hussein refused UNSCOM weapons inspectors access to certain sites, as the provisions of UN Resolution 687 outlined. Hussein argued that U.S. involvement in the inspections was the problem. The Clinton administration suggested that diplomacy was their main instrument in solving the crisis, but reserved the right to use force. Implicit in the administration's argument for the use of force was that the administration had the authority to do so. In an address at Tennessee State

University, Secretary of State Madeleine Albright stated, "We will work for that peaceful solution as long as we can. But if we cannot get such a solution—and we do believe that the time for diplomacy is running out—then we will use force."[23] Days before, in a statement before the House International Relations Committee, Albright remarked, "Let no one miscalculate. We have authority to do this, the responsibility to do this, the means and the will."[24]

By the end of February, however, UN Secretary-General Kofi Annan had negotiated a diplomatic solution to the crisis. The Clinton administration responded by sponsoring a successful resolution in the UN Security Council. Resolution 1154 explained that Iraq would face the "severest consequences" if it failed to comply with UNSCOM.[25] President Clinton made clear that the UN Security Council's decision authorized the use of force against Iraq, despite opposition from other members of the UN Security Council. In remarks the day after the UN Security Council vote on Resolution 1154, Clinton stated, "The Government of Iraq should be under no illusion. The meaning of 'severest consequences' is clear. It provides authority to act if Iraq does not turn the commitment it has now made into compliance."[26]

In December 1998 Clinton attacked Iraq after a series of diplomatic conflicts over UNSCOM. In an address to the American public, Clinton explained that Iraq had been given numerous opportunities to comply and must face the "consequences of defying the U.N."[27] In a letter to Congress, Clinton justified the attacks citing UN Security Council Resolutions 678 and 687, authorizing "all necessary means" to ensure Iraqi compliance. He also referred to the power granted to the president under Public Law 102–1, which authorized President Bush to use force against Iraq in 1991.[28]

Clinton's actions toward Iraq established a pattern that continued into the George W. Bush administration. First, the Clinton administration took action with little congressional consultation. In fact, Congress remained relatively silent on each occasion. Some of this silence can be attributed to public approval of Clinton's actions. For example, in the 1993 case, 61 percent of the public approved of the action taken.[29] Second, the Clinton administration claimed unilateral powers under the commander in chief clause of the Constitution and UN Security Council authorizations. Justifying the attacks based on UN Security Council authorization broadly defined presidential and U.S. power.

The Clinton Administration and Osama bin Laden

The Clinton administration's abuse of war powers with regard to Iraq paled in comparison to its abuse of war powers in its decision to strike the alleged terrorist bases of Osama bin Laden. The threat of terrorism became a more prominent foreign policy concern in the 1990s. In 1998, President Clinton unilaterally authorized air strikes against alleged terrorist sites. These strikes were not only conducted unilaterally, but also were executed without prior authorization from the United Nations.

Although terrorism was not considered a central threat to U.S. interests when Clinton took office, it quickly became one. By the end of the Clinton administration's first term the federal building in Oklahoma City had been bombed, the World Trade Center had been victimized by terrorists, and U.S. troops were killed in Saudi Arabia when terrorists exploded a car near a military complex. These events, among others, pushed terrorism to the center of U.S. interests. Like its predecessors, the Clinton administration attempted to deal with terrorism through multilateral, diplomatic channels. Despite these efforts, however, terrorists struck the U.S. embassies in Kenya and Tanzania on August 7, 1998. These attacks were soon attributed to Osama bin Laden and his terrorist network, al Qaeda.

Following the Soviet withdrawal from Afghanistan in 1989, Osama bin Laden established training camps for Islamic radicals from across the world. Bin Laden had been a wealthy financier of the resistance to the Soviet Union in Afghanistan. Returning to his native Saudi Arabia, bin Laden targeted U.S. and Saudi interests. In 1991 Saudi Arabia expelled him to Sudan where Sudan's radical Islamist regime supported him. In 1996 he retreated back to Afghanistan on the eve of the Taliban's seizure of power. In 1997 from his hidden caves in the mountains of Afghanistan, CNN's Peter Arnett interviewed bin Laden. He declared a jihad against the United States for its support of Israel, U.S. military presence in Saudi Arabia, the home to the holiest shrines of Islam, Mecca and Medina, and "other acts of aggression and injustice" in Muslim countries.[30]

When the U.S. embassies in Kenya and Tanzania were bombed, 300 people were killed, including 12 Americans, and nearly 5,000 people were injured. Six days later, the Clinton administration responded with tomahawk missile attacks on alleged bin Laden bases in Afghanistan and Sudan. In an address to the nation, President Clinton provided four justifications for the attacks:

> I ordered this action for four reasons: first, because we have convincing evidence these groups played the key role in the Embassy bombings in Kenya and Tanzania; second, because these groups have executed terrorist attacks against Americans in the past; third, because we have compelling information that they were planning additional terrorist attacks against our citizens and others . . . ; and fourth, because they are seeking to acquire chemical . . . and other dangerous weapons.[31]

In his letter to congressional leaders notifying them of the attack, he added:

> The United States acted in exercise of our inherent right of self-defense consistent with Article 51 of the United Nations Charter. These strikes were a necessary and proportionate response to the imminent threat of future terrorist attacks against U.S. personnel and facilities. . . . I directed these actions pursuant to my constitutional authority to conduct U.S. foreign relations and as Commander in Chief and Chief Executive.[32]

Not only did Clinton rely on the UN Charter and his powers as commander in chief for his actions, but he also suggests that these actions were an inherent right of his power as chief executive. This sounds familiarly like Hamilton's argument that foreign policy was an executive function and the powers of declaring war and ratifying treaties bestowed on Congress were "exceptions out of the general 'executive power' vested in the President."[33] Clinton was relying on the Hamiltonian interpretation of the Constitution. If we accept the notion that bin Laden was planning a second attack, the president was acting on behalf of the country's defense to repel the attack. His successor, George W. Bush, would incorporate these notions into U.S. foreign policy, vastly expanding the powers of the presidency in foreign affairs.

THE BUSH ADMINISTRATION: INCREASING RISKS, INCREASING POWER

In the George W. Bush administration, the war on terrorism and policy toward Iraq are intertwined. This became clear after the September 11, 2001, terrorist attacks on the United States. On that day, terrorists struck the World Trade Center Twin Towers and the Pentagon, killing thousands. Following these attacks, Bush made clear his intentions vowing, "Terrorism against our nation will not stand."[34] He further argued, "War has been waged against us by stealth and deceit and murder," granting the president full authority to defend against the threat.[35] The policy would eventually become the Bush Doctrine, including not only terrorist groups, but rogue states.

On September 12, the UN Security Council adopted a resolution condemning the attacks, declaring that they constituted a "threat to international peace and security." In addition, the resolution recognized the "inherent right of individual or collective self-defense in accordance with the Charter."[36] On September 28, the UN Security Council unanimously adopted a historic resolution directed toward combating terrorism and states that support, harbor, provide safe haven to, supply, finance, help recruit, or aid terrorists. The resolution required cooperation of all member states in a wide range of areas.[37] Resolution 1373 established a comprehensive legal framework for addressing the threat of international terrorism. It also provided a basis for the Bush Doctrine.

On October 7, the U.S. ambassador to the United Nations, John Negroponte, delivered a letter to the president of the UN Security Council stating that the United States, together with other states, had "initiated actions in the exercise of its inherent right of individual and collective self defense." These actions were taken against al Qaeda terrorist camps and military installations in Afghanistan, which had a "central role in the attacks." The letter went on to state that the United States "may find that our self-defense requires further actions with respect to other organizations and other States."[38] This letter was the birth of the Bush Doctrine, which asserted the right of the United States to use military force in "self-defense" against any state that aids, harbors, or supports international terrorism, and it had profound implications. Most significantly, Ambassador Negroponte's letter left open the possibility that a state may intervene in anticipatory self-defense, without UN Security Council authorization, in another state that is alleged to be aiding, harboring, or supporting terrorism. Secretary of Defense Donald Rumsfeld later added:

> The only way to deal with the terrorists . . . is to take the battle to them, and find them, and root them out. And that is self-defense. And there is no question but that any nation on Earth has the right of self-defense. And we do. And what we are doing is going after those people, and those organizations, and those capabilities wherever we're going to find them in the world, and stop them from killing Americans.[39] . . . That is in effect self-defense of a preemptive nature.[40]

In his January 2002 State of the Union address, Bush, referring to North Korea, Iran, and Iraq, argued, "States like these, and their terrorist allies, constitute an axis of evil, arming to threaten the peace of the world. . . . America will do what is necessary to ensure our nation's security. . . . I will not wait on events while dangers gather. I will not stand by as peril draws closer and closer."[41] With this statement, the president made clear his intentions to wage war when he felt preventing threats to the United States was necessary. The United States had been attacked, and Bush believed his actions did not require congressional authority or consultation.

Although Bush had a strong argument for unilaterally exercising the decision to use force with regard to the terrorist attacks on September 11, he used that argument to extend his authority and shift U.S. foreign policy. Throughout the spring and summer 2002, the Bush administration devised its strategy for approaching the world. The national security strategy that emerged in September 2002 represents the most sweeping transformation in U.S. foreign policy since the beginning of the cold war. The strategy sets forth three tasks: "We will defend the peace by fighting terrorists and tyrants. We will preserve the peace by building good relations among great powers. We will extend the peace by encouraging free and open societies on every continent."[42]

These tasks have profound implications for the Bush administration's foreign policy. More significantly, the strategy links terrorists with tyrants, the axis of evil and its allies, as sources of danger in the world. Since September 11, it argues, the United States no longer makes a "distinction between terrorists and those who knowingly harbor or provide aid to them." Furthermore, the Bush administration articulates that it does not believe that traditional U.S. strategies such as containment and deterrence will be effective against these new threats. According to the strategy, these terrorists and tyrants are seeking weapons of mass destruction to threaten U.S. security. Faced with this elevated threat to U.S. interests and the American way of life, the strategy argues, "America will act against such emerging threats" and will not "let our enemies strike first."[43]

The national security strategy establishes a doctrine of preemption, relying on the argument that:

> nations need not suffer an attack before they can lawfully take action to defend themselves against forces that present an imminent danger of attack. . . . Our priority will be first to disrupt and destroy terrorist organizations. . . . We will disrupt and destroy terrorist organizations by . . . identifying and destroying the threat before it reaches our borders . . . we will not hesitate to act alone, if necessary, to exercise our right of self-defense by acting preemptively against such terrorists, to prevent them from doing harm against our people and our country. . . . [O]ur best defense is a good offense. . . . This strategy will turn adversity into opportunity.[44]

In addition, the strategy links action against rogue states to action against terrorists, expanding preemption:

> [N]ew and deadly challenges have emerged from rogue states. . . . These states' pursuit of, and trade in, [weapons of mass destruction have] become a looming threat to all nations. We must be prepared to stop rogue states and their terrorist clients before they . . . threaten or use

> weapons of mass destruction against the United States. . . . [T]he United States can no longer solely rely on the reactive posture as we have in the past.[45]

The new strategy is proactive, rejecting the reactive strategies of containment and deterrence; its proactive stance is the basis for expanded presidential power. The strategy suggests that due to the nature of the threat a president may act alone to start a war against a perceived aggressor. The strategy presents an incontestable moral claim that in certain situations preemption is preferable to doing nothing and relies on Article 51 of the U.N. Charter for its legitimacy. In fact, the entire strategy is based on the presumption that a president can and must act to prevent future attacks on the United States or U.S. interests. Although such a policy may have its merits, it denies the necessity for congressional action of any kind in the use of force.

The irony of this policy is that although it does not require international support, the Bush administration has sought international support for it, using the United Nations and international law to justify the implementation of the national security strategy. On September 13, 2002, Bush addressed the UN General Assembly in New York City. He linked U.S. strategy to the purposes of the United Nations and justified using force against rogue states such as Iraq:

> The United Nations was born in the hope that survived a world war, the hope of a world moving toward justice, escaping old patterns of conflict and fear. The founding members resolved that the peace of the world must never again be destroyed by the will and wickedness of any man. . . . After generations of deceitful dictators and broken treaties and squandered lives, we dedicated ourselves to standards of human dignity . . . and to a system of security defended by all. Today, these standards and this security are challenged. . . . Above all, our principles and our security are challenged today by outlaw groups and regimes that accept no law of morality and have no limit to their violent ambitions.[46]

Bush proceeded to make clear that the new doctrine of preemption, and the United Nations' relevancy, would be tested in Iraq. "In one place—in one regime—we find all these dangers in their most lethal and aggressive forms, exactly the kind of aggressive threat the United Nations was born to confront."[47] Bush proceeded to lay out the case for using force against Iraq, which, he argued, had made a series of commitments to the United Nations, dating back to 1991. Furthermore, Iraq repeatedly failed to meet its commitments. Thus, preventing Iraqi aggression and securing the interests of the world from the Iraqi threat was left to the United States and the United Nations:

> Delegates to the General Assembly, we have been more than patient. We've tried sanctions. We've tried the carrot of oil for food and the stick of coalition military strikes. But Saddam Hussein has defied all these efforts and continues to develop weapons of mass destruction. The first time we may be completely certain he has . . . nuclear weapons is when . . . he uses one. We owe it to all our citizens to do everything in our power to prevent that day from coming. The conduct of the Iraqi regime is a threat to the authority of the United Nations and a threat to peace. Iraq has answered a decade of UN demands with a decade of defiance. . . . If Iraq's regime defies us again, the world must move deliberately, decisively to hold Iraq to account. . . . The Security Council resolutions will be enforced, the just demands of peace and security will be met, or action will be unavoidable.[48]

The administration consequently negotiated a new UN Security Council resolution. The intent of that resolution was to prepare the way toward military action in Iraq. Resolution 1441 passed the UN Security Council unanimously on November 8, 2002, with a 15–0 vote in support of the resolution, and laid out what Iraq had to do to avoid war. The resolution cited Iraq in "material breach of its obligations under relevant resolutions." Furthermore, it offered Iraq "a final opportunity to comply with its disarmament obligations." In its final phrases, the resolution warned Iraq that it would face "serious consequences" because of continued violations of the UN Security Council resolutions.[49]

Iraq responded to Resolution 1441 by inviting UN weapons inspectors back into the country. Throughout late 2002 and early 2003, the weapons inspectors, headed by Hans Blix and Mohammed el Baredei, pursued their task while the world watched and the United States continued to make its case that Iraqi failure to comply would be met with swift action. In January 2003 Bush stated:

> We're confronting the threat of outlaw regimes who seek weapons of mass destruction. . . . In the case of Iraq, the world has already spoken with one voice. The Iraqi regime has a duty under Security Council resolutions to declare and destroy all of its weapons of mass destruction. That's what the world has said. That's what the United States expects from Saddam Hussein. The Iraqi regime is a grave threat to the United States. . . . The Iraqi regime has used weapons of mass destruction. . . .

> Four years ago, UN inspectors concluded that Iraq had failed to [account] for large Stockpiles of chemical and biological weapons. . . . In last month's declaration, Iraq again failed to account for those weapons. . . . Saddam Hussein was given a path to peace. Thus far, he has chosen the path of defiance. . . . We certainly prefer voluntary compliance by Iraq. . . . Yet, if force becomes necessary to disarm Iraq of weapons of mass destruction and enforce the will of the United Nations, if force becomes necessary to secure our country and to keep the peace, America will act deliberately, American will act decisively, and America will prevail. . . .[50]

And in his State of the Union speech, Bush reiterated that the United States would use force if Iraq failed to comply with UN resolutions. "The world has waited twelve years for Iraq to disarm . . . let there be no misunderstanding: If Saddam Hussein does not fully disarm . . . we will lead a coalition to disarm him."[51]

Bush, like Clinton before him, stressed the importance of the United Nations and used UN resolutions as a basis for using force against Iraq. On February 6, 2003, Bush referred to Iraqi noncompliance with UN resolutions as a basis for using force. In addition, he challenged the United Nations to act or face the possibility of becoming irrelevant:

> Twelve years after Saddam Hussein agreed to disarm and ninety days after the Security Council passed Resolution 1441 by a unanimous vote, Saddam Hussein was required to fully cooperate in the disarmament of his regime. He has not done so. Saddam Hussein was given a final chance. He is throwing that chance away. . . . On November 8, by demanding the immediate disarmament of Iraq, the United Nations Security Council spoke with clarity and authority. Now the Security Council will show whether its words have any meaning. Having made its demands, the Security Council must not back down when those demands are defied and mocked by a dictator. . . . The United States, along with a growing coalition of nations, is resolved to take whatever action is necessary to defend ourselves and disarm the Iraqi regime.[52]

Bush continued to emphasize Iraqi noncompliance with UN resolutions throughout February and into March, despite failed diplomatic attempts to receive further UN support for action. On March 19, citing continued Iraqi noncompliance with international law, Bush announced that a coalition of thirty-five countries, led by the United States, began their attack on Iraq. "Our nation enters this conflict reluctantly," he told the American people, "yet our purpose is sure. The people of the United States and our friends and allies will not live at the mercy of an outlaw regime that threatens the peace with weapons of mass murder."[53]

Following just over one month of warfare, the Iraqi regime crumbled and U.S. troops occupied Baghdad, Iraq's capital. With rebuilding efforts under way in Iraq, Bush immediately began efforts to focus on another member of the axis of evil—Iran, thus extending the Bush Doctrine of preemption. It is clear that the doctrine is firmly in place and presidential power will remain strong as long as U.S. foreign policy continues to emphasize and expand the war on terrorism.

IS CURBING THE IMPERIAL PRESIDENCY POSSIBLE?

Presidential abuse of war powers is not a new phenomenon. Since World War II, however, presidential war power has vastly expanded and increased. Despite the constitutional questions that presidential war power raises, it is most likely to remain a problem for a variety of reasons. First, Congress is designed to be the primary check on presidential war powers. Since World War II, however, Congress has been rather ineffective in checking presidential war powers. In some cases, Congress not only fails to combat presidential war power, but also even voluntarily surrenders its legislative functions. In both the Clinton and George W. Bush administrations, Congress never declared war, but actively supported the actions each president took.

Second, contemporary presidents do not believe they need congressional approval and have substituted congressional approval with international legal sanction. Presidents Clinton and George W. Bush both relied on international legal authority in the form of UN Security Council resolutions to pursue military force. This suggests that presidents must no longer garner congressional approval when pursuing war, but must now acquire international support and must meet obligations under international law. This, as the George W. Bush case suggests, opens up the door to an even greater expansion of presidential authority and power in the use of force.

Both presidents relied on Article 51 of the UN Charter, the inherent right of self-defense, to enhance and justify their own and U.S. power. In addition, they both used UN Security Council resolutions as authority for action. This pattern will continue to expand presidential power. As long as the American public and Congress accept the United Nations as providing necessary authority for the use of force, presidents will no longer need congressional authorization.

Third, and perhaps most important, the American public and media have virtually accepted presidents' unilateral use of force. Practice has led most to believe that Congress does not and should not play a significant role in the process. The media age has contributed to this image by increasing the stature of presidents vis-à-vis Congress. As during the Clinton administration, Bush's high popularity ratings, which have until recently consistently been in the 60 percentile, make it unlikely that Congress will challenge him.

Ultimately, presidential war power remains strong and will continue to remain strong. Presidents will not willingly give up this power, and Congress is not actively trying to take this power away. Instead of cooperation between the executive and legislative branches of government, the imperial presidency has triumphed. Presidents increasingly take unilateral steps to involve the U.S. military in operations abroad and have substituted the United Nations and international law for congressional sanction of their actions.

NOTES

1. Arthur M. Schlesinger Jr., *The Imperial Presidency* (Boston: Houghton Mifflin, 1989), p. viii.

2. See James M. Scott, ed., *After the End: Making U.S. Foreign Policy in the Post–Cold War World* (Durham, N.C.: Duke University Press, 1998); James M. Lindsay, *Congress and the Politics of U.S. Foreign Policy* (Baltimore: Johns Hopkins University Press, 1994); and Randall B. Ripley and James M. Lindsay, eds., *Congress Resurgent: Foreign and Defense Policy in Capitol Hill* (Ann Arbor: University of Michigan Press, 1993).

3. This term comes from Richard E. Neustadt, *Presidential Power and the Modern Presidents: The Politics of Leadership from Roosevelt to Reagan* (New York: Free Press, 1990).

4. U.S. Congress, *Report of the Congressional Committees Investigating the Iran-Contra Affair. With supplemental Minority, and Additional Views*, 100th Congress, 1st sess. (1987), p. 467.

5. John Tower, "Congress versus the President: The Formulation and Implementation of American Foreign Policy," *Foreign Affairs* (Winter 1981–1982): 229–46.

6. Robert Bork, "Erosion of the President's Power in Foreign Affairs," *Washington University Law Quarterly* 68 (1990): 694–701.

7. *U.S. v. Curtiss-Wright Export Corp. et al.*, 299 U.S. 304 (1936).

8. "Authority of the President to Repel the Attack in Korea," *Department of State Bulletin* (July 31, 1950), p. 173.

9. In Jean Edward Smith, *George Bush's War* (New York: Holt, 1992), p. 227.

10. George Bush, "Remarks at the Texas State Republican Convention in Dallas, Texas," *Public Papers of the President* 1 (June 20, 1992): 995.

11. *Articles of Confederation*, November 4, 2002, http://encarta.msn.com/encnet/refpages/RefArticle.aspx?refid=761567227&pn=2#s15 (accessed ???).

12. James Madison, Alexander Hamilton, and John Jay, *The Federalist Papers*, ed. Isaac Kramnick (New York: Penguin Books, 1987), p. 402.

13. See Article I, Section 8, of the *U.S. Constitution*.

14. Charles A. Lofgren, "War-Making under the Constitution: The Original Understanding," *Yale Law Review* (March 1972): 685.

15. John Locke, "Of Prerogative," in *Two Treatises of Government*, ed. Peter Laslett (New York: Cambridge University Press, 1997), pp. 374–80.

16. *The Founders Constitution*, http://press-pubs.uchicago.edu/founders/documents/92_2_2-3s14.htm (accessed October 3, 2005).

17. *The Founders Constitution*, http://press-pubs.uchicago.edu/founders/documents/92_2_2-3s15.htm (accessed October 3, 2005).

18. *Talbot v. Seeman*, 5 U.S. 1 (1801).

19. Bill Clinton, "Letter to Congressional Leaders on the Strike on Iraqi Intelligence Headquarters," *Public Papers of the President* (June 28, 1993), p. 940.

20. Bill Clinton, "Address to the Nation on the Strike on Iraqi Intelligence Headquarters," *Public Papers of the President* (June 26, 1993), pp. 938–39.

21. Bill Clinton, "Remarks Announcing a Missile Strike on Iraq and an Exchange with Reporters," *Public Papers of the President* (September 3, 1996), p. 1469.

22. Bill Clinton, "The President's Radio Address," *Public Papers of the President* (September 14, 1996), pp. 1566–67.

23. Madeleine Albright, "Remarks at Tennessee State University," Office of the Spokesman, U.S. Department of State (February 19, 1998).

24. Madeleine Albright, "Statement before the House International Relations Committee," Office of the Spokesman, U.S. Department of State (February 12, 1998).

25. *U.N. Security Council Resolution 1154*, S/RES/1154 (1998).

26. Bill Clinton, "Remarks on Signing a Memorandum on Standards to Prevent Drinking and Driving," *Public Papers of the President* (March 3, 1998), p. 317.

27. Bill Clinton, "Address to the Nation Announcing Military Strikes on Iraq," *Public Papers of the President* (December 16, 1998), p. 2182.

28. Bill Clinton, "Letter to Congressional Leaders on the Military Strikes against Iraq," *Public Papers of the President* (December 18, 1998), pp. 2195–96.

29. Richard L. Berke, "Raid on Baghdad," *New York Times* (June 29, 1993), p. A7.

30. Osama bin Laden, *Interview with Peter Arnett*, CNN, March 1997, www.anusha.com/osamaint.htm (accessed January 3, 2003).

31. Bill Clinton, "Remarks in Martha's Vineyard, Massachusetts, on Military Action against Terrorist Sites in Afghanistan and Sudan," *Public Papers of the President* (August 20, 1998), p. 1460.

32. Bill Clinton, "Letter to Congressional Leaders Reporting on Military Action against Terrorist Sites in Afghanistan and Sudan," *Public Papers of the President* (August 21, 1998), p. 1464.

33. See Corwin, *The President's Control of Foreign Relations* (Princeton, N.J.: Princeton University Press, 1917), chap. 1.

34. George W. Bush, "Remarks by the President after Two Planes Crash into World Trade Center," www.whitehouse.gov (September 11, 2001) (accessed January 3, 2003).

35. George W. Bush, "President's Remarks at National Day of Prayer and Remembrance," www.whitehouse.gov (September 14, 2001) (accessed January 3, 2003).

36. *U.N. Security Council Resolution 1368*, S/RES/1368 (2001).

37. *U.N. Security Council Resolution 1373*, S/RES/1373 (2001).

38. www.usinfo.state.gov (October 7, 2001) (accessed April 8, 2003).

39. Donald H. Rumsfeld, *Interview with Wolf Blitzer*, CNN, October 28, 2001. Available at www.defenselink.mil/news (accessed October 28, 2001).

40. Donald H. Rumsfeld, *Remarks outside ABC-TV studio*, October 28, 2001. Available at www. Defenselink.mil/news (accessed October 28, 2001).

41. George W. Bush, "Address before a Joint Session of the Congress on the State of the Union," *Weekly Compilation of Presidential Documents* 38 (January 29, 2002), p. 135.

42. *The National Security Strategy of the United States of America*, September 21, 2002, www.whitehouse.gov (accessed January 3, 2003).

43. *National Security Strategy*.

44. *National Security Strategy*.

45. *National Security Strategy*.

46. George W. Bush, "Address to the United Nations General Assembly in New York City," *Weekly Compilation of Presidential Documents* (September 13, 2002), pp. 1529–30.

47. Bush, "Address to the United Nations," p. 1530.

48. Bush, "Address to the United Nations," pp. 1531–32.

49. *U.N. Security Council Resolution 1441*, S/RES/1441 (2002).

50. George W. Bush, "Remarks to the Troops at Fort Hood in Killeen, Texas," *Weekly Compilation of Presidential Documents* (January 3, 2003), pp. 24–25.

51. George W. Bush, "Address before a Joint Session of the Congress on the State of the Union," *Weekly Compilation of Presidential Documents* (January 31, 2003), p. 116.

52. George W. Bush, "Remarks on the Iraqi Regime's Noncompliance with United Nations Resolutions," *Weekly Compilation of Presidential Documents* (February 6, 2003), pp. 164–65.

53. George W. Bush, "President Bush Addresses the Nation," *Lexington Herald-Leader* (March 20, 2003), p. A13.

ELEVEN

Clinton's Other Infidelity: Signing, Ignoring, and Disobeying Helms-Burton

Patrick J. Haney, Maureen P. Haney, and Walt Vanderbush

In March 1996, after the Cuban Air Force shot down two planes members of the group Brothers to the Rescue piloted,[1] President Clinton signed into law the Cuban Liberty and Democratic Solidarity Act (known as LIBERTAD for short or Helms-Burton for its sponsors).[2] The bill seemed moribund when it went to Conference Committee before the shooting. The central components of the bill that passed the House of Representatives in September 1995—Title III, which allowed American citizens to sue in U.S. courts companies that "traffic" in confiscated property,[3] and Title IV, which denied entry visas to the United States for such companies' executives and their families[4]—had been stripped from the Senate version in October.[5] But the shooting that killed three U.S. citizens and one permanent resident brought the bill back to life in an even stronger form. Titles III and IV were put back in the bill, and a new component was added: codification into law of all parts of the embargo that executive order had previously been established.[6] The president received six-month waivers for the enforcement of Title III[7] and Clinton signed the bill.

The passage of Helms-Burton would seem to be the last word on Cuba policy, but it has not turned out that way. In 1998 Pope John Paul II visited the island and President Clinton relaxed numerous restrictions on Cuba.[8] And in January 1999 he announced a second set of unilateral policy initiatives toward Cuba[9]—including increased remittances and even a baseball game against Cubans with the Baltimore Orioles.[10] In that same month Clinton also exercised the Title III waiver for the sixth time. In addition, the Clinton administration largely ignored the enforcement of Title IV. The president essentially acted as if the codification part of Helms-Burton did not exist. A combination of influences including institutional power, electoral interests, and foreign policy concerns—with important forces lobbying in the background—led the Clinton administration to try to regain ground and the power it willingly signed away in Helms-Burton through a strategy of presidential disobedience.

We focus on the steps the Clinton administration took on Cuba policy in the period following Helms-Burton. To understand why Clinton took the substantive policy moves he did in 1998 and 1999, moves that arguably went beyond what Helms-Burton would allow, one needs to see them as not just policy initiatives but also as part of a strategy to take back power over U.S. foreign policy that was signed away in Helms-Burton. The Clinton record of waiving parts of Helms-Burton, generally ignoring others, and creating "licensing" power where none seemed to exist are not just examples of presidential infidelity, but they are also part of an ongoing struggle between the branches for control over U.S. foreign policy toward the island. This case highlights many of the institutional advantages that the executive enjoys in this struggle even when operating from a position of apparent—if self-imposed—weakness. The power tools the Clinton administration applied in this case, from signing statements to enforcement discretion to legislative reinterpretation, show how tough a competitor a determined executive can be in the struggle between the branches for control over foreign policy.

A BRIEF HISTORY OF HELMS-BURTON

The LIBERTAD, which ultimately emerged from Congress and the President signed "in the name of the four men who were killed,"[11] presented a clear statement of U.S. policy toward Cuba and included unambiguous language that tightened, expanded, and codified the embargo. It drove a complicated road to passage, however.[12] In early 1992 Representative Robert Torricelli (D-N.J.) and Senator Bob Graham (D-Fla.) introduced the Cuban Democracy Act (CDA) in their respective chambers.[13] The CDA attempted to increase economic pressure on Cuba by shutting off trade with foreign subsidiaries of U.S. multinationals and by making entering U.S. ports more difficult for ships that had visited Cuba, thus closing the de facto loosening of the embargo that followed the Cuba economy's opening to the rest of the world after the fall of the Soviet Union. The CDA had a "second track" that tried to reach out to the Cuban people by making communication and family visits to Cuba easier.[14] The Bush administration opposed the CDA, but changed its position to support the bill following presidential candidate Bill Clinton's acceptance of it while campaigning in Florida.[15] That bill became law a few weeks before the 1992 presidential election.

A new move to tighten and expand the embargo of Cuba further came from the Congress in early 1995 in the form of the LIBERTAD, or Helms-Burton, which began to take shape at the direction of Senator Jesse Helms (R-NC), the new chair of the Senate Foreign Relations committee.[16] On the House side, beyond the sponsorship of Rep. Dan Burton (R-IN), the three Cuban-Americans on Capitol Hill were particularly active: Lincoln Diaz-Balart (R-FL), Robert Menendez (D-NJ), and Ileana Ros-Lehtinen (R-FL). When the Bill was presented it included several controversial components.[17] Title III would give U.S. citizens the right to sue in U.S courts foreign companies that traffic in stolen property in Cuba. Title IV would have denied visas to executives of companies (and their families) who traffic in confiscated properties in Cuba.

The Clinton administration opposed Helms-Burton, seeing it as unnecessary because of the existing CDA and as unwise because of the way it would limit the president's flexibility in foreign affairs. Nevertheless, the House passed Helms-Burton 294–130 on September 21. Moving Helms-Burton through the Senate, however, proved more difficult. Unable to move the bill, the Senate removed Title III and Title IV.[18] The eviscerated bill seemed dead as it went to conference—at least before two Brothers to the Rescue planes were shot down by the Cuban Air Force on February 24, 1996.[19] Out of these ashes a new life emerged for Helms-Burton.

In the postshooting atmosphere, the advantage clearly shifted to Congress. At a strategy meeting on Capitol Hill the next day Titles III and IV were put back in the bill. A new measure was added to Title I as well at the insistence of Diaz-Balart: codification of the embargo into law.[20] From the perspective of the bill's congressional supporters, Clinton now had no choice but to accept Helms-Burton in any form.[21] Even the President's special advisor for Cuba policy, Richard Nuccio, admitted that, "Castro created a veto-proof majority for the Helms-Burton bill."[22] In the meeting with administration representatives that followed a deal was struck that Clinton would sign the bill but in return a waiver would be included in Title III. The administration's efforts to get a waiver for Title IV and to remove the codification provision failed; Clinton signed Helms-Burton on March 12, 1996. Although Clinton could waive Title III, the ultimate question of Cuba policy—the embargo—was codified into law. Helped along by the Cuban Air Force and congressional activism, Helms-Burton seemed to mark a key shift in foreign policy power by transferring control over the embargo to Congress. The following details how President Clinton tried over time to at least loosen these bonds if not slip them altogether.

CLINTON STRIKES BACK

President Clinton's responses to Helms-Burton fell into three areas: (1) waiving Title III, (2) sparingly enforcing Title IV, and (3) expanding licensing powers to pursue unilateral policy initiatives toward Cuba. The Clinton administration justified its actions, arguing that the use of the Title III waivers was necessary to build international support for a democratic transition in Cuba.[23] Presumably the limited enforcement of Title IV was also not to anger allies. The administration also argued that the limited licensing power granted to the president in Helms-Burton can be construed broadly to allow wide discretion to alter the shape of the embargo.[24] In addition, the president argued that he took many of the components of Helms-Burton as "precatory,"[25] or as an entreaty, rather than as a requirement. Our view is that each of these steps is probably outside the domain of the legislation Congress passed and that the president signed and were taken at least in part to reassert presidential power over foreign policy in general and Cuba policy in particular.

The waiver mechanism in Title III was added in the conference committee after the shooting and allows the president to waive or suspend the right to bring suit for six-month periods if the president determines "that such suspension is necessary to the national interests of the United States and will expedite a transition to democracy in Cuba."[26] The conference committee report is very clear about the intent of the waiver provision. The committee specifically rejected a usual "national security interests" waiver proposal the Executive branch made because it wanted the issue of a democratic transition to Cuba to be a central feature of the decision to exercise the waiver.[27] This was a higher standard than most waivers, and the report goes on to note:

> In the judgment of the committee of conference, under current circumstances the President could not in good faith determine that the suspension of the right of action is either "necessary to the national interests of the United States" or "will expedite a transition to democracy in Cuba." In particular, the committee believes that it is demonstrably not the case that suspending the right of action will expedite a transition to democracy in Cuba.[28]

Frankly, the drafters of Helms-Burton did not think Clinton would use the waivers because they did not think the president could show progress toward a democratic transition in Cuba, nor did they think he would risk the political costs of the waiver in Florida so close to the 1996 elections.[29] Helms himself, following Clinton's first use of the waiver in July 1996, argued angrily that he had intended the bill to be "Clinton Proof."[30]

In July 1996 Clinton announced that he would allow Title III to come into force, but that he would exercise the waiver, thereby preventing suits from going forward.[31] Clinton continued to waive Title III throughout his presidency. Clinton's use of the waiver provisions of Title III seems to many to be beyond the plain language and clear intent of Helms-Burton. The act and the accompanying conference committee report make clear that suspension of the right of action was meant to be used only if the president believes it is in the interests of the United States to do so *and* if the waiver is an instrumental part of facilitating a democratic transition in Cuba. Clinton's use of the waiver signals more of an interest in working with allies and in flexing presidential power than in obeying the clear spirit and mandate of Title III.

Title IV instructs the secretary of state and attorney general to prevent any third country national from entering the United States if that person has trafficked in confiscated property in Cuba to which a U.S. national has an existing claim. The provision applies to executives, principals, or major shareholders in a corporation trafficking, and for good measure the spouse and minor children are to be excluded as well. The clear intent of Title IV was to deter further economic activity in Cuba by foreign companies and to induce divestment by companies currently doing business on the island.[32]

Contrary to Clinton's assertion that Title IV has been the subject of "aggressive implementation,"[33] Title IV was applied quite selectively during the Clinton years. The primary enforcement targets were executives of the Canadian firm, Sherritt International Corporation. In July 1996 seven members of that company received official letters from the U.S. government informing them that they and their family members would not be allowed to enter the country legally.[34] Other warning letters were sent to executives at the Mexican firm Grupo Domos and the Italian company Stet International.[35] Grupo Domos, which was a partner in the Cuban telephone company, eventually relinquished its stake therein; the weak peso and other financial difficulties Domos faced was probably as important as the threat Helms-Burton posed in the Mexican company's decision to withdraw from the island.[36] Stet, also a telecommunications company, "immunized" itself against Helms-Burton by agreeing to compensate ITT for their confiscated assets.[37] By March 1999 a Department of State official testified in the House of Representatives that only officials with Sherritt International Corporation (fifteen by now) and the Israeli BM Group were being excluded from the United States as a result of Title IV.[38] Given that initial estimates ran from 100 to 200 joint ventures that were trafficking in confiscated property,[39] the small number of companies targeted suggests that the Clinton administration practiced a de facto waiver of Title IV.

The president was given some limited licensing power to revise sanctions on family remittances and travel to Cuba that were in effect when Helms-Burton came into force. In Section 112 of the act, in "sense of the Congress" language, the president is given the authority under certain circumstances to reinstitute licenses (1) to allow people in the United States to send money to their families in Cuba, and (2) to allow travel to Cuba by U.S. residents who have family members in Cuba.[40] The reinstitution of remittances is premised on reforms in Cuba to allow small businesses to operate freely; the reinstitution of family travel is based on the Cuban government's release of political prisoners and the recognition of fundamental freedoms such as the right of association.

Clinton used the limited licensing power granted in Section 112 of Helms-Burton to relax several restrictions placed on access to Cuba imposed following the Brothers to the Rescue shooting. The first of these steps preceded Pope John Paul's 1998 visit to the island and included: (1) resuming licensing direct humanitarian charter flights to Cuba; (2) establishing new licensing arrangements to permit Cuban Americans and Cuban families living in the United States to send humanitarian remittances of up to $300 per quarter to their families in Cuba, as was permitted until 1994; and (3) facilitating licensing for the sale of medicines and medical supplies and equipment to Cuba.[41]

In January 1999 Clinton announced a second set of unilateral actions, including increased support for Radio- and TV-Marti.[42] He also announced: (1) expanding remittances by allowing any U.S. resident to send limited funds to individual Cuban families and independent organizations; (2) expanding people-to-people contact through two-way exchanges among academics, athletes, scientists, and others; (3) authorizing the sale of food and agricultural inputs to independent nongovernment entities such as family restaurants, religious groups, and private farmers; (4) authorizing charter passenger flights to cities in Cuba other than Havana and from some cities in the United States other than Miami; and finally, (5) endeavoring to establish direct mail service to Cuba.[43]

Clinton acknowledged that he is prevented "from lifting the embargo without the support of Congress."[44] Still, his moves in March 1998 and in January 1999 can be seen as going beyond that which Helms-Burton permitted. The plain language of the act with respect to licenses speaks in terms only of family travel and remittances. The president's actions go well beyond these limitations and stand in contradiction to clear prohibitions in the bill. After the 1998 reforms, a congressional staffer said, "it was not clear that Clinton has the authority himself to allow direct flights, since the ban is covered under the legislation, which does not allow special waivers [for flights]."[45] At that same time, Rep. Diaz-Balart said, "We are not going to let Clinton proceed along the path of normalization."[46] Following the January 1999 reforms, Rep. Ros-Lehtinen said, "We want to know where is the legal controlling authority that authorizes them to change the law. The way we read Helms-Burton, they do not have any such authority."[47] The Cuban Americans in Congress have not been able to get the administration to present in writing their argument on this point, and preliminary discussions are currently under way about how to sue Clinton on this issue.[48]

In his written signing statement[49] of Helms-Burton, although not in his verbal remarks, Clinton argued that he saw the bill's codification provision—Section 102(h)—as too rigid.[50] He also argued that he would treat various parts of Helms-Burton as precatory, or as an entreaty, thus "not derogating from the President's authority to conduct foreign policy."[51] He argued, "While I support the underlying intent of these sections, the President's constitutional authority over foreign policy necessarily entails discretion over these matters."[52] Clinton only used such language twelve times in signing statements during his two terms.[53]

By invoking a term such as *precatory* as he signed Helms-Burton, however, Clinton provided a signal of his likely infidelity on Helms-Burton. Perhaps Congress should have anticipated this, but Congress had made its intent clear in the bill. Clinton's steps on Titles III and IV, while irksome to many in Congress and we think questionable given the clear language of Helms-Burton and the conference committee report, are not nearly as significant as the use of licenses as a way to erode Congress's codification of the embargo. Alan J. Kreczko, special assistant to the president and legal advisor for the National Security Council during that period, reports that Clinton's language emerged less from the administration's concern about Cuba policy than it did from a "preserve the president's institutional prerogatives policy."[54] Such language set the stage for Clinton's future moves that would be as much about regaining power as they were about policy toward the island. The balance of this chapter assesses the history of case law in the foreign policy and trade policy area as it applies to Clinton's interpretation of Helms-Burton as part of an effort to understand the roots of Clinton's Cuba policy actions.

A CASE AGAINST CLINTON'S ACTIONS

The Clinton administration attempted to justify its actions, and by them to reclaim power in this area, by categorizing Helms-Burton as precatory and by manipulating the act's plain language. Although Clinton described

Helms-Burton as precatory based on his interpretation of the presidential prerogative in foreign affairs, his understanding of that prerogative—and the case law that provides its underpinnings—is flawed. Rather, the history of case law in this area, beginning with *United States v. Curtiss-Wright Export Corporation*[55] and its progeny, supports the notion that the actions the Clinton administration took on Cuba policy are at best invalid. Moreover, Clinton's argument that the licensing provision in Section 112 authorizes him unilaterally to change various facets of U.S. policy toward Cuba is of dubious validity given the clear intent of Congress to the contrary. Rather, the Clinton administration has interpreted a minor, very narrow provision that provides for some relaxing of restrictions quite broadly, in such a way as to reclaim ground willingly signed away in March 1996.

In the written Helms-Burton signing statement, Clinton expressed his intention to interpret the act as "not derogating from the President's authority to conduct foreign policy."[56] He argued, "While I support the underlying intent of these sections, the President's constitutional authority over foreign policy necessarily entails discretion over these matters. Accordingly, I will construe these provisions to be precatory."[57] The "constitutional authority" the president refers to is no doubt drawn from the history of case law in the foreign policy area, beginning with *Curtiss-Wright* and continuing through to the modern-day trade legislation cases. Clinton, like other presidents, read these cases as authorizing broad-scale presidential prerogative—even in the face of clearly expressed congressional will to the contrary. Whereas Clinton was perhaps correct in understanding these cases to stand for general presidential preeminence in foreign affairs, he failed to take into account the role of Congress in the foreign policy process, a role that even the Supreme Court has emphasized as important and that continues to stand as an important check on presidential power in this area.

The history of presidential-congressional relations in foreign affairs has been well documented.[58] Throughout that history, the U.S. Supreme Court had, on the whole, seemed to strike a balance in favor of the legislature when faced with interbranch conflict on issues relating to foreign policy up until its 1936 landmark decision in *Curtiss-Wright*.[59] In that case, the Court instead announced that the president, not Congress, was to be seen as the "sole organ of the nation" in foreign affairs.[60] According to the majority, the president was not reliant on the Constitution for his foreign affairs powers, but rather was vested with such powers simply by virtue of his role as head of state.[61] The Supreme Court has also taken steps to curtail the expansive power it provided for in *Curtiss-Wright*. In *Youngstown Sheet and Tube Co. v. Sawyer* (1952), the Court took the opportunity provided by President Truman's seizure of U.S.

steel mills to hold that unless the president is enforcing laws made by Congress, his actions must be carried out pursuant to some power granted to him by the Constitution.[62] This puts *Youngstown* in marked contrast to *Curtiss-Wright*; the latter has come to stand for the idea of presidential dominance in foreign policy, whereas the former represents a return to the separation-of-powers principle and a curtailment of presidential power.[63]

Although the majority in *Youngstown* denounced Truman's actions as extraconstitutional and invalid, Justice Jackson's concurrence has, throughout the years, received the most attention for significantly limiting the power of the president in foreign affairs. Justice Jackson establishes three zones of presidential authority vis-à-vis Congress: one in which the president acts "pursuant to the express or implied authorization of Congress" and thus enjoys the greatest amount of power; a second in which the president acts but the Congress remains silent, commonly dubbed the "zone of twilight"; and a third in which the president acts contrary to the "express or implied will of Congress" and thus enjoys the least amount of power. Under the *Youngstown* analysis, presidents who choose to act in direct conflict with the expressed will of Congress risk upsetting the delicate "equilibrium established by our constitutional system."[64]

Thus although Clinton was correct to the extent that he understood his role to be one of conducting the foreign policy of the United States, he is incorrect in assuming that he could unilaterally determine what that foreign policy is in a situation where, as with Helms-Burton, Congress has clearly spoken on the matter. According to constitutional law scholar Laurence Tribe:

> Although the President alone can act in foreign affairs, the content of presidential options is defined partly—and increasingly—by congressional enactments and limited by constitutional strictures. Hence, while it may be symbolically correct to say that the President is the sole national "actor" in foreign affairs, it is not accurate to label the President the sole national policy maker.[65]

Curtiss-Wright is perhaps Clinton's best weapon in asserting the primacy of the executive in foreign affairs, yet even that case may not be as strongly in support of presidential prerogative as it first appears. In *Curtiss-Wright* the Court was dealing with was a president acting in conjunction with Congress, not one acting in contradiction to Congress.[66] A delegation of power from Congress to the president is markedly different than a situation in which, as in Helms-Burton, the executive instead attempts to alter the law unilaterally as Congress had enacted it. In his influential concurrence in *Youngstown*, Justice Jackson was careful to point out that *Curtiss-Wright* involved, "not the question of the President's power to act without congressional authority, but the question of his right to act under and in accord with an Act of Congress."[67] When presented with a situation in which the president has unilaterally altered enacted policy, *Curtiss-Wright* hardly seems applicable, and other Supreme Court precedents, including *Youngstown*, would seem more relevant. Applying Justice Jackson's three-zone analysis, Clinton's recent actions about Cuba would find him in zone three—acting contrary to the established will of Congress and thus finding his power at its lowest ebb.[68]

Helms-Burton is a curious mix of trade and foreign policy legislation. For forty years, the backbone of U.S. policy toward Cuba has been the embargo, and the stated goal of Helms-Burton is to continue and strengthen that embargo. The struggle between Congress and the president for control of Cuba policy must thus be viewed in the trade legislation context. This context makes the Cuba case so unique: although power struggles between the branches have been extensively debated in the past, these debates took place largely in the war powers context or about other crisis situations. Here, however, we have no crisis and no real threat from Cuba.

One of the first cases to deal with the relative powers of Congress and the president in the trade legislation context was *Little v. Barreme* in 1804.[69] In that case, Congress enacted legislation authorizing the president to order the seizure of U.S. ships en route to French ports. The president, however, ordered that ships traveling both to and from French ports could be seized. A ship's captain found himself the subject of litigation for carrying out the president's orders. The Supreme Court held the captain liable, notwithstanding the fact that he had acted in accordance with a presidential order. According to the majority opinion, Congress had taken care in the statute to specifically identify ships sailing "to" French ports, and thus in ordering the seizure of vessels to or from French ports, the president was reconstructing the language of the legislation. Implicit in the Court's opinion is the notion that once Congress has spoken clearly on an issue, such as by enacting legislation, the president is not at liberty to rewrite that legislation according to his own views on the wisdom of that particular policy.

Similarly in the 1953 case of *United States v. Guy W. Capps, Inc.*,[70] the Fourth Circuit Court invalidated presidential action that contradicted a statute. In that case, the president issued an executive agreement between the United States and Canada dealing with the importation of vegetables that would have conflicted with a statute Congress enacted on that same issue. Refusing to uphold the executive agreement, the Court explained, "the power to regulate foreign commerce is vested in Congress, not in the executive or the court."[71] As late as 1986 the Supreme Court reiterated its commitment to congressional preeminence in matters relating to international trade in the case of *Japan Whaling Ass'n v. American Cetacean Society*.[72] In that case, Congress authorized the president, at his discretion, to prohibit the importation of fish products from other nations that failed to comply with international whaling quotas. When Congress realized that the president was not going to exercise that power, it amended the statute to remove the "discretionary" language in an effort to force the president's hand. When Japan continually refused to comply with the quotas and the president, acting through the secretary of commerce, still refused to comply with the amended statute, certain wildlife groups filed suit. Although ultimately upholding the secretary's actions as furthering the goals of the legislation,[73] the Court was nevertheless clear that the president, "may not act contrary to the will of Congress when exercised within the bounds of the Constitution. If Congress has directly spoken to the precise issue in question, if the intent of Congress is clear, that is the end of the matter."[74] There, however, a 5–4 majority of the Court found the administration's actions as a reasonable construction of the statutory language and legislative history and thus was willing to give the president broad discretion.[75] The majority held that it would allow such discretion "unless the legislative history of the enactment shows with sufficient clarity that the agency construction is contrary to the will of Congress."[76] One would be hard-pressed to find such ambiguity in the text or history of Helms-Burton, however.

Clearly, Congress has the power to control commerce and is the dominant force in trade legislation. The Constitution grants to Congress the power to regulate tariffs and foreign commerce, whereas the president enjoys no comparable authority to direct international trade. According to Theresa Wilson: "In the area of foreign commerce . . . Congress is given more respect by the courts. While Congress will be allowed to delegate its foreign commerce power to the president if it so chooses, the courts have held that power over foreign commerce ultimately rests with the legislative branch and with that branch alone."[77] The cases outlined herein suggest that when Congress has clearly spoken on a matter involving trade, the president is limited to conducting U.S. foreign policy according to that mandate. Like the president in *Little v. Barreme*, Clinton attempted to reconstruct an otherwise clear congressional enactment. The fact that this enactment is premised on the embargo, a type of trade legislation, means that the president is instead constrained by the choices Congress has constitutionally made.

The administration's view of codification differs from the view on Capitol Hill. James Dobbins, special assistant to the president and senior director for Inter-American Affairs of the National Security Council staff, argued that although "Helms-Burton codified the embargo," it also "codified the president's licensing power; that is it codified a process by which there was an embargo to which exceptions could be granted on a case-by-case basis, by the president, in cases in which is was deemed consistent with U.S. policy."[78] The administration admits that under codification in Section 102(h) all restrictions on Cuba were frozen, however, they point to language in another section, Section 112, to develop their wide licensing power. Titled Reinstitution of Family Remittances and Travel to Cuba, that section provides:

> It is the sense of the Congress that the president should—(1)(A) before considering the reinstitution of general licenses for family remittances to Cuba, insist that, prior to such reinstitution, the Cuban government permit the unfettered operation of small businesses fully empowered with the right to hire others to whom they may pay wages and to buy materials necessary in the operation of the businesses . . . and (2) before considering the reinstitution of general licenses for travel to Cuba by individuals resident in the United States . . . insist on such actions by the Cuban government as abrogation of the sanction for departure from Cuba by refugees, release of political prisoners, recognition of the right of association, and other fundamental freedoms.[79]

The administration read this to imply that the president can make adjustments with licenses not just in these areas but across the full range of Cuba policy short of the embargo. Yet based on the plain language of this section, as well as language contained in other parts of Helms-Burton, Clinton's argument is dubious at best.

First, the plain language of this section makes clear that the licensing provisions apply only to family remittances and travel. Congress was explicit in detailing that "before considering the reinstitution of general licenses for family remittances" and "before considering the reinstitution of general licenses for travel to Cuba," the president is to ensure that the Cuban government is taking certain steps. Yet, as discussed previously, Clinton's initiatives have thus far gone well beyond family remittances and travel to include things such as direct mail service to Cuba and sale of food and other agricultural goods to nongovernment entities. Clinton's actions were clearly beyond the realm of permissible policy changes. Although Congress may have offered the president one small loophole in dealing with the Cuban people, it clearly did not intend to offer him the opportunity to rewrite Cuba policy wholesale.

Second, many of Clinton's initiatives thus far have dealt in large part with foreign commerce between Cuba and the United States. As we explained about the trade legislation cases, however, Congress, not the president, has the ultimate power in that area. With regard to the regulation of foreign commerce, the president is charged only with taking care that "the Laws be faithfully executed." In this case, however, Clinton arguably failed—by ignoring the plain language and instead attempting to unilaterally regulate foreign commerce in contradiction with Congress's intent.

Third, Section 112 is couched in nonbinding, sense of the Congress language. Hanging such a broad assertion of authority on such a weak component of Helms-Burton, especially a component that actually tries to restrict presidential initiatives, is not tenable for the president. Contrast this with the other provisions of Helms-Burton that are not written in loose sense of the Congress language and that strongly assert and codify sanctions on Cuba. Furthermore, even if the president wished to use the narrow license found here to build the foundation for a broad licensing authority, he could not do so in the face of prohibitive language elsewhere in the bill.

Fourth, even if a court were to deviate from the plain language of Helms-Burton, the legislative history makes clear that Congress did not intend to grant to the president broad-scale licensing powers.

> The conference committee modified the definition of "economic embargo of Cuba" to include all statutes or regulations relating to trade, travel, and transactions involving Cuban assets imposed under [the Foreign Assistance Act, the Trading with the Enemy Act, the Cuban Democracy Act, the Food Security Act, or any other provision of law]. *It is the intent of the committee that this definition be interpreted broadly, in part, in order to ensure that the suspension or termination of any economic sanctions on Cuba be pursuant only to the authority granted in section 204 of this Act.*[80]

Section 204, to which the report refers, provides that the president may suspend the embargo, "upon submitting a determination to the appropriate congressional committees . . . that a transition government in Cuba is in power."[81] Clinton's actions thus are not covered under either the plain language of the licensing provision or the suspension provision of Section 204.

Thus whereas Clinton was correct in asserting that Congress contemplated allowing the president to alter Cuba policy, they did so only in clearly defined circumstances: with regard to family remittances and travel, and on a determination that democratic change was taking place in that country. Finally, although some flexibility is built into the enforcement of the embargo, this flexibility actually conflicts with the initiatives President Clinton took. According to the conference committee report, "it is not the intent of this section to prohibit executive branch agencies from amending existing regulations to *tighten* economic sanctions on Cuba."[82] Thus the president's actions to strengthen the embargo against Cuba or to increase pressure on the Cuban government would be sanctioned by Congress, whereas actions taken to decrease the effects of the embargo are clearly not. In arguing that his initiatives are in accordance with the licensing provisions of LIBERTAD, Clinton sorely misconstrued the plain language of Section 112. And even a perfunctory analysis of the legislative history reveals that Congress had no intention of allowing the president to alter set policy unilaterally. Together with the various other rationales presented in this section, Clinton's initiatives clearly are in derogation of Helms-Burton and, as such, are an invalid exercise of the presidential prerogative.

CONCLUSION: PRESIDENTIAL DISOBEDIENCE AND EXECUTIVE POWER

Although reasonable debate exists about the policy impact of the steps President Clinton took following Helms-Burton, the more noteworthy significance of these actions—the precatory language in the written signing statement, the waivers on Title III, relative nonenforcement of Title IV, and the licensing initiatives—relates to the issue of who controls policy toward Cuba. To understand why Clinton would go to such (questionable) lengths to elude the strictures of a law he signed one must take into account not only the president's policy interests but also his institutional interests.[83] Clinton tried to regain strategic and institutional powers in ways that the Constitution and the case law it has spawned cannot fully explain. Clinton's expanded use of licensing power seems to be clearly beyond the bounds of what Congress intended. His waivers of Title III probably stretch the language of the bill beyond what is reasonable, and his little enforcement of Title IV, although understandable given international concerns, also seems to contradict what Congress called for in the bill. Without the shooting of the Brothers to the Rescue planes, Helms-Burton would perhaps not exist at all—almost certainly not in its current form. But it does; and Clinton signed it. No matter what one may think of the wisdom (or the lack thereof) of the legislation, Clinton's steps that followed since its signing are striking. Clinton's relationship with an intern and subsequent impeachment will no doubt go down in history, but we argue that his other infidelity will have far more lasting implications for the relationship between the president and Congress in the area of foreign policy.

In recent books, Louis Fisher[84] and Gordon Silverstein[85] each make compelling arguments that since World War II the president has garnered significant unilateral control over much of foreign policy and war powers, often with the unwitting (and even witting) help of Congress. Cuba policy largely fit into this trend during the cold war, but in the 1990s Cuba policy became more domesticated. It became less a security issue and more a trade issue, and more the subject of an increasingly assertive Congress. Congress has acted to retain significant authority over Cuba policy. President Clinton showed the limits of congressional action and the strength of the executive following Helms-Burton—the kind of strength that Fisher and Silverstein document.

The case of Clinton after Helms-Burton supports the view that presidents rely on executive authority to make policy unilaterally in ways traditional analyses of presidential power can fail to appreciate.[86] Presidents often find ways to get around Congress when they are highly motivated, as Clinton certainly was in this case. Helms-Burton stands as an impressive example of congressional activism on Cuba policy and on trade policy more generally, but it also highlights the limits of congressional activism[87] and the strength of the executive, even in an area where Congress has acted clearly to try to constrain the president.

NOTES

1. See Larry Rohter, "Exiles Say Cuba Downed Two Planes and Clinton Expresses Outrage," *New York Times*, February 25, 1996, p. 1. See also Carroll J. Doherty, "Planes' Downing Forces Clinton to Compromise on Sanctions," *Congressional Quarterly Weekly Reports* 54 (March 2, 1996): 565–66.

2. 22 U.S.C. 6021ff. (HR 927, PL #104–114, March 12, 1996).

3. *Congressional Record* 141 (September 21, 1995): H9375–76.

4. *Congressional Record* (September 21, 1995): H9376–77.

5. See Patrick J. Kiger, *Squeeze Play: The United States, Cuba, and the Helms-Burton Act* (Washington, D.C.: Center for Public Integrity, 1997), p. 55.

6. U.S. Congress, Committee of Conference, *Report*, pp. 104–468, *Cuban Liberty and Democratic Solidarity (LIBERTAD) Act of 1996*, 104th Cong., 2nd sess., March 1, 1996 (Washington, D.C.: U.S. Government Printing Office), p. 11.

7. Committee of Conference, pp. 39–40.

8. William Jefferson Clinton, "Statement on Cuba," *Weekly Compilation of Presidential Documents* 34 (March 20, 1998): 475–76.

9. William Jefferson Clinton, "Statement on United States Policy toward Cuba," *Weekly Compilation of Presidential Documents* 35 (January 5, 1999): 7–8.

10. See, for example, Tim Weiner, "U.S. Ready to Ease Some Restrictions in Policy on Cuba," *New York Times*, January 5, 1999: online; Thomas W. Lippman, "U.S. Ready to Play Ball with Cuba: Clinton to Ease Trade Embargo, Using Orioles as Unofficial Envoys," *Washington Post*, January 5, 1999, p. A1.

11. William Jefferson Clinton, "Remarks on Signing the Cuban Liberty and Democratic Solidarity (LIBERTAD) Act of 1996," *Weekly Compilation of Presidential Documents* 32 (March 12, 1996): 478.

12. For a detailed history, see Kiger, *Squeeze Play*; Patrick J. Haney and Walt Vanderbush, "The Helms-Burton Act: Congress and Cuba Policy," in *Contemporary Cases in U.S. Foreign Policy: From Trade to Terrorism*, Ralph G. Carter, ed. (Washington, D.C.: Congressional Quarterly Press, 2002).

13. 22 U.S.C. 6001ff.

14. See David Rieff, "Cuba Refrozen," *Foreign Affairs* 75 (July/August 1996): 62–75; Richard Nuccio, "Cuba: A U.S. Perspective," in *Transatlantic Tensions: The United States, Europe, and Problem Countries*, Richard N. Haass, ed. (Washington, D.C.: Brookings, 1999).

15. See, for example, "Bush Gives Support to Cuba Bill," *Miami Herald*, May 6, 1992, p. A1; Christopher Marquis, "Bush Vira a Favor de Plan Contra Cuba," *Nuevo Herald*, May 6, 1992, p. 1A. Indeed, although Clinton did not win Florida in 1992, he did gain nearly three times as many Cuban-American votes as did the Democratic presidential candidate Michael Dukakis in 1988, and Clinton carried Florida in 1996. (And many argue Gore won Florida in 2000!)

16. See Kiger, *Squeeze Play*, chap. 5; Dick Kirschten, "Raising Cain," *National Journal*, July 1, 1995, pp. 1714–17; Walt Vanderbush and Patrick J. Haney, "Policy Toward Cuba in the Clinton Administration," *Political Science Quarterly* 144 (Fall 1999): 387–408.

17. H.R. 927, Report No. 104–202, Part I. July 24, 1995.

18. *Congressional Record*, 1995: S15584–S15589; see also Jim Lobe, "U.S.-Cuba: Senate Republicans Throw in Towel on Cuba Sanctions," *Inter Press Service* (October 18, 1995); Kiger, *Squeeze Play*, p. 55.

19. See Carl Nagin, "Backfire," *New Yorker*, January 26, 1998, pp. 30–35.

20. Rep. Lincoln Diaz-Balart (R-FL), telephone interview with Patrick J. Haney, July 2, 1998.

21. Dan Fisk argues, "the shootdown left the Clinton Administration politically naked: they were shown to have no Cuba policy, no contingencies for such things. LIBERTAD was now the only game in town." Dan Fisk, telephone interview with Patrick J. Haney, June 16, 1998. Another House staff member noted that the shooting "changed everything," and left the administration in "no position to bargain." Steve Vermillion, from the office of Rep. Lincoln Diaz-Balart, telephone interview with Patrick J. Haney, June 19, 1998.

22. Quoted in Carroll J. Doherty, "Planes' Downing Forces Clinton to Compromise on Sanction," *Congressional Quarterly Weekly Report* 54 (March 2, 1996): 565.

23. See William Jefferson Clinton, "Statement on Action on Title III of the Cuban Liberty and Democratic Solidarity (LIBERTAD) Act of 1996," *Weekly Compilation of Presidential Documents* 34 (July 16, 1998): 1398.

24. See Special State Department Briefing on U.S.-Cuba Relations, January 5, 1999.

25. See William Jefferson Clinton, "Statement on Signing the Cuban Liberty and Democratic Solidarity (LIBERTAD) Act of 1996," *Weekly Compilation of Presidential Documents* 32 (March 12, 1996): 479–80.

26. Public Law, Cuban Liberty and Democratic Solidarity Act of 1996, 306(c)(1)(b), pp. 104–14.

27. Committee of Conference, *Report*, p. 65.

28. Committee of Conference, *Report*, p. 65.

29. Steve Vermillion, telephone interview with Patrick J. Haney, February 8, 1999.

30. Jesse Helms, "Helms Slams Decision to Waive Cuba Provision," congressional press releases, July 16, 1996.

31. William Jefferson Clinton, "Statement on Action on Title III of the Cuban Liberty and Democratic Solidarity (LIBERTAD) Act of 1996," pp. 1265–66.

32. Committee of Conference, p. 66.

33. William Jefferson Clinton, "Statement on Review of Title III of the Cuban Liberty and Democratic Solidarity (LIBERTAD) Act of 1996," *Weekly Compilation of Presidential Documents* 35 (July 16, 1999): 1383.

34. See John M. Kirk and Peter McKenna, *Canada-Cuba Relations: The Other Good Neighbor Policy* (Gainesville: University Press of Florida, 1997), pp. 168–69; Carla Anne Robbins and Jose de Cordoba, "Sherritt Officials to Be Barred from U.S.," *Wall Street Journal*, July 11, 1996, p. A11.

35. See John Pearson, "Just Who's Getting Punished Here?" *Business Week International Editions*, June 17, 1996, p. 28.

36. See Larry Rohter, "Mexican Conglomerate Abandons Cuban Phone Venture," *New York Times*, June 30, 1997, p. D2.

37. Guy de Jonquie'res, "Keeping the Lid On Helms-Burton: US and EU Warn that Talks May Prove Complicated," *Financial Times*, July 31, 1997, p. 4.

38. Michael E. Ranneberger, Coordinator for the Office of Cuban Affairs, "Statement before the Subcommittee on Western Hemisphere of the House International Relations Committee," Federal News Service, March 24, 1999.

39. Craig Auge, "Title IV of the Helms-Burton Act: A Questionable Secondary Boycott," *Law and Policy in International Business* 28 (1997): 575–92.

40. 22 U.S.C. 6042.

41. William Jefferson Clinton, "Statement on Cuba," pp. 475–76.

42. In related actions, the administration reached an agreement in mid-1998 to let Cuban airliners fly over the United States on routes to Canada. The agreement was reached days before the United Nation's International Civil Aviation Organization was due to rule on the dispute, a ruling the United States was expected to lose. See Christopher Marquis, "Cuba May be Allowed to Fly over U.S. Territory," *Miami Herald*, June 17, 1998, p. A1. The United States expected to lose the case because the "national security exception" would most likely not be upheld, given that the U.S. Defense Department itself admitted that Cuba posed no significant threat to the United States. See the report at <http://www.defenselink.mil/pubs/cubarpt.htm>. Also, after announcing the 1999 initiatives, Clinton scuttled a plan to assemble a bipartisan commission on US-Cuba policy that enjoyed wide support. See, for example, Thomas W. Lippman, "Group Urges Review of Cuba Policy," *Washington Post*, November 8, 1998, p. A10.

43. William Jefferson Clinton, "Statement on United States Policy Toward Cuba," *Weekly Compilation of Presidential Documents* 35 (January 5, 1999): 7–8.

44. William Jefferson Clinton, "Remarks and a Question and Answer Session

at a Democratic National Committee Dinner in New York City," *Weekly Compilation of Presidential Documents* 34 (January 8, 1998): 27.

45. Quoted in Steven Erlanger, "U.S. to Ease Curbs on Relief to Cuba and Money to Kin," *New York Times*, March 20, 1998, p. 2.

46. Quoted in Christopher Marquis, "U.S. to Cut Sanctions on Cuba," *Pittsburgh Post-Gazette*, March 20, 1998, p. A1.

47. Quoted in Juan O. Tamayo, "Eased Cuba Sanctions Questioned," *Miami Herald*, January 7, 1999, p. A12.

48. Steve Vermillion, from the office of Lincoln Diaz-Balart, telephone interview with Patrick J. Haney, February 8, 1999; see also Tamayo, "Eased Cuba Sanctions."

49. See Kristy L. Carroll, "Whose Statute Is It Anyway? Why and How Courts Should Use Presidential Signing Statements When Interpreting Federal Statutes," *Catholic University Law Review* 46 (Winter 1997): 475–522; Chris Kelley, *The Unitary Executive and the Presidential Signing Statement*, Ph.D. diss., Miami University, 2003.

50. William Jefferson Clinton, "Statement on Signing the Cuban Liberty and Democratic Solidarity Act."

51. Clinton, "Statement on Signing the Cuban Liberty and Democratic Solidarity Act."

52. Clinton, "Statement on Signing the Cuban Liberty and Democratic Solidarity Act."

53. According to a search of the online version of the *Weekly Compilation of Presidential Documents*. For comparison, according to a Lexis-Nexis Academic Universe Search of the Public Papers of the President, President Bush used the term *precatory* ten times.

54. Alan J. Kreczko, Telephone interview with Patrick J. Haney, June 18, 2002.

55. 299 U.S. 304 (1936).

56. Clinton, "Statement on Signing the Cuban Liberty and Democratic Solidarity Act," p. 479.

57. Clinton, "Statement on Signing the Cuban Liberty and Democratic Solidarity Act."

58. See, for example,Gordon Silverstein, *Imbalance of Powers: Constitutional Interpretation and the Making of American Foreign Policy* (New York: Oxford University Press, 1997); Harold Koh, *The National Security Constitution* (New Haven, Conn.: Yale University Press, 1990); Louis Fisher, *Presidential War Power* (Lawrence: University Press of Kansas, 1995).

59. See, for example, Theresa Wilson, "Who Controls International Trade? Congressional Delegation of the Foreign Commerce Power," *Drake Law Review* 47 (1998): 141–76.

60. Justice Sutherland, writing for the majority, apparently took the "sole organ" language from an argument Justice Marshall gave before the House of Representatives on March 7, 1800. Some scholars have argued, however, that Justice Sutherland misinterpreted Justice Marshall's statement and in so doing fundamentally altered its meaning. See Charles A. Lofgren, "*United States v. Curtiss-Wright Export Corp.*: An Historical Reassessment," *Yale Law Journal* 83 (1973): 1–32. Justice Marshall was referring to presidential authority carried out pursuant to congressional delegation and not inherent presidential power. See also Louis Fisher, "Foreign and

Defense Policy," in *Presidential Policymaking: An End-Of-Century Assessment*, Steven A. Shull, ed. (Armonk, N.Y.: Sharpe, 1999), pp. 249–50.

61. *Curtiss-Wright*, 299 U.S. 317–319.

62. See *Youngstown*, 343 U.S. 587–89.

63. See Harold H. Koh, *The National Security Constitution: Sharing Power after the Iran-Contra Affair* (New Haven, Conn.: Yale University Press, 1990); Anthony Simones, "The Reality of *Curtiss-Wright*," *Northern Illinois University Law Review* 16 (1996).

64. See *Youngstown*, 343 U.S. 637–38.

65. Laurence H. Tribe, *American Constitutional Law*, 2d ed. (Mineola, N.Y.: Foundation Press, 1988), p. 219.

66. See, for example, Michael J. Glennon, "Two Views of Presidential Foreign Affairs Power: *Little v. Barreme* or *Curtiss-Wright?*," *Yale Journal of International Law* 13 (1988): 307; Koh and Yoo, "Dollar Diplomacy/Dollar Defense: the Fabrics of Economic National Security Law," *International Lawyer* 26 (1992): 715–62.

67. See *Youngstown*, 343 U.S. at 635 n. 2 (emphasis added).

68. This category remains in tact after some alterations were made to the scheme in *Dames and Moore v. Regan* (1981).

69. 6 U.S. (2 Cranch) 170 (1804).

70. 204 F.2d 655 (1953).

71. Ibid, 658.

72. 478 U.S. 221 (1986).

73. The Secretary's actions here were to enter into an agreement with Japan in which Japan agreed to certain whaling limits and promised to end commercial whaling by 1988.

74. 478 U.S. 221 (1986), 233.

75. 478 U.S. 221 (1986), 233. See also Wilson, "Who Controls International Trade?" p. 162; Gordon Silverstein, "Judicial Enhancement of Executive Power," in *The President, The Congress, and The Making of Foreign Policy*, Paul E. Peterson, ed. (Norman: University of Oklahoma Press, 1994); Gordon Silverstein, *Imbalance of Powers*.

76. 478 U.S. 221 (1986), 233.

77. Wilson, "Who Controls International Trade?" p. 163.

78. Quoted in "Special State Department Briefing on US-Cuba Relations," Federal News Service, January 5, 1999. See also Tamayo, "Eased Cuba Sanctions;" Thomas W. Lippman, "U.S. to Ease Some Curbs against Cuba," *Washington Post*, March 20, 1998, p. A1.

79. See 22 U.S.C. 6042 section 112.

80. Committee of Conference, p. 44 (emphasis added).

81. 22 U.S.C. 6064 at section 204.

82. 22 U.S.C. 6064, at section 204.

83. See Walt Vanderbush and Patrick J. Haney, "Clinton, Congress, and Cuba Policy between Two Codifications: The Changing Executive-Legislative Relationship in Foreign Policy Making." *Congress and the Presidency* 29 (Autumn 2002): 171–94.

84. *Congressional Abdication on War and Spending* (College Station: Texas A&M Press, 2000).

85. Silverstein, *Imbalance of Powers*.

86. Kenneth R. Mayer, *With the Stroke of a Pen: Executive Orders and Presidential Power* (Princeton, N.J.: Princeton University Press, 2001).

87. That the House would impeach Clinton over Monica but not for this defiance perhaps says something about how serious Congress is about controlling foreign policy. See Barbara Hinckley, *Less than Meets the Eye: Foreign Policy Making and the Myth of the Assertive Congress* (Chicago: University of Chicago Press, 1994).

Conclusion

Christopher S. Kelley

The past thirty years of presidential "executing" has come to fruition with the George W. Bush administration. Since the difficult election of 2000, the president has asserted broad prerogatives over energy meetings held in the vice president's office, through 2003 has made over 100 constitutional exceptions in legislation that he has signed into law, has used executive orders to make presidential records secret all the way back to the Reagan administration, and, after the September 11 attacks, has altered our military doctrine in such a fundamental way that it places firm control over war into the hands of the president. And this does not even begin to scratch the surface of unilateral action in the Bush administration.

This book had two major objectives. The first was to direct presidential scholars to alternative ways to study the presidency other than focusing on the nuances associated with the modern presidency. Chapter 1 argued this point in which Professor Pious asserted a more holistic view of the presidency that returned to the constitution where true political power originates. Pious argued that rather than an either/or approach, we should be looking to wed a variety of approaches that will help us understand the presidency. As such we have seen authors who have used public law, presidential rhetoric, and presidential cycles to explain presidential action in a particular area.

The second objective, which was a subset of the first, was to use the period since the Nixon administration to highlight the advantages of studying the presidency through the lens of raw constitutional and political power. This period has been highly contentious in which the president has been forced to govern during a particularly hostile political environment. This period has forced presidents to be creative in the pursuit of policy and to be aggressive in the defense of presidential prerogatives.

Both of these objectives were satisfied. Each of the chapters focused on the period from Nixon to the present to explore and explain the ways in which presidents have returned to constitutional roots to exercise power.

The book had at least three major themes: The first theme is to understand how difficult containing a president who is committed to a course of action is. If you imagine trying to dam a raging river, you will understand that damming the river in one spot often leads to the formation of tributaries that work around the choked spot in the river. The same is true with the use of executive power. When Congress seeks to challenge a president in an area that it can make a strong case for congressional prerogatives, the president will find a way to work around the challenge. For example, as Kelley showed in chapter 4 on the use of presidential signing statements, when President George H. W. Bush was forced to sign the Civil Rights Act of 1991, he was able to work out an alternative legislative history that favored both his political position and a key constituency—the business community. In a second example, Cairo highlighted the fact that when faced with a challenge over the war power, the president was able to use international treaties to circumvent the congressional prerogative over war.

A second major theme was the construction of devices that would enable the president to control his policy preferences and to protect the institutional prerogatives of the office. For example, the Reagan administration used the executive order to establish administrative oversight of policy implementation and then used the signing statement to direct executive branch agency heads on how to implement legislation. The president has also developed ways to protect the pocket veto in an attempt to ensure that the last word on a piece of legislation is his. Furthermore, the president has established the "rhetorical" branch, which is meant to coordinate the administration's message to a variety of important political actors: executive branch agency heads, the leadership of Congress, or heads of state. Additionally, the president has also turned to the courts as a mechanism to ensure that the road to achieving his policy preferences is wide open. As Thomas argued in chapter 8, legal scholars have often deemed the focus on the Reagan appointees to the Supreme Court a failure because Reagan failed to overturn the *Roe* decision. However, if we look at the appointees in a political rather than a legal way, you can see that the issues closest to the president—a limited government and a return to federalism—were achieved by the Reagan appointees to the Supreme Court.

These unique devices have also been used to protect the institutional prerogatives of the executive branch. First, we should again note that during the Reagan administration the president began aggressively to assert his right to interpret the Constitution independently, a practice referred to as "departmentalism." Thus we should not be surprised that the volume of aggressive assertions of prerogatives also begins with the Reagan administration and carries forward to the George W. Bush administration. The number of constitutionally oriented signing statements increases with the Reagan administration, as the president signals to the Congress and the courts that he is taking his oath to protect the Constitution seriously. Furthermore, the expansive view of executive privilege picks up in the first Bush administration and continues through the George W. Bush administration. The George H. W. Bush administration sought to use executive privilege to protect information from Congress, whereas the Clinton administration expanded its use in an effort to protect wrongdoing by the president because he also sought to use it to protect all White House internal communications.

Finally, the third major theme of the book is the importance of establishing precedence for actions. In chapter 2, Barilleaux stressed the importance of precedent to the evolution of presidential power, which is something that clearly comes forward in many chapters. Precedent is important to give a president something to refer to when he is embarking on a risky action that tests the outer boundaries of presidential power. The importance of precedent, or at least the recognition by the president that it is important, dates back to the Jefferson administration. Jefferson asserted prerogatives over foreign policy as well as the establishment of the two-term presidency by pointing to the actions of the Washington administration. In a constitutional sense, precedent is very important for the courts to rely on when a presidential action is challenged. If the courts can determine a pattern of action that has not been met with a challenge by other political actors, most importantly the Congress, the tendency is to decide in favor of the president.

One of the key insights provided by Dodds in chapter 3, for example, was the incremental way in which presidents from Nixon through Clinton used the executive order to assert control over the executive branch agencies. By the time Clinton came to the White House, he was able to include not just the executive branch agencies but also the independent regulatory agencies without interference from the Congress.

In chapter 6, Spitzer explores just how important precedent is in the development of the pocket veto. The Reagan and the Bush administrations, for example, asserted the right to use the pocket veto during a session of Congress (intrasession) by applying it to little-noticed bills not to draw any unwarranted attention to its actions. Because the bills tended to be noncontroversial, Congress had little incentive to challenge the use of the pocket veto. Thus when the president would use it later in an instance that did draw congressional attention, the president could claim a past practice of usage.

And finally, Rozell shows us in chapter 5 just how protective of precedent the president is by exploring the reasons why the George W. Bush administration has asserted executive privilege over information from the Clinton Department of Justice. The impulse is to wonder why the Bush administration would exert energy trying to protect potentially damaging information on his Democratic predecessor. Although this may seem to be an obvious choice, Rozell explains why it is the wrong one. Had the Bush administration handed to the Congress the information it sought (even though it was a fellow Republican in the Congress who made the request), it would have set the precedent for future congressional requests regarding information from the executive branch—in essence, it would have set a precedent that would have given Congress an advantage over the president.

This edited volume will conclude where it began—with the Pious chapter. Professor Pious urges us to make use of the variety of tools at our disposal to come to as complete an understanding of presidential power as we can. As Professor Pious argues in the opening chapter, presidential power lies within executive branch officials who often make decisions outside of the explicit language of the Constitution. The success of those decisions rests with whether these decisions are considered legitimate. Throughout this edited volume, the authors examined the variety of ways in which these decisions are made as well as how the president can rely on their being considered legitimate.

The political environment continues to become more polarized, not less. Added to this are the pressures that the president must face from the international environment—pressures that take the form of foreign governments targeting the electoral base of the president in the form of tariffs (as the European Union recently did in response to the Bush steel tariff policy) or devastating attacks by nonstate actors that we saw on September 11. Each set of problems will not necessarily be resolved by bargaining and persuasion, but rather by constitutional creativity. I hope that this book will serve as a starting point in our quest to understand the nature of presidential power.

Contributors

RYAN J. BARILLEAUX

Ryan J. Barilleaux is currently chair of the Department of Political Science at Miami University (Ohio). Professor Barilleaux received his Ph.D. from the University of Texas. He is the author of several books on the presidency, including *Power and Prudence: The Presidency of George H. W. Bush*, *The Post-Modern Presidency*, and *The President as World Leader*. Professor Barilleaux is also currently the editor-in-chief of the *Catholic Social Science Review*.

MICHAEL CAIRO

Michael Cairo received his Ph.D. from the University of Virginia. He has taught at Virginia Commonwealth University, Southern Illinois University at Carbondale and the University of Wisconsin—Stevens Point. He is currently an assistant professor of political science at Georgetown College in Georgetown, Kentucky. Dr. Cairo's research interests include U.S. diplomacy and the foreign policy process. His publications include articles on civil control of the military and the role of local actors in foreign policy.

GRAHAM G. DODDS

Graham G. Dodds is an assistant professor of political science at Concordia University in Montreal, Canada. Professor Dodds received his Ph.D. from the University of Pennsylvania. He has published articles on presidents and the media, Hobbes, and political apologies. His dissertation was an examination of the presidential use of executive orders.

PATRICK J. HANEY

Patrick J. Haney is associate professor of political science at Miami University in Oxford, Ohio. His research interests focus on U.S. foreign policy, crisis decision making, and U.S.–Cuba policy. He is the author of *Organizing for*

Foreign Policy and coauthor with Walt Vanderbush of papers on U.S.–Cuba policy that have recently appeared in *Political Science Quarterly*, *International Studies Quarterly*, and *Congress and the Presidency*. He also recently contributed a chapter on using films to learn about foreign policy to *The New International Studies Classroom: Active Teaching, Active Learning*, edited by Jeffrey S. Lantis, Lynn M. Kuzma, and John Boehrer.

MAUREEN P. HANEY

Maureen P. Haney is a senior associate at Frost Brown Todd LLC in Cincinnati, Ohio whose practice is focused in large part on media and First Amendment issues, general commercial litigation, probate litigation, and appellate work. In the First Amendment and media arena, she regularly counsels firm clients on newsgathering, prebroadcast and prepublication issues, defends clients in defamation proceedings, and otherwise works—often on an emergency basis—to represent clients in obtaining access to courtrooms, court hearings, and public records, as well as in quashing or otherwise responding to subpoenas. Ms. Haney is a published author, an adjunct instructor of electronic media law at the University of Cincinnati, and is active on numberous bar association committees and organizations

CHRISTOPHER S. KELLEY

Christopher S. Kelley is currently a visiting assistant professor at Miami University (Ohio) where he teaches courses on American government, the American presidency, and mass media, and American politics. His primary area of research is on the development of presidential power since the Reagan administration and how it has applied to the presidential signing statement. Professor Kelley has published in the areas of presidential power and the president-media relationship.

KEVIN J. McMAHON

Kevin J. McMahon received his Ph.D. from Brandeis University (Waltham, Mass.) and is an assistant professor of political science at Trinity College (Hartford, Conn.). His most recent book is *Reconsidering Roosevelt on Race*. His article "Constitutional Vision and Supreme Court Decisions: Reconsidering Roosevelt on Race" appears in *Studies in American Political Development*, and he has coauthored a chapter in *Leveraging the Law: Using Courts to Achieve Social Change*.

RICHARD M. PIOUS

Richard M. Pious holds the Adolph and Effie Ochs Chair in American Studies at Barnard College (New York City), where he has taught since 1973, and he has been chair of the Department of Political Science since 1999. He is also a professor at the School of International and Public Affairs, and the graduate faculties, both schools of Columbia University, where he has taught since 1968. His books include *The American Presidency* (1979); *The President, Congress and the Constitution* (1984); *American Politics and Government* (1986); and *The Presidency* (1996). He edited the centennial volume of the Academy of Political Science, *The Power to Govern* (1982) and its subsequent volume, *Presidents, Elections and Democracy* (1992). He has also published articles in numerous journals. Dr. Pious has been a consultant to several presidential election campaigns, an advisor to congressional committees dealing with presidential war powers, a consultant to foreign governments, and a source for journalists writing about the presidency for leading news magazines. He has also been on panels that rate the presidents for the *New York Times Magazine* and the *Chicago Sun-Times*.

MARK J. ROZELL

Mark J. Rozell is professor of public policy at George Mason University in Virginia. He is the author of numerous studies on the U.S. presidency including *Executive Privilege: Presidential Power, Secrecy, and Accountability*, 2nd edition (University Press of Kansas, 2002).

ROBERT J. SPITZER

Robert J. Spitzer received his Ph.D. from Cornell University (Ithaca, N.Y.), and is Distinguished Service Professor of political science at the State University of New York, College at Cortland. His books include *The Presidency and Public Policy*, *The Right to Life Movement and Third Party Politics*, *The Bicentennial of the U.S. Constitution*, *President and Congress*, *Media and Public Policy*, *The Politics of Gun Control*, *The Right to Bear Arms*, *The Presidential Veto*, and *Politics and Constitutionalism*, also published by State University of New York Press. He is also series editor for the book series American Constitutionalism for State University of New York Press. Spitzer is the author of nearly 200 articles and papers appearing in many journals and books on a variety of U.S. political subjects. He currently serves as president of the Presidency Research Group of the American Political Science Association.

GEORGE THOMAS

George Thomas teaches constitutional law and theory at Williams College, Williamstown, Mass. He has published on the relationship between politics and the law in U.S. constitutional development. His work has appeared in the *Oklahoma Law Review*, *Polity*, and *Presidential Studies Quarterly*. His current project, Contesting Constitutional Meaning, examines how constitutional meaning is contested and shaped in the political arena.

WALT VANDERBUSH

Walt Vanderbush is associate professor of political science at Miami University in Oxford, Ohio. His research interests focus on Latin-American political economy and U.S.–Latin-American relations. He has published recent articles on the Mexican political economy in the *Journal of Interamerican Studies and World Affairs* and *Economic Development Quarterly*. He is also the coauthor with Patrick Haney of several papers on U.S.-Cuba policy. Vanderbush and Haney are currently finishing a book on U.S. policy toward Cuba called *The Rise and Fall of the Cuban Embargo*.

KEVAN M. YENERALL

Kevan M. Yenerall, Ph.D., associate professor of political science at Clarion University, teaches courses in American politics, international relations and politics and film. He is the co-author of *Seeing the Bigger Picture: Understanding Politics Through Film and Television* (Peter Lang Press, 2004), and has published articles, essays and book chapters dealing with the presidency, parties and elections, the media, and human rights. Forthcoming projects and publications include *The Cultural Pulpit Presidency: Rhetoric and Executive Power in the Clinton White House* (SUNY Press) and an edited volume on pop culture and politics. Dr. Yenerall serves as chair of the Popular Culture and Politics section of the Northeastern Political Science Association, and resides in Pittsburgh with Nee and Max.

Index